Port Washington, N.Y.

IRA J. FRIEDMAN, INC.

1969

JOAN D. BERBRICH

THREE VOICES
FROM
PAUMANOK

THE INFLUENCE OF LONG ISLAND
ON
James Fenimore Cooper
William Cullen Bryant
Walt Whitman

1

EMPIRE STATE HISTORICAL PUBLICATIONS SERIES No. 81

Manufactured by
Taylor Publishing Company
Dallas, Texas

To
Dorothy Berbrich,
my mother,
who has taught me
to love and appreciate
Long Island

Introduction

New England has had its literary historians, as have the Southwest, the Middle West, the Deep South, and the Pacific Coast. But seldom, if ever, have critical eyes rested meaningfully on the little strip of land that juts out from Manhattan's shores into the Atlantic and that bears the prosaic name, "Long Island."

Unlike the areas mentioned above, Long Island does not breed one type of man; it does not wrestle with one major problem; it is not characterized by one type of landscape, or by one personality trait, or by one point of view. This very versatility, which has protected it from literary critics and historians in the past, provides a fascinatingly complex background for the study of writers who have lived on this island and whose work bears its imprint. Three such writers are James Fenimore Cooper, William Cullen Bryant, and Walt Whitman. All three knew Long Island well.

Long Island is a strip of land 120 miles long and 30 miles wide. Her physical features are astonishingly varied: she offers prairies, forests, waterways, and sand dunes as well as apartment houses and heavily-populated residential sections. She probably has more housing developments per square mile than any other similar area in the United States, yet her inhabitants talk knowingly of duck farms, deep-sea fishing off Montauk, and children getting lost in the woods. She brags equally about being near the theatres and concert stages of New York City and of the deer-hunting, wild rabbits, and still-flourishing menhaden industry on her south shore.

Long Island also boasts a long and colorful history. It includes the early settlements of Southold and Southampton in 1640, the birth of the Secret Service in the Revolutionary War, the development of the whaling industry in the early 19th century, and the growth of aviation in the 20th century.

This variety — geographical, social, and historical — has been (and still is) vitally important to the literary works that have been by-products of this Island culture. One expects to find certain qualities in the writers of almost any geographical section. There are certain attitudes, certain concepts common to the writers who lived in Concord or Cambridge in the 19th century, as there are other attitudes and concepts common to the writers of New Mexico in the 20th century. This is not true of Long Island. During her history she has shown dozens of different "faces" to dozens of different writers. Each has taken from her according to his needs. This is especially true of the three writers discussed in this work.

James Fenimore Cooper found Sag Harbor, an important whaling port, in the second decade of the 19th century. He promptly succumbed to the whaling fever that ran high in the town. Young and energetic, Cooper spent much of the next three years exploring eastern Long Island and sailing up and down the Sound. The material that he gathered he would draw upon for the rest of his life.

William Cullen Bryant, seeking a sanctuary away from the City, found Roslyn, still Hempstead Harbor then. Ensconced in his beloved Cedarmere, surrounded by sloping green lawn and blossoming dogwood, Bryant found the serenity he craved. Editorials he wrote in Manhattan; poems he wrote on Paumanok!

Walt Whitman didn't have to find Long Island; it found him ...for Walt was born on the Island. As an infant, he knew the sound of the surf in his ears and the feel of wet sand beneath his toes. As a boy, he knew the fun of clamming and eeling, of setting out lobster-pots and of listening, wide-eyed, to tales of a whale chase. As a man, he knew his heritage: from family and from birthplace. And these experiences, in time, *became* his poetry.

Three writers with wholly different personalities — yet each found on Long Island raw material for creation. Each took from the Island what he needed; each gave back literary works that have endured.

*   *   *   *   *

But there is a second reason, too, for the existence of this book. We live today in a world of constant change. Apparently permanent values are being questioned; old certainties are being cast aside. Our new mobility is a glittering plaything, an irresistible toy that both threatens and attracts. Only in the last few years have we begun to realize that this splendid bauble has at least one cutting edge: it separates us from our past. We have become a rootless people — a tribe of wandering Ishmaels — at home everywhere but finding a home nowhere. This is especially true of Long Island.

Too long we have thought of ourselves as an adjunct of New York City. Too long we have thought of our history as beginning in the 1940's with the mushrooming housing developments. It is time now to uncover our past...and, in so doing, to provide "instant" heritage for the millions of people who now call themselves "Long Islanders."

*   *   *   *   *

While working on this volume, I received help from more sources than I can here acknowledge individually, from family and friends, from colleagues and students; but I would like to offer special thanks to a few: to the librarians at the Huntington Historical Society, the Huntington Public Library, the Hempstead Public Library, the Mineola Memorial Library, the Sag Harbor Library, the Nassau County Museum in Salisbury, the Bryant

Library in Roslyn, the Long Island Division of the Queensbor-
ough Public Library, and the Long Island Historical Society in
Brooklyn; to my sister, Anne Marie Levin, who spent long hours
in typing the original manuscript; and to Professor Gay Wilson
Allen of New York University, one of the leading Whitman
scholars in this country, who was generous both with his materials and with encouragement.

Contents

PART TWO
William Cullen Bryant

PART THREE
Walt Whitman

CONTENTS

THREE
VOICES
OF
PAUMANOK

PART ONE
James Fenimore Cooper

I

Cooper on Long Island

In 1819, the whaling ship, the *Union,* set forth on its maiden voyage, sailing out of Sag Harbor. The 262-ton whaler was the first ship of its type to be owned and financed by a group of shareholders. James Fenimore Cooper, watching it leave the harbor, must have felt a special sense of pride and responsibility, for it was, in many ways, his creation. He himself held the largest number of shares, had recruited most of the crew, had selected the captain, and had supervised preparations. He had even initiated the system of shareholding in this field.

To readers who know Cooper only through *The Leatherstocking Tales,* there is an apparent incongruity in this episode. One normally thinks of him following a trail in the woods, rowing on an inland lake, or playing lord of the manor; yet a study of his life indicates that this whaling venture was almost inevitable.

Born in Burlington, New Jersey, in 1789, James Fenimore Cooper was taken, while still a child, to Cooperstown, New York. Here, on the shores of Lake Otsego, he spent most of his childhood, playing in the woods and absorbing frontier adventures told by the men who had experienced them. He was a bright lad, but he lacked self-discipline, a fact proved by his unsuccessful career at Yale. When he was 17, he signed on the merchantman, the *Sterling.* Almost at once he loved the sea and the excitement of foreign ports when the ship touched land in England and along the Mediterranean coast. Most of all, he loved the excitement and danger of life at sea. He learned to fear impressment by the English, and he learned the helplessness felt by the crew of a merchantman pursued by an armed felucca. In 1808 he enlisted as a midshipman in the United States Navy. But this was a disappointment. Although he saw some sea service on the *Vesuvius* and the *Wasp,* he spent most of the three years at a desk or at a recruiting station.

When he married Susan De Lancey in 1811, he resigned from the Navy. He had grown bored with desk jobs and with the red tape connected with any government service. His future life must have seemed uncertain. Burdened with the responsibilities of marriage, he could hardly return to a life at sea. The obvious choice was to manage his wife's family estate in Westchester. This he did, for several years. It was a boring existence for a young man who had grown up amid excitement and danger, but there was one compensation. He now had the time and opportunity to visit his wife's relatives on Long Island.

The De Lanceys were an old and established family. They were as well-known in the New York-Westchester area as the Coopers were up near Otsego Lake. The various branches of the family were scattered all over Long Island. His wife's cousin, Mrs. Charles T. Dering, lived in Sag Harbor; and Miss Anne Nicoll, another cousin, lived on Shelter Island. Her mother's family, the Floyds, owned land in Mastic; and there were rather tenuous connections with the "Tangier" Smiths and the Townsends. All of these relatives held enviable social positions, and this in itself must have appealed to the class-conscious Cooper. During these Westchester years, the young couple made frequent trips to these Long Island relatives; their . favorite destination seemed to be Sag Harbor or nearby Shelter Island.

According to the historian, James Truslow Adams, it was on Shelter Island that the famous challenge was made that started the writing career of James Fenimore Cooper.[1] The story is well known: Cooper, reading an English novel one day, threw it down in disgust and claimed he could write a better one. His wife promptly challenged him; and in answer to the challenge, Cooper wrote his first novel, *Precaution.* It was not a very good novel, but it must have suggested to Cooper one possible escape from the routine life of a gentleman-farmer.

A second possible escape occurred to him during one of his visits to Shelter Island. Shelter Island was the Dering family estate, inhabited only by the Derings and their dependents. Here, between 1811 and 1819, Cooper and his wife spent much time during the summer and autumn months, leading a "sort of semi-aquatic life, which had great attraction for a young man who was still a seaman at heart." The island was well equipped for all kinds of activities. There were fishing smacks, sailboats, and rowboats, and an occasional sloop. Fishing, shooting, and fowling parties were held frequently, and in these events "Cooper took his place with great zest."[2]

General Sylvester Dering was the familial ruler of Shelter Island's eight thousand acres. The island had come into the family in the preceding generation when his father, Thomas Dering of Boston, had married Mary Sylvester. The Sylvesters had been living on the island since 1656. The Nicolls, another well-known family in the area, had bought one-fourth of Shelter Island from the Sylvesters in 1695. For over one hundred years, the two families remained on friendly terms but did not inter-marry. Then, in the early 19th century, Charles Thomas Dering (son of the General) married Elizabeth Floyd Nicoll. At about the same time, Charles's sister Margaret married Elizabeth's brother, Richard F. Nicoll, thus establishing a dual bond between the two families. The Floyds, maternal ancestors of Elizabeth and Richard, had married earlier into the Nicoll family. Susan De Lancey Cooper's mother was Elizabeth Floyd of Mastic; and her cousin, Elizabeth Floyd Nicoll, as already stated, was the wife of Charles Thomas Dering. Hence all four families were related to Susan Cooper, and through her to James Fenimore Cooper.[3]

These family and inter-family relationships form a complicated pattern, but one well worth tracing; it indicates that, in 1819, Cooper and his wife found themselves not among strangers, but among friendly relatives. Wherever they traveled on the eastern half of the Island — in Sag Harbor, Shelter Island, Gardiner's Island, Mastic, Brookhaven, Southampton — they were assured of a warm welcome and assistance. It explains a fact that is otherwise almost incredible: that the Coopers were accepted by the natives of Sag Harbor and its environs. The inhabitants of eastern Long Island, like their New England forebears, tended to create a closed society; few were accepted until they had lived in the area for several generations. The Coopers, though "aliens," were accepted almost immediately because their relatives included members of the four first families. This made it possible for Cooper to gain an intimate knowledge of the geography, industry, religion, and social mores of the area. Such knowledge was important to Cooper the man, but it was to become still more important to Cooper the writer.

The residents of Shelter Island were in almost constant communication with Sag Harbor, the nearest town and an important port of the whaling industry. Charles T. Dering and James Fenimore Cooper were of about the same age, and when Dering went to Sag Harbor on business, Cooper often went with him. Before long, he was a familiar figure in the town, "visiting the different ships, making acquaintance with their captains and mates, and hearing the details of their adventures."[4]

In 1819, Sag Harbor was one of the leading whaling ports in the United States. Her whaling fleet during that period numbered almost fifty ships "valued with their outfit at nearly a million of dollars, and employing more than a thousand seamen."[5] Whale-oil, whalebone, and ambergris had made Sag Harbor prosperous. The houses were large and comfortable, and most of them were equipped with widows' walks where wives could keep a look-out for seafaring husbands. The houses were elaborately furnished with scrimshaw (hand-carved whalebone) and exotic articles brought back from foreign ports. One-legged captains gathered often on street corners and in front of general stores to swap yarns of whaling ships. That Cooper was caught up in the town fever is attested to by his daughter Susan:

> During his visits to Shelter Island the young man from
> Otsego, still a sailor at heart...was much interested

in hearing the details of those whaling voyages, and
much amused with the whaling spirit pervading the
whole community at Sag Harbor.[6]

The amusement soon gave way to real interest, and in 1819
Cooper was ready to enter the competition. He and Dering
combined their capital; and when that did not suffice, the two
men "put in practice" the sale of shares in the ship *Union*.[7]
It was the first time this method had been used in the whaling
industry. There was no lack of purchasers, but Cooper intel-
ligently retained the largest share for himself, and thus was able
to assume management of the ship. He and Dering planned the
maiden voyage, chose the officers, enlisted a crew, and outfitted
the ship. He was really a part of Sag Harbor now, holding business discussions in Fordham's Tavern, walking the deck of his
whaler while it was in port, and conferring with Captain Jonathan
Osborne of Wainscott whom he had chosen to handle their
vessel.

Captain Osborne was a good choice. He was an expert harpooner who had over 150 whales to his credit. He could boast
(and often did) that he was one of the few men who had survived after being entangled in a line with a whale on the other
end. Osborne had been a whaling master for years, and he had
fascinating tales to tell. It is easy to believe that some of these
stories later found their way into the pages of Cooper's sea novels.

Did the *Union* bring her owner the fortune he expected?
Today, a century and a half later, it is impossible to know with
certainty. Adams tells us that the *Union* made several voyages
to Brazil between 1819 and 1822, but with little success.[8] However, Harry Sleight in his *History of Whaling* claims that the
Union made fourteen voyages with cargoes worth $350,000, and
Paul Bailey substantiates this claim.[9] Cooper sold out his share
in 1822; and since no whaler could possibly have made fourteen
voyages in three years, it is probable that the *Union* made most
of those voyages *after* 1822. It is also probable that Cooper
received for his efforts very small dividends in oil and whalebone,
but he did receive dividends of a more enduring nature: he

gained the experience of owning and outfitting a whaler; he learned something of whaling itself, its skills and terminology; and he became acquainted with the kind of men who worked whaling ships.

From his letters it is possible to trace Cooper's enthusiasm and involvement in this whaling venture. To Andrew Thompson Goodrich, bookseller and publisher, he wrote on May 31, 1820 that he wanted fast answers to some questions regarding publication of the novel *Precaution* because "I am in hourly expectation of my whaler and wish the work off my hands before she comes in..."[10] In another letter to Goodrich on July 2, 1820, he wrote: "I hourly expect the *Union* in, and must go to Sag-Harbor as soon as I hear of her arrival."[11] His "hourly expectation" continued for seventeen days; then he wrote triumphantly: "I have this moment heard of the arrival of my ship the *Union* at Sag Harbor."[12] His somewhat exultant tone and the possessiveness of "my ship" may be forgiven a young investor who is on the brink of tasting his first success. He continued with a request that Goodrich obtain from Mr. Jennings (proprietor of City Hotel, New York City) a bundle of papers marked "Ship *Union* — 1819" and rush them to him.

Meanwhile, on July 17, Cooper had received a letter from Dering informing him of the *Union's* arrival with one thousand barrels of whale oil and 220 barrels of spermaceti, not a good cargo for a vessel of her tonnage.[13] Cooper went out to Sag Harbor and there hired two sloops to take part of the cargo to Boston. For this he received $2,533.14. The second voyage of the *Union* brought in 28,485 gallons of whale oil and 6,585 gallons of spermaceti. Cooper's share for this second voyage amounted to $7,000 or $8,000. Most of this money was reinvested in fitting out the *Union* for her next trip.[14]

To James Fenimore Cooper, 31 years of age, aristocratic by birth, pragmatic by breeding, this whaling episode must have been deeply satisfying. It gave him an opportunity to take part in sea adventures again, though this time the experience was a vicarious one. It proved his business acumen, since the *Union* was at least moderately successful in her quest and since the shareholding system (which he had originated) was effective enough to be adopted by other whaling masters. It also gave him a chance to play at being a nautical authority. Years later, his daughter spoke fondly of her father's "grand appearance in the magnificent uniform of a colonel in the New York militia and of his playing master of the *Union*, the whaler in which he had a part interest."[15]   Surely the culmination of his joy came on those days when his ship, temporarily idle, could be taken under his own command and sailed freely up and down the Sound. On one occasion, he sailed the *Union* clear across the Sound to Newport.[16]   It must have been experiences like this that enabled the novelist to write the detailed maritime descriptions that delight readers of his sea novels. He could describe in vivid detail the Sound, its coast, and its navigational hazards because he knew them. In an unexpected way, the three-year whaling adventure eventually paid full dividends to the young novelist. In the three decades that followed this experience, Cooper utilized in his novels his first-hand knowledge of (1) navigation in the Long Island Sound, (2) whaling lore, (3) the geographical and social characteristics of the area, (4) the virtues and vices of the inhabitants, and (5) the history of the area.

II

The Sea and Ships

Navigation of Long Island Sound

Daniel Webster called it "the Mediterranean of the Western Hemisphere,"[1] but Captain John S. Blank, who had had experience on the Great Lakes, the St. Lawrence, the Irish Sea, the English Channel, and the coast of China, called it "one of the toughest runs in the world."[2] These two quotations depict accurately the two faces of Long Island Sound. To the landlubber, it is serene and beautiful; to the experienced mariner, it is teeming with perils and unseen hazards. Since World War II and the use of radar, the Sound has become safe for all kinds of navigation, but in the two hundred years before that, it demanded seamen with grit, consummate skill, and daring. A ship leaving the Battery off the Manhattan coast met its first major challenge at Hell Gate. This strait was aptly named. Its narrow, tortuous channel is dotted with jagged rocks, turbulent whirlpools, and swift cross-currents. Guiding a ship through Hell Gate in the early 19th century must have been akin to guiding a ship between Scylla and Charybdis in Homer's time.

James Fenimore Cooper knew Hell Gate well, and it fascinated him. It is best described in an early novel, *The Red Rover*, in which the "heroic" tailor, Homespun, boasts to the youth Pardy:

"I've been something of a traveler, too, Pardy.

12

Twice have I been overland to Boston, and once have
I sailed through the Great Sound of Long Island, down
to the town of York. It is an awful undertaking, the
latter, as it respects the distance, and more especially
because it is needful to pass a place that is likened, by
its name, to the entrance to Tophet.

"I have often heard the spot called 'Hell Gate'
spoken of; and I may say, too, that I know a man
well who has been through it twice; once in going to
York, and once in coming homeward.

"He had enough of it, as I'll engage! Did he tell
you of the pot which tosses and roars as if the biggest
of Beelzebub's fires was burning beneath, and of the
hog's back over which the water pitches, as it may
tumble over the Great Falls of the West?"[3]

Even the name "Hell Gate" fascinated Cooper. He hated the
early 19th century tendency toward euphemism. The traditionalist
in him liked the "old" names, and especially in his later novels
he grew querulous when old names were changed to new. In
Jack Tier, Mrs. Budd (an American Mrs. Malaprop) and Captain
Spike, a marine ruffian, engage in a conversation on this point.
Mrs. Budd points out that "Hell Gate" is almost obscene, that
"Hurl Gate" is vulgar, but that "Whirl Gate" is quite accept-
able. Captain Spike is honestly affronted by this false delicacy,
and Rose, Mrs. Budd's niece, reminds her aunt that too much
"genteelity" is in itself vulgar.[4] The point seems sufficiently
made, but Cooper — evidently fearing that his readers might miss
his meaning — comes back almost forty pages later with a comment reiterating his stand:

As for ourselves, we are still so old-fashioned as to
say, and write, Hell-Gate, and intend so to do, in spite
of all the Yankees that have yet passed through it, or
who ever shall pass through it, and that is saying a
great deal. We do not like changing names to suit their
uneasy spirits.[5]

After the passage through Hell Gate came the East River which
required navigational feats in its own right. In 1900, Captain

Henry Nickerson claimed that navigating a Sound steamer through
the East River "tries the nerves of the most experienced boatmen
and gives them many hours of anxiety. Great experience is
required and only men of cool disposition are fit for the business."[6] Cooper realized this a half-century earlier in *Jack Tier*.
The *Molly Swash,* under Captain Spike, has come through Hell
Gate into the last reach of the 'river,' and the author comments:
"Still the navigation at the entrance of this end of the Sound
was intricate and somewhat dangerous, rendering it indispensable
for a vessel of any size to make a crooked course."[7] Rather
typically, Cooper is not content to let the *Molly Swash* face only
natural dangers. A government revenue steamer has preceded her
through Hell Gate and is now awaiting her. When she approaches,
the steamer hails her, then shoots a warning at her. Spike
refuses to answer (he has a guilty conscience) and sets sail
rapidly, pushing the brig on toward the Stepping-Stones. A few
hours later they pass the light at Sands' Point, one of the earliest
landmarks on the Sound. Cooper once again shows his knowledge
of Sound navigation. Through the narrow and twisting waterways
leading to Sands' Point, the smaller sailing brig could make
better time than the revenue steamer. After Sands' Point, in the
open water of the Sound proper, the steamer would inevitably
have the advantage. Spike realizes this and suggests to Mulford,
his mate, that they pull in to the north shore of the Island and
let the steamer pass them by. Mulford reminds him that this
maneuver will necessarily be seen by the other vessels in the
vicinity. Spike agrees, but has an additional thought:

> "What you say is true enough, Mr. Mulford ... But
> here is Hempstead Harbor a few leagues ahead; if we
> can reach *that* before the blackguards close, we may do
> well enough. It is a deep bay, and has high land to
> darken the view. I don't think the brig could be seen
> at midnight by anything outside, if she was once fairly
> up that water a mile or two."[8]

No alternative plan being offered, Captain Spike keeps the brig under the western side of the harbor, and the crew of the *Molly Swash* watch triumphantly as the revenue ship steams by.

The next morning "when the light of day is just beginning to chase away the shadows of night," the *Molly Swash* inches toward the entrance of the estuary "to enable the lookouts aloft to ascertain that the coast was clear . . ." They study the horizen and see some lines of smoke. Some of the men are fearful that the steamer may be returning, but Spike, after studying the smoke carefully, determines (by a kind of magic not rare in Cooper's novels) that the smoke comes from a Providence or Stonington steamer, heading west with the Boston train. The next fifty miles or so are relatively smooth sailing, and by four o'clock, the *Swash* approaches the Race on the last of the ebb.

The Race is the main channel leading from Long Island Sound to Block Island Sound and thence to the Atlantic Ocean. Even in fine weather, it is not without its hazards. The name of this channel, The Race, derives from the velocity of its current which is normally from three to five knots, occasionally reaching six knots during spring tides. McAdam, a student of the Sound, adds: "Eastward lay a diabolical region of lusty winds, tremendous seas, shoals, shallows, and restricted channels where pinpoint navigation was a necessity." [10]   This is the area toward which the *Swash* is sailing, and despite a "staggering southwest wind," the brig sails easily through the Race and out into clear water. Montauk is only three hours away and already in sight, and the revenue steamer is nowhere visible. For a little while, success seems sure.

However, nothing is sure, especially in a Cooper sea-novel. As they approach Montauk, they see not one light, but two. Spike, who knows the waters well, declares: "If there is anything like a second, it must be a sail. Montauk has but one light." [11]   He keeps the *Molly Swash* moving swiftly on her ordained course:

> Montauk was by this time abeam, and the little brigantine began to rise and fall, on the long swells of the Atlantic, which now opened before her, in one vast sheet of green and rolling waters. On her right lay the

termination of Long Island; a low, rocky cape, with its
light, a few fields in tillage for the use of those who
tended it. It was the "land's end" of New York, while
the island that was heaving up out of the sea, at a
distance of about twenty miles to the eastward, was
the property of Rhode Island, being called Block
Island. Between the two, the *Swash* shaped her course
for the ocean.[12]

Now they are close enough to Montauk to spy a sail, but the
indomitable Spike refuses to accept the evidence of his eyes:
"Sail! Impossible, sir. What should a sail be doing in there, so
near Montauk — no man ever saw a sail there in his life."[13]
Even the most sanguine spirit must eventually succumb to proof,
and Spike at last admits that there *is* a sail and that it must be
another revenue cutter hiding behind the point waiting for the
Molly Swash. The apparent plan is for the cutter to approach
the *Swash* from one angle, while the revenue steamer, anchored
near Block Island, approaches it from the opposite direction, thus
catching the brig in a kind of pincer movement. Spike knows
his waters, however, and taking advantage of his small size and
consequent speed, he maneuvers the brig out of sight, around
one end of the island, doubling back rapidly and darting out
into the open waters. His start is so great now that the cutter
and the steamer temporarily give up the chase.

Pretty much the same territory is covered in *The Water-Witch*.
Fantastic though much of it is, this novel takes on a startling
realism when the "Skimmer of the Seas" guides his ship through
Hell Gate, across the Sound between the Connecticut and the
Long Island shores, and settles her successfully off Montauk.
Resting at anchor near his native island, the young captain
watches the British *Coquette* and a French ship engage in battle.
Again Cooper's nautical knowledge is valuable as he manipulates
the *Coquette* through tricky channels and past treacherous reefs.
That the *Coquette* is finally lost is the result of the fortunes of
war, not of faulty navigation.

Stephen Spike and the "Skimmer of the Seas" are not the only
captains to consider Montauk as a symbol of safety. Montauk

Point is a favored haven for several other naval heroes in Cooper novels. Her channels and reefs provide a 19th century substitute for the *deus ex machina*. In *Miles Wallingford,* the young hero leaves Clawbonny, his family estate, and shortly after finds himself pursued by a British ship. Fearing impressment, Wallingford skillfully plans his escape:

> The south side of Long Island tending a little to the north of east, I ordered the ship to be steered east by south, which, with the wind at south-southwest, gave me an opportunity to carry all our studding-sails. The soundings were as regular as the ascent on the roof of a shed, or on that of a graded lawn; and the land in sight less than two leagues distant. In this manner we ran down the coast . . . In less than an hour, or when we were about four leagues from Sandy Hook Light, the Englishman wore short round, and made sail to cut us off . . . (By the next morning) I had the satisfaction of seeing Montauk a little on my lee-bow, at sunrise. [14]

Finding the British ship still near-by and still menacing, Wallingford is tempted to stop and face her squarely. But Moses Marble, his first mate, fears impressment more than reefs and persuades the youthful captain to let him guide the *Dawn* around Montauk. He boasts complacently: "Though New York born, as it now turns out, I'm 'down east' edicated, and have got a 'coasting pilot' of my own in my head." [15] Wallingford agrees, Marble succeeds, and the *Dawn* slips cheerfully away from her opponent by using a channel known only to the first mate.

This nautical knowledge of the area was utilized again in *The Sea Lions,* one of Cooper's later novels. The ship, the *Sea Lion,* is ready to leave its home port for the Antarctic, and the author grasps the opportunity to declaim briefly on its problems:

> There are two passages by which vessels enter or quit Long Island Sound, at its eastern termination. The main channel is between Plum and Fisher's Islands, and, from the rapidity of its currents, is known by the

name of the Race. The other passage...lies to the
southward of the Race, between Plum Island and
Oyster Pond Point, and is called by the Anglo-Saxon
appellation of Plum Gut.[16]

The ship progresses easily through the desired channel. For hours,
the light on Montauk "...was the sole beacon for these bold
mariners, who rounded it about midnight, fairly meeting the long,
rolling swell of the broad Atlantic. Then the craft might be said
to be at sea for the first time."[17]

Second only to his knowledge of Long Island Sound is Cooper's knowledge of Sandy Hook and the waters to the south of
Long Island. Sandy Hook is the major setting of *The Water-
Witch.* It is, Cooper explains, either a peninsula or an island,
depending on the tide, and in this novel the Alderman's Cove
is on the inner side of this peninsula-island. This location pro-
tects it from the force of the Atlantic Ocean, and provides a
perfect refuge for ships caught in gale winds or unruly currents.
It also provides an excellent hiding-place for the *Water-Witch,* a
privateer engaged in the illegal importation of luxury goods from
foreign countries. Near the beginning of the novel, the Alderman,
his niece Alida, and a stranger (later found to be the "Skimmer
of the Seas," captain of the *Water-Witch*) are on a ferry. Nearby is the *Coquette,* a British ship under the command of Captain
Ludlow, suitor for the hand of Alida. Ludlow is under orders
from his Majesty's Government; the stranger, realizing this,
wonders out loud as to the nature of Ludlow's next duty. Alderman Beverout, with characteristic subtlety, suggests an answer:

> "There is a report among the boatmen of the South
> Bay, that something was seen yester'night off the outer
> side of Long Island!"
> "I'll answer for the truth of that rumor, for having
> come up with the evening flood, I saw it myself."
> "Der duyvel's luck! and what dost take it to be?"[18]

And the answer (to confound those critics who have accused
Cooper of having no sense of humor) was the simple rejoinder —

"The Atlantic Ocean..." The Alderman, of course, had been fishing for information about the illicit *Water-Witch*, but its sharp-witted owner, retaining his anonymity, adeptly turned the rumor into riddle.

*   *   *   *   *   *

Whaling Lore

Closely associated with Cooper's knowledge of Sound navigation was his knowledge of whaling. He was, for the most part, deadly serious about whaling; after all, he had invested much of his money and most of his youthful dreams in this 19th century industry. But the rewards were rich, if not those anticipated in 1820. Before the end of his writing career, he was to use the knowledge he had gained in Sag Harbor in five novels of the sea.

His first sea novel, *The Pilot,* written in 1823, is enriched by its youthful author's memories of whaling. In this novel is the delightful Long Tom Coffin, "as romantic a figure as ever trod a deck." Warren Walker, in a recent biography of Cooper, traces the Coffin ancestry to a Massachusetts family, famous in American maritime history, that dominated first Nantucket, then New Bedford, and finally Sag Harbor.[19] It would be presumptuous, however, to assume a direct relationship between Long Tom Coffin of *The Pilot* and the Coffins of Sag Harbor since there is no certain evidence of this, but surely it is permissible to infer that the following vivid description of Long Tom was the direct result of Cooper's close acquaintance with many professional whalemen on Long Island:

> ...he stood nearly six feet and as many inches in his shoes...there was a forward inclination about his head and shoulders that appeared to be the consequence of habitual confinement in limited lodgings...his enormous hands furnished a display of bones and sinews which gave indication of gigantic strength...his harsh visage, the sharp, prominent features of which were completely encircled by a set of black whiskers, that

began to be grizzled a little with age. One of his hands grasped, with a sort of instinct, the staff of a bright harpoon . . . [20]

In this novel, Lt. Barnstable, Long Tom Coffin, and young Merry are Americans on an American frigate hovering near the English coast line. The Revolutionary War has already started, and the two countries are avowed enemies. Barnstable, Coffin, and Merry are sent in a whaleboat to the English shore to find a certain pilot (who, at the end of the novel, turns out to be John Paul Jones!). Shortly after landing, they stumble upon a fat ox. Tom, almost automatically, raises his harpoon. "...let Captain Barnstable but say the word, and I'll drive the iron through him to the quick; I've sent it to the seizing in many a whale, that hadn't a jacket of such blubber as that fellow wears."[21] Tom's eagerness is temporarily dampened by Barnstable's reminder that they are not now engaged on a whaling voyage and that everything, therefore, is not, perforce, fair game.

A few minutes later, Barnstable is accosted by an insolent young lad who is really Barnstable's sweetheart, Katherine Plowden, in disguise. The lad laughs at him pertly, and Barnstable — drawing on his creator's experience — swears roundly: "Now, by all the whales in the sea . . . but you are merry out of season, young gentleman."[22]

About 150 pages then cover land-happenings, and at last the men are once again in the whaleboat, returning to the frigate. They are in very real danger of pursuit, and they know it. An almost inevitable death-penalty awaits them if they are caught. A few minutes later, the stillness is broken by a heavy rush of air and a dash of water. Coffin identifies the source immediately as a whale: " . . . here is his spout not half a mile to seaward; the easterly gale has driven the creatur' to leeward, and he begins to find himself in shoal water." The men, forgetting their pursuers, heatedly discuss a more accurate identification of the whale. Barnstable thinks it's a finback, but Tom knows better; he knows it's a right whale because he saw its spout: "He threw up a pair of as pretty rainbows as a Christian would wish to look at. He's a real oil-butt, that fellow!"[23]   That problem settled, they try determinedly to ignore the whale and to continue their way to the frigate, but their whaleboat is equipped with half a whale line, Tom is equipped with a harpoon, and they decide (against all probability and reason) to give chase. This episode is totally irrelevant to the story and makes no sense from a military point of view, but its inclusion becomes understandable when one remembers that only three years before, Cooper had been involved in whaling and here merely succumbed to the desire to use his fascinating new knowledge. The next five pages are devoted to a description of the whale, his movements, and the chase, and they are among the liveliest pages in the novel. Note this description of the approach:

> Their approach was utterly unnoticed by the monster of the deep, who continued to amuse himself with throwing the water in two circular spouts high into the air, occasionally flourishing the broad flukes of his tail with a graceful but terrific force, until the hardy seamen were within a few hundred feet of him, when he suddenly cast his head downward, and, without an apparent effort, reared his immense body for many feet above the water, waving his tail violently, and producing a whizzing noise, that sounded like the rushing of winds.[24]

The monster then disappears, but Tom knows he'll soon be up for air. A Coffin is always right when it comes to whales, and in a few moments the huge animal again appears, casting half its length up out of the water. The men eagerly pull their boat alongside the whale, and Tom buries the iron in the blubber of their ancient foe. Cooper, knowing his whales, comments that the monster, not realizing his own strength, flees from his puny persecutors. Again the whale sounds; the line grows taut; then the "terrified and wounded victim" rises again. This time he drags the boat in his wake. Soon Tom, seeing the jetting fluid streaked with red blood, shouts in exultation: "Ay, I've touched the fellow's life! It must be more than two foot of blubber that stops my iron from reaching the life of any whale that ever sculled the ocean!''[25]

The whale surrenders, lies quietly for a moment, then is convulsed in its death throes:

> From a state of perfect rest, the terrible monster threw its tail on high, as when in sport, but its blows were trebled in rapidity and violence, till all was hid from view by a pyramid of foam, that was deeply dyed with blood. The roarings of the fish were like the bellowing of a herd of bulls... As life departed, the enormous black mass rolled to one side; and when the white and glistening skin of the belly became apparent, the seamen well knew that their victory was achieved.[26]

The chase is over, and it is successful. The men, with typical New England thrift, look regretfully at the carcass: it will probably drift to land and serve only to aid their enemies with oil.

Suddenly this irrelevant episode is over; the *Alacrity*, an enemy ship, looms into sight. Barnstable, with self-anger now, aware of his delinquency as a leader, explodes: "Damn the whale! but for the tow the black rascal gave us, we should have been out of sight of this rover!"[27]   All is well in the end, however, for just in the nick of time, they are picked up by their ship, the *Ariel*.

Perhaps it is unfair to label this episode as totally irrelevant; it does help us to understand Tom Coffin, sturdy and practical, ready to fight whale or foe at any time under any circumstances; and it does help us to understand Lt. Barnstable, impulsive, sometimes thoughtless, often immature, but always boyishly brave.

In *The Pilot,* Cooper's whaling experience used him, in the sense that his recent memories trampled on his art; a few years later, a more skilled artist, he used the experience, shaping it into a brief and ironic simile. In *The Water-Witch,* Alderman Beverout, finding that his niece Alida has disappeared and suspecting her of eloping, mutters: "Women and vagaries!... Their conceits are as uncertain as the profits of a whaling voyage."[28]   One senses here the wry, backward look of the mature man who has learned to laugh at his own earlier mistakes.

Whales could be useful, too, by providing illuminating contrasts to the forests and inland lakes of western New York. In the early novel, *The Pioneers,* Benjamin (a seafaring man) and some friends are getting ready to go fishing in lake Otsego. Benjamin has some doubt as to the probable fruitfulness of this task:

> " ...just listen to the philosophy of the thing. Would it stand to reason, that such fish should live and be catched in this here little pond of water, where it's hardly deep enough to drown a man, as you'll find in the wide ocean, where, as everybody knows, that is, everybody that has followed the seas, whales and grampuses are to be seen, that are as long as one of the pine trees on yonder mountain?" [29]

Sheriff Jones, a native of the area, reminds him that some of the pines measure two hundred feet. But Benjamin is undaunted: "Haven't I been there, and haven't I seen? I have said that you fall in with whales as long as one of them there pines; and what I have once said I'll stand to!"

In the 1838 novel, *Home as Found,* a similar discussion takes place. Captain Truck, who knows the ocean, and the "commodore," who knows only the local lake, are in the middle of a rather heated argument. The commodore has been bragging about his "sogdollager," an especially large and intelligent fish with which he had feuded for half a century. Truck replies:

> "I make no doubt your 'sogdollager' is scaly enough; but what is the use in wasting words about such a trifle? A whale is the only fish fit to occupy a gentleman's thoughts. As long as I have been at sea, I have never witnessed the taking of more than three whales." [30]

The commodore is temporarily deflated, for "if there were anything in the world for which (he) entertained a profound but obscure reverence, it was for a whale." Truck, unfortunately for the glory of ocean-going mariners, cannot resist further boasting. He looks up at the surrounding pine trees and—like Benjamin—

declares confidently that he has seen whales as long as these pine trees are high. The commodore, more clever than Sheriff Jones, asks him how high he thinks the pines are; Truck guesses about forty feet, maybe more. When the commodore tells him that the pines are one hundred to two hundred feet high, Captain Truck admits defeat and the honor of western New York is vindicated.[31]

Evidently the passing years modified Cooper's memories of the power and importance of the whale. Certainly in *The Pathfinder*, two years after *Home as Found,* the sea-faring character, Cap, fares even worse than did Captain Truck. Cap too finds it difficult to believe that anything really good is to be found inland. However, his opponent, Natty Bumppo, is hard to impress. When Cap says defiantly, "Now, I dare say that there isn't such a thing as a whale in all your lake, Master Path-finder!" Natty is content to reply: "I never heard of one, I will confess..."[32]   Cap tries bravely to induce an argument, but Natty refuses to rise to the bait, and the argument dies before it is well started.

In the above three novels, Cooper's use of his whaling experi-ence was incidental, but four years later, in *Afloat and Ashore,* he again interjected a whaling episode into the main plot of the story. The captain of the ship has been lost, leaving Moses Marble as acting captain. Marble is another Ishmael, a wanderer, without home or friends. Assisting Marble is the young hero, Miles Wallingford. In the middle of the Pacific Ocean, two thou-sand miles from the western coast of South America, Captain Marble suddenly spies a deserted American whaleboat and sets out to secure her. Fog and a storm separate Marble from his ship, and he is given up for lost. Miles takes over as acting captain. When they meet again, some time later, Marble is in the whaleboat and the whaler is standing near-by. The detailed and professional description proves that Cooper had not forgotten his whaling lore:

> The boat was American-built, had a breaker of water,
> the oars, and all the usual fittings in it; and the painter
> being loose, it had probably been lost, when towing in

the night, in consequence of having been fastened by *three* half-hitches.[33]

Twenty pages later, Cooper refers to the whaler again. It may be seen now, in the distance, with its boat lying near it. About a mile to windward is a dead whale, with another boat, waiting for the approach of the ship. As Wallingford's ship pulls away, a last glimpse shows the whaler starting the serious business of "cutting in" the fish.

Unlike the whaling episode in *The Pilot,* this whaling incident is handled in an efficient, business-like manner. It lacks the color and excitement of a Tom Coffin harpooning a whale and commenting succinctly on its reactions, but it is — as its predecessor was not — an integral part of the story. Moses Marble is a fine broth of a man, a downeaster, with no education and no home training. He follows his instincts (as Tom Coffin would have followed his) by setting out alone to take a deserted whaleboat; but this very action dramatizes his personal inability to command a ship. He has neither the foresight nor the sense of responsibility necessary in a good captain, and he himself recognizes this when he refuses to take the ship back from Miles Wallingford. This incident gives us then an understanding of Marble's character, and elevates — in a fairly logical manner — Miles Wallingford to a position of high command. It also prepares us to see the real relationship between these two men: Wallingford is the natural leader, a man of good birth and education, and Marble is the loyal follower, a little rough but always cheerful and willing.

This whaling episode satisfies two other needs in the story: it provides a realistic atmosphere through the use of down-to-earth details that Cooper knew so well how to write, and it provides subject-matter that contrasts and highlights the conflicts with other ships that immediately precede and follow the incident. Here again, Cooper has used his material instead of letting it use him.

In *Jack Tier,* four years later, Cooper referred to whaling only once, this time in much the same way he had used it in *The Water-Witch.* Stephen Spike, captain of the *Molly Swash,* has

been studiously avoiding a revenue steamer that has been pursu-
ing them. Since the United States is involved in war with Mexico,
Spike claims that the steamer may really be a Mexican in disguise. The mate, Mr. Mulford, handsome, brave, and rather
pedantic, is discussing this with pretty Rose Budd, in whom he
has a non-academic interest. He tells her: "I can see no sufficient
reason, beyond native antipathy, why Captain Spike should wish
to avoid any craft, for it is humbug his dread of a Mexican, and
least of all, here, in Long Island Sound. All that story about
Jones is a tub of whales." And Rose, who returns his admiration
and interest, retorts drily: "Thank you for the allusion; my aunt
and myself being the whales."[34]   The humor is rather forced,
but the whale metaphor is skillfully used.

The most interesting of Cooper's late novels is *The Sea Lions,*
published in 1849. This novel—a conglomeration of religion,
sealing, and greed—was written when Cooper was already irritable
and unhappy, disillusioned with American democracy and shocked
by youthful irreverence. For this brain-child of his sixtieth year,
Cooper returned to happier memories—to Sag Harbor and its
environs. The first section of the novel takes place in Oyster
Pond, a town on the northern fork of Long Island, just across
the bay from Sag Harbor and Shelter Island. Young Roswell
Gardiner, who is to captain Deacon Pratt's schooner in its quest
for seals and gold, spends considerable time in recruiting a crew
and preparing his vessel for sea. His recruiting takes him to Sag
Harbor, across the Sound to Stonington, Connecticut, and to
other maritime villages along the coast. This was familiar territory
to Cooper, for he had checked in at the same towns when he
was recruiting *his* crew for his whaler, the *Union.* Even the time
is the same, for *The Sea Lions* opens in 1819, the year that
Cooper became involved in his whaling venture. The exactness
and abundance of detail in this part of the novel is not surprising; evidently Cooper was indulging in a little nostalgia,
perhaps re-reading his records and journals, certainly returning
in spirit to a more hopeful day.

The *Sea Lion* is at last outfitted and ready to start its journey.
Its purpose is two-fold: to collect seals in the Antarctic and gold

in the West Indies. Forty-six days from Montauk, a sudden cry
rings through the ship — "a spout! a spout!" Seals and gold are
forgotten as the crew (and Cooper, too) turn to their first and
most loved occupation — whaling. First there is an enthusiastic
description of the whaling equipment which the ship possesses
and which is now readied: lines, lances, harpoons, and quarter-
boats. Then there is a discussion of the whale as a species that
is unmatched even in Melville. The right whale throws up two
high-arched jets of water; the spermaceti, a single, low, bushy
one. The right whale has no regular teeth; the spermaceti is
equipped with regular grinders. Cooper reminds the reader that
one does not, with impunity, attack a whale with its young; this
provides the greatest danger. [35]

Young Roswell Gardiner, who has grown up in whaling
territory, knows exactly which whale to choose: an old bull, too
clumsy and tired to hold out for long, yet sure to yield a hundred
barrels of oil. The chase begins, and the old bull is harpooned
and tied. Meanwhile, the *Sea Lion II* (a rival ship captained by
Daggett of Martha's Vineyard which hopes to share the profits
of *Sea Lion I*) sends out its whaleboat. By accident, Daggett's
line passes into the mouth of Gardiner's whale. A long dispute
ensues as to who is the proper owner of the whale, but legal
and moral right finally grant it to Gardiner. The whale is tried
and casked, and at the *Sea Lion's* next port of call sent home
to Deacon Pratt in Oyster Pond. News of this exploit throws the
quiet little town into an uproar. Mary, Pratt's niece, dreams
admiringly of the young and heroic Roswell; the greedy Deacon
is delighted with this unexpected and extra dividend; and the
whole town is proud that a little schooner like the *Sea Lion*,
setting out from its own shores, was able to take a hundred-
barrel whale and send home its "ile." [36]

The rest of the novel is concerned with sealing and the inhabitants of Oyster Pond. Two years after writing this novel,
James Fenimore Cooper died; in those two years he did not
again handle whales or whaling in his writing. In one very real
sense, therefore, the chase and capture of the leviathan in *The
Sea Lions* is the swan-song to three years of the writer's youth.

*   *   *   *

General Sea Influence

Only recently has Cooper as a novelist of the sea been granted
serious study by critics; yet the sea is the foremost element in
his writing. Out of thirty-three novels, eleven deal almost exclusively with the sea, and another six utilize, either as subject-
matter or as metaphor, their author's nautical knowledge. Even
The Leatherstocking Tales, with settings far inland, have salty
touches.

In *The Deerslayer,* the reprobate Thomas Hutter was once a
sea-pirate, and his rigidly-guarded chest is found to contain a
mathematical instrument used by seamen. When Judith and
Hetty, Hutter's "daughters," are in a boat fleeing from the
Indians, Cooper carefully explains that the Indians are following
at two hundred yards "in their wake," and that this makes the
pursuit "a stern chase" which is proverbially, "a long chase." [37]

The cockney, Benjamin Penguillan, in *The Pioneers,* spent most
of his life at sea, and now that he is a major-domo in the Temple
home, he spices his conversation with sea phrases and analogies.
When someone wonders how a man can find his way through
the woods, Benjamin replies: " . . . look aloft, sir, look aloft. The
old seamen say that the devil wouldn't make a sailor, unless he
looked aloft." [38]   When Miss Temple returns home and a servant
fears impending changes, Benjamin remarks philosophically: "Life
is as unsartain as the wind that blows . . . and nothing is more
vari'ble than the wind . . . unless you happen to fall in with the
trades, d'ye see, and then you may run for the matter of a
month at a time, with studding-sails on both sides, alow and
aloft, and with the cabin-boy at the wheel." [39]   Benjamin knew
he was fortunate in his youthful training, and one of his comments (satirical though it was) reminds one of Cooper's love for
the sea. Benjamin said: "The sea . . . is a great advantage to a
man, in the way of knowledge, for he sees the fashions of
nations, and the shape of a country." [40]

Another old salt, Cap in *The Pathfinder,* is more belligerent and less philosophical then Benjamin. Cap, who has spent many years on the ocean, feels only contempt for the forest, trees, Indian ambushes, and landsmen's phrases. But the acme of his contempt is saved for Oswego Lake, which measures a good twenty leagues from shore to shore. "This, then, is what you call your lake?" Cap demands when they catch their first glimpse of the blue waters. "I say, is this really your lake?" They assure him that it is, and in the next few moments he depicts it pithily as "a bit of a pond," "a scuttle-butt," and even a mere "stripe of water."[41]   Later he almost destroys the whole party when he takes command of the *Scud,* a cutter designed for lake waters, and tries to use on it navigational methods learned on the ocean. This near-disaster only proves to Cap that the lake is no true sea, and he is no more modest after the incident than he was before.

In *The Prairie,* Cooper uses the sea but once. Here there is no marine braggart, no jokes that hinge on sea terminology, but only one tremendous sea-simile. He is describing the western prairie:

> The earth was not unlike the ocean, when its restless waters are heaving heavily, after the agitation and fury of the tempest have begun to lessen. There was the same waving and regular surface, the same absence of foreign objects, and the same boundless extent to the view. Indeed so very striking was the resemblance between the water and the land, that, however much the geologist might sneer at so simple a theory, it would have been difficult for a poet not to have felt that the formation of the one had been produced by the subsiding dominion of the other. Here and there a tall tree rose out of the bottoms, stretching its naked branches abroad, like some solitary vessel; and, to strengthen the delusion, far in the distance appeared two or three rounded thickets, looming in the misty horizon like islands resting on the waters.[42]

Here the sea, imaged in an alien element, conveys the dual nostalgia of Natty Bumppo and James Fenimore Cooper. As

Natty, an old man now, stares hungrily at this last, unopened expanse of frontier which symbolizes so many scenes of his past life, Cooper visualizes the swells and billows of his own remembered youth.

This note of nostalgia is important in Cooper; it accounts for the frequent interjection of maritime characters and phrases in stories in which one would least expect to find them. It accounts for *Homeward Bound,* which started as a novel of social criticism and ended as a tale of adventure at sea. The sea is, by far, the most common element and the most powerful force in Cooper's writing. It proves again the old adage — "that the child is father to the man."

III

The Land and the People

The Geographical and Social Characteristics of the Area

Near the beginning of his writing career, James Fenimore
Cooper, standing on a hill in Westchester, looked across the
valley at the blue waters of Long Island Sound. He described
what he saw:

> An island more than forty leagues in length lies oppo-
> site the coasts of New York and Connecticut. The arm
> of the sea which separates it from the main is techni-
> cally called a sound, and in that part of the country
> *par excellence, The Sound.* This sheet of water varies
> in its breadth from five to thirty miles.[1]

Near the end of his writing career, after a thirty years' acquaintance with the Island, he wrote this:

> Every one at all familiar with the map of America
> knows the position and general form of the two islands
> that shelter the well-known harbour of the great em-
> porium of the commerce of the country. These islands
> obtained their names from the Dutch, who called them
> Nassau and Staten; but the English, with little respect
> for the ancient house whence the first of these appel-
> lations is derived, and consulting only the homely taste
> which leads them to a practical rather then (sic) to a
> poetical nomenclature in all things, have since virtually

31

dropped the name of Nassau, altogether substituting
that of Long Island in its stead.[2]

The second quotation is more academic than the first, and shows
a more detailed geographical and historical knowledge of the
area, but both share a "tone." Together, they indicate the true
nature of Cooper's attitude toward Long Island, similar in many
ways to his attitude toward all America. He loved it, visited it
frequently, kept thinking about it, and continued to use it in his
novels; but always there is the note of sarcasm, the raised eye-
brow, the patronizing glance. Always he was the aristocratic
landowner, the gentleman farmer, firmly ensconced in the family
manor at Cooperstown; but also he was the rather brash young
man who had married Susan Augusta De Lancey, knowing full
well that the De Lanceys occupied a higher position socially than
did his own family. Perhaps these facts resulted in the ambiva-
lence in his attitude toward the island and its inhabitants. He
respected the De Lancey relations: the Nicolls, the Derings, the
Floyds; and looked down upon the "people"; yet he admired
the adventurous and was bored by the stay-at-homes. Since the
adventurous most often came from the people, and the respectable were usually sedentary, it is small wonder that Cooper was
never able to resolve these contradictory elements.

He was most at ease in describing the town of Sag Harbor.
This village, in which he had pursued youthful dreams, he
remembered until the end of his life. It never ceased to fascinate
him. He remembered the houses, the streets, the Fordham tavern
— *the feeling:*

> As a whaling town, Sag Harbour is the third or fourth
> port in the country, and maintains something like that
> rank in importance. A whaling haven is nothing with-
> out a whaling community... It is as indispensable that
> a whaler should possess a certain esprit de corps, as
> that a regiment, or a ship of war, should be animated
> by its proper spirit... Success in taking the whale was
> a thing that made itself felt in every fibre of the

prosperity of the town; and it was just as natural that the single-minded population of that part of Suffolk should regard the bold and skillful harpooner, or lancer, with favour, as it is for the belle at a watering-place to bestow her smiles on one of the young heroes of Contreras or Churubusco. His peculiar merit, whether with the oar, lance, or harpoon; is bruited about, as well as the number of whales he may have succeeded in "making fast to," or those which he caused to "spout blood." [3]

It was, for the most part, a rather ordinary little town. In 1820, its total population included 1,646 people. There were only about two hundred houses, most of which had been built after the Revolution. Almost all of the inhabitants were working people, and most of them earned a living by catching whales and codfish. Families were large, and sons expected to follow in their fathers' footsteps. Boys went to sea on whalers as soon as they were old enough to help. Cooper used the word "amphibious" to describe people like the Sag Harborites: "sailors without being seamen," he said.[4] They were good and they knew their work, but they were not true professionals.

Sag Harbor was more than a town, both to the people of the area and to Cooper himself. It was the pulsing heart of the whaling industry, and in its heyday commanded the loyalty of sailors for a hundred miles around. Cooper, in speaking of Oyster Pond, said that its true maritime character, "as well as that of all Suffolk, was derived from the whalers, and its proper nucleus was across the estuary, at Sag Harbour."[5] When Cooper thought of Sag Harbor, he thought of whaling and temporarily forgot the foibles and human defects that so often aroused his anger. Whatever the cause, Sag Harbor is the only town to escape completely the satirical lash of the Cooper pen.

This small whaling port of the past still cherishes the famous writer who here began his writing career. On July 4, 1879, Sag Harbor Park was officially opened with elaborate ceremony. Some youthful, would-be poet had written a poem for the occasion, commemorating its great days, both in whaling and in literature:

Here boldly to sail
In pursuit of the whale
Was honored in every station,
And his capture and spoil
Represented in oil,
Was the thought of the whole population.

For no maiden would look
On a young man who took
To a land life of torpor and stupor,
When the scene was here laid
Of the "Sea Lions" raid,
Of our national novelist, Cooper.[6]

This poem goes on to describe how busy the town was then, and how quiet it is now when the whaling days are gone forever.

For Oyster Pond, Cooper had less affection and keener observation. Its geographical location is best described in Cooper's own words:

Long Island forks at its eastern end, and may be said to have two extremities...(one is Oyster Pond Point, the other Montauk)... Within the fork lies Shelter Island, so named from the snug berth it occupies... Between Shelter Island and the longest or southern prong of the fork, are the waters that compose the haven of Sag Harbour, an estuary of some extent; while a narrow but deep arm of the sea separates this island from the northern prong, that terminates at Oyster Pond.[7]

Cooper's geography is right; his history errs slightly, for Shelter Island gained its name not only from its snug berth but also from the shelter it provided for Quakers who were fleeing from persecution in the mid 1660's. In The Sea Lions, Cooper refers to the heights on Shelter Island and the bluffs towards Riverhead; he comments that these might seem unimportant in Switzerland, but here on Long Island they possessed a certain majesty. Any native Long Islander knows what he meant.

Cooper then describes the town, Oyster Pond:

> Plain, but respectable dwellings, with numerous out-
> buildings, orchards, and fruit-trees, fences carefully
> preserved, a pains-taking tillage, good roads, and here
> and there a 'meeting-house' gave the fork an air of
> rural and moral beauty. [8]

Deacon Pratt, one of the main characters in *The Sea Lions,* is
a childless widower and a tight-fisted sinner. With him lives his
niece, Mary Pratt, an orphan since she was ten years old.

The Deacon owns three small farms and a one-horse chaise.
The house in which they live is of wood, "as is almost uniformly
the case in Suffolk." It is two stories high, with five windows in
the front. "The siding was of unpainted cedar-shingles; and,
although the house had been erected long previously to the
Revolution, the siding had been renewed but once ... " Before the
house, stretches a two-acre garden, full of flowers and shaded by
four rows of cherry-trees; and near the edge of the lawn stands
a fine apple orchard. From a window in the second story, one
can see the Sound in one direction and Peconic Bay in the other.

Cooper was happy with the Oyster Pond of 1819, but less so
with the Oyster Pond of 1849, when he was writing *The Sea
Lions.* By then it had become the terminus of the Long Island
Railroad, and as such, was the key link in the new New York-
Boston route. This, said the irate Cooper, "put an end to all
its seclusion, its simplicity, its peculiarities, and we had almost
said, its happiness." [9] But change of any kind was anathema to
this author-traditionalist. He did not like it when they changed
Sterling to Greenport nor when they changed Oyster Pond to
Orient. As already seen, he had been annoyed when they called
Hell Gate, Hurl Gate, and when Nassau gave way to Long
Island. On the other hand, he was charmed with the pronunci-
ation of what he called "old-fashioned" English; he loved to
hear Holmes's Hole called "Hum'ses Hull," Gardiner's Island
called "Gar'ner's Island," and Oyster *Pond* called "Oyster
Pund." [10] This rustic speech seemed, to Cooper, proof that the

people were not being kept "in leading strings by pedagogues," that they were stoutly maintaining their old freedom and their simplicity.

Cooper had spent the summer of 1825 at Sunswick, near Hallett's Cove and opposite Blackwell's Island, in a farmhouse owned by his friend, Colonel George Gibbs.[11] In *Jack Tier,* as the *Molly Swash* prepares to go through Hell Gate, the author stops the story to note Blackwell's new penitentiary and a hamlet of villas called Ravenswood "though there are neither wood nor ravens to authorize the name." This "Ravenswood" was formerly "Sunswick," which satisfied the Gibbses and Delafields but which was not "elegant enough for the cockney tastes of these latter dates..."[12] He notes with satisfaction that the vulgar Captain Spike prefers the new Grecian temples to the old-fashioned and respectable residences, but soon sours again when he remembers that Hallett's Cove is Hallett's Cove no longer, but is now *Astoria.* "This Astoria was a very different place (from the one in Oregon), and is one of the many suburban villages that are shooting up, like mushrooms in a night, around the great Commercial Emporium."[13]

That phrase, "Commercial Emporium," annoyed Cooper throughout his life. He could not see how anyone could use so redundant a phrase. He was equally disturbed by these mushrooming suburbs. In this new move toward modernity, he saw a breakdown in the old way of life:

> Even in the American towns, the old observances are giving way before the longings or weaknesses of human nature; and Sunday is no longer what it was. I have witnessed scenes of brawling, blasphemy, and rude tumult in the suburbs of New York, on Sundays, within the last few years...[14]

Another cause for disturbance, even in Oyster Pond in 1819, was the great haste "in getting rid of the dead."[15] The funerals were short and simple, and this was as it should be; but they followed with an almost indecent speed upon the last breath.

Still, the simplicity was correct, and Cooper noted with approval that when Mary Pratt inherited $30,000 from her uncle, it did — in that place, at that time — constitute real wealth.[16]

If the little towns on Long Island had been able to stand still, if all of America had stood still, Cooper might have been a happy man; but the "new world" was a changing world, and this Cooper could not endure. The people of Cooperstown dared to sue the family that had given their name to the town; the courts granted him legal right, but mocked him with their nominal awards; the newspapers had grown mutinous. All the sweet things had turned sour; the dreams had become nightmares; and the hamlets of eastern Long Island were rocked by the clatter of railroads and the din of conductors' cries of "Greenport" and "Orient."

*   *   *   *

The Inhabitants of Long Island

As the whaling industry and the coastal towns had fascinated Cooper, so too did some of the inhabitants. The influence of the first two is clearly evident in his writing, but the "human" influence is considerably more nebulous. It has been further obscured by rival contentions and unsubstantiated "proof."

The character that can most directly be traced to a Long Island origin is Dr. Ebenezer Sage, in *The Sea Lions*. When Daggett, the Vineyard seaman, is dying, Deacon Pratt reluctantly yields to Mary's pleading that Dr. Sage be summoned.[17]   Dr. Sage is a physician of "merited celebrity" in old Suffolk and he resides in Sag Harbor. At Mary's request, Roswell Gardiner takes the whaleboat across the bay to Sag Harbor, picks up Dr. Sage, and brings him back to Oyster Pond. He is "a shrewd, observant, intelligent man, who had formerly represented the district in which he lived in Congress."[18]   He is too shrewd and observant to satisfy Deacon Pratt, who fears he will learn Daggett's secret, but since there is no other physician in the area, there is no choice. Dr. Sage examines the patient, announces his end is near and that nothing can be done for him. He also manages to pry the patient's name out of the old Deacon and — much to that gentleman's disgust — promptly sends a message to Daggett's relatives in the Vineyard. Dr. Sage's part in the novel is a small one, but it is pivotal, since it is that message that alerts the Daggetts and eventually results in their outfitting *Sea Lion II* to compete with the Deacon's schooner.

This Dr. Sage is no fictitious character. For some reason not now clear, Cooper chose to transfer this man, complete with name, from real life into his novel.[19]   According to historical records, Ebenezer Sage was born in Chatham, Connecticut, in 1755. He attended Yale College and became a physician. In 1784 he settled in East Hampton. From 1809-1817, he was a member of Congress representing Suffolk County, and in 1821 he was a delegate to the Convention for amending the Constitution of the State of New York. He was married to Ruth Smith, a daughter of Dr. William Smith of Southampton and a descendent of Richard Smith who had settled in Smithtown in 1663. By this marriage, Dr. Sage became related to the "Bull Smiths," one of the oldest families on Long Island. His son, John, was born in East Hampton in 1789, the same year in which Cooper was born.[20]

Now, from 1801 to 1834 (with interruptions for his political activities), Dr. Sage practiced medicine in Sag Harbor. Since his two terms in Congress had ended in 1817 and he was not elected delegate to the Convention until 1821, he must have been in residence in Sag Harbor during 1819 and 1820. This places him accurately for his role in *The Sea Lions* and also places him in Sag Harbor in exactly those years when Cooper himself sojourned there. Dr. Sage (or the Honorable Ebenezer Sage — he was known by both titles) built a house, which is still standing, at the rear of the Masonic Hall in Sag Harbor. Here he often acted as host to the brothers Sylvester and Henry Dering, to Thomas Dering of Shelter Island, to Ezra L'Hommedieu, and to the Reverend Lyman Beecher.[21]   Sag Harbor at this time had fewer than two thousand inhabitants and the names listed above formed a large

part of the "elite" of the area. Since Cooper's wife was related
—to the Derings and since Cooper himself was in partnership with
a Dering, it seems highly probable that Cooper knew, perhaps
quite well, Dr. Sage. He may have known even better the son,
Dr. John Sage, who was exactly his age and may have shared
many of his interests.

From this point on, one is necessarily dealing with theory. The
simplest theory is that Cooper, needing a doctor in the story he
was writing, plucked Dr. Sage out of thirty-year-old memory and
inserted him into the novel. A second theory, more gratifying and
almost as probable, is that Cooper, remembering the medical and
political figure that he had once admired, chose deliberately to
immortalize him in this small but important role. One strong
reason for preferring the second theory is that Cooper deliberately
retained the correct name of the physician, contrary to his usual
literary custom.

Dr. Sage died in 1834 and was buried in Oakland Cemetery,
Sag Harbor. A citizen of the town later declared: "He was a
man of elevated character and utterly above the craft and chi-
canery which too often characterized politicians." [22]

Another character, Long Tom Coffin in *The Pilot*, is less easily
explained. There can be no question that Long Tom is a member, figuratively at least, of the famous Coffin whalers of Nantucket, New Bedford, and Sag Harbor. But was he an actual
Coffin, or did Cooper merely associate the famous name with
another man's portrait? Samuel Adams Drake, as long ago as
1875, thought he had settled the problem by identifying Reuben
Chase, the Nantucket-born midshipman of the *Bon Homme
Richard,* as the model for Coffin; W.B. Shubrick Clymer, in a
biography of the author, suggested Mr. Irish, the first mate of
the *Sterling,* as a prototype; the French student Marcel Clavel
believed that Philadelphia Bill of the *Sterling* was a more likely
candidate; and in his doctoral dissertation, John H. Clagett—
attempting to solve three mysteries at one time—proposed Stephen
Stimpson, another member of the crew of the *Sterling,* as a
source for Coffin, Moses Marble (in *Afloat and Ashore*) and
Stephen Stimson (in *The Sea Lions*).[23] Meanwhile, two Long

Islanders, H.P. Hedges and Anna Mulford, both long-time residents of Sag Harbor, were equally sure that the original of Long
Tom Coffin was Captain Jonathan Osborne of Wainscott. Captain
Osborne, it will be remembered, had been chosen by Cooper to
command the *Union* during the three years he was part-owner.
Osborne was "one of the most noted of the whaling captains
that sailed then from Sag Harbor." He was also an expert with
the harpoon and had over 150 whales to his credit.[24]   Unfortunately, this is about all we do know of him. It is a pretty
theory, but like all the other theories about Long Tom's origin,
it lacks sure substantiation and must remain a theory.

Roswell Gardiner, the young master of the schooner in *The
Sea Lions,* is quite clearly a Long Island character;[25] however,
it seems unnecessary to seek his prototype. He is probably an
amalgam of Cooper's knowledge and enjoyment of local history
and of his acquaintance with numerous young whalers in Sag
Harbor. There is nothing remarkable about young Roswell: he
is young, good-looking, a bit of a free-thinker, and a competent
man at the helm. Cooper describes him as being an expert at
whaling and sealing and adds that Gardiner accepted Pratt's
offer only because he was at the time without a berth—"Had
it only been a year or two later, when speculation took hold of
the whaling business in a larger way, he would not have had
the least difficulty in obtaining a ship." The one distinguished
fact about this seaman is his name. He is the descendent, though
not in the direct line, of Lion Gardiner:

> That engineer who had been sent to the settlement of
> the lords Saye and Seal, and Brook, since called
> Saybrook, near two centuries before, to lay out a town
> and a fort. This Lyon Gardiner had purchased of the
> Indians the island in that neighborhood, which still
> bears his name. This establishment on the island was
> made in 1639.[26]

In 1819, the island was still in the possession of the Gardiner
family, though the deed had passed through nine pairs of hands.
This fact in itself must have pleased Cooper, who placed high

value on family lineage and family holdings. The Roswell Gardiner of the novel is a member of a "branch" rather than of the "tree proper," and is not on familiar terms with the lord of the manor. A modest man, he comments:

> There never was any LORD Gardiner among us...
> though it was a fashion among the east-enders to give
> that title to the owner of the island. My ancestor who
> first got the place was Lyon Gardiner, an engineer in
> the service of the colony of Connecticut.[27]

If one looks for a prototype of this seaman, one need turn no further than to his creator. The young Roswell Gardiner and the young James Fenimore Cooper shared many things: both were proud of family ancestry and the family manor; both were young rebels who found the call of the sea irresistible; both were free-thinkers with respect to organized religions, but both believed firmly in the existence of a Supreme Deity. After their three-year adventure in Sag Harbor, Susan Cooper, distrusting her husband while he was within sight and smell of salt water, encouraged the movement of the small family to the Cooperstown estate in upper New York.[28] In this inland area, with the only water safe Otsego Lake, she hoped her husband would forget his first love and settle down. In *The Sea Lions,* Mary (who had become Gardiner's wife after his return from the Antarctic) urges her husband to leave Oyster Pond to move to a town in western New York. The author says, knowingly:

> Mary had an important agency in bringing about his
> migration. She had seen certain longings after the
> ocean, and seals, and whales, in her husband; and did
> not consider him safe, as long as he could scent the
> odours of a salt marsh. There is a delight in this
> fragrance that none can appreciate as thoroughly as
> those who have enjoyed it in youth; it remains as long
> as human senses retain their faculties.[29]

Surely there is more than coincidence operating here. When

Cooper wrote *The Sea Lions* in 1849, he was returning nostalgically to his Sag Harbor days of thirty years before, and he must have been returning, too, to his own youth. In Roswell Gardiner, he depicted much of himself: his vitality, his eagerness, his love for adventure, and his dreams.

If this is coincidence, then there is a third coincidence in *Miles Wallingford,* in which the young hero (also proud of his ancestry, attracted by the sea, rebellious against academic work and convention) signs on board a ship, and later returns home to marry his sweet Lucy. After their marriage she immediately takes him off to Clawbonny, his family estate, which is safely inland and hence far from temptation.[30]

A third character with possible roots on Long Island is Natty Bumppo. The proposed candidate this time is Captain David Hand of Sag Harbor. Hand was quite a man even in his unconventional era. During the Revolutionary War, he was a seaman in privateers and vessels of the navy. By the time he was twenty years of age, he "had seen Washington, been a prisoner of war five times, and was one of the exchanged prisoners from the Jersey prison ship."[31] He had five wives, and survived them all. He was a friend of Henry Packer Dering, who in turn was a friend of Dr. Ebenezer Sage, so it is quite probable that Cooper knew Hand. One day Dering took Captain Hand and another friend, David Gelston, to Gardiner's Island for some deer-hunting. Hand, who was normally a pretty good shot with a rifle, either lost control of his weapon or else mistook his friend for a deer. At any rate, he shot David Gelston, wounding him fatally.[32] If he *is* the prototype for Natty Bumppo, this anecdote should be quickly forgotten!

Captain David Hand died in 1840, at the age of 81. He was buried in Oakland Cemetery, Sag Harbor. The epitaph on his gravestone, inscribed at his direction, reads:

Behold ye living mortals
passing by

> How thick the partners of
> one husband lie.[33]

Shortly after *The Pioneers* was published in 1823, natives of
Sag Harbor found no difficulty in recognizing Captain David
Hand in the character of Natty Bumppo.[34]   The description of
the personal appearance and peculiar laugh of Natty Bumppo
was the basis of their identification. Here, in Cooper's own
words, is a description of Natty (alias David Hand) Bumppo:

> His face was skinny and thin almost to emaciation;
> but yet it bore no signs of disease; — on the contrary,
> it had every indication of the most robust and enduring
> health. The cold and the exposure had, together, given
> it a color of uniform red. His gray eyes were glancing
> under a pair of shaggy brows, that overhung them in
> long hairs of gray mingled with their natural hue; his
> scraggy neck was bare, and burnt to the same tint
> with his face . . . [35]

And of his laugh:

> . . . here Natty stretched out his long neck and straight-
> ened his body as he opened his mouth, which exposed
> a single tusk of yellow bone, while his eyes, his face,
> even his whole frame seemed to laugh, although no
> sound was emitted except a kind of thick hissing, as
> he inhaled his breath in quavers.[36]

The evidence, after careful reading, seems slim. Certainly the
description of Natty's appearance could fit hundreds of old men
who have led eventful, outdoor lives. The description of Natty's
laugh, however, deserves further consideration. The carefully
listed details — a single tusk of yellow bone, the thick hissing,
above all, the silent laugh — are individual and not common.
Since Cooper considered them important enough to repeat many
times throughout *The Pioneers,* and since the same characteristics
are applicable to David Hand as attested to by Sag Harborites
who knew him, there seems a strong possibility that Cooper

had known Hand, had remembered him, and had incorporated some of his features into those of his favorite character.

In the interest of scholarly truth and sanity, it should be noted that Cooper, in his 1850 preface to *The Deerslayer,* discussed this point:

> The author has often been asked if he had any original in his mind, for the character of Leather-Stocking. In a physical sense, different individuals known to the writer in early life, certainly presented themselves as models, through his recollections: but in a moral sense this man of the forest is purely a creation. [37]

There is much good sense in that paragraph, and many of the truths stated therein are applicable to the characters developed by any writer. Certainly Natty Bumppo is *not* David Hand: Natty had no wife, Hand had five; Natty was no seaman, David was; Natty fought only briefly in the Revolution in the van of Mad Anthony's army, Hand was involved in the fighting for years; Natty knew his way through a forest, Hand would probably have gotten lost. They did share some characteristics: both were individualists who cared little for what other people thought; both were handy with a rifle (though Natty appeared to be a better shot); both were garrulous; both shared certain physical features and a now-famous silent laugh. On this evidence, the case rests.

That many minor characters in other Cooper novels rely to some extent on people he knew on Long Island cannot and need not be denied. In *The Wing-and-Wing,* Captain Cuffe of the British frigate, the *Proserpine,* speaks with admiration of Ralph Willet Miller, the officer who commanded the ship to which Nelson shifted his pennant, at the battle of Cape St. Vincent. In a footnote, Cooper adds that Miller was an American whose relatives still resided in New York; that he got the name *Willet* from the first English mayor, a gentleman from whom are descended many of the old families on Long Island. [38] In *The Water-Witch,* Tom Tiller, "the Skimmer of the Seas," is described as a native of Long Island who has spent most of his life on his own privateer, flaunting cheerful challenges at the British Royal Navy. Characters like Deacon Pratt in *The Sea Lions*, Captain Spike in *Jack Tier*, Lt. Barnstable in *The Pilot*, and Moses Marble in *Miles Wallingford* all may owe some of their features, some of their habits, to Long Island forebears. But how much? And to what degree? The answers to these questions are shrouded in uncertainty, as they must be; for all writers have built-in melting furnaces where the people they meet are dissolved, mixed with others, and re-created into the characters that appear in their novels.

* * * * *

The History of the Area

The Spy, published in 1821, was influenced by Cooper's knowledge of the whaling industry in Sag Harbor; and this knowledge was the rather direct result of Cooper's friendship with his wife's relatives on Long Island. These same relatives influenced Cooper in the writing of this novel in still another way: in their political allegiances and family legends. Mrs. Cooper, it will be remembered, was a De Lancey, and the De Lanceys — almost to a man — were Loyalists during the Revolution. So were many of their friends, the Nicolls, the Floyds, and the Townsends.

One De Lancey headed the brigade originally planned for the defense of Long Island. In the 1778 invasion of the North Shore by New England men, most of these Loyalist troops were withdrawn — even DeLancey's.   This withdrawal meant that the Loyalists on the Island were temporarily undefended, and easy targets of rebel attack and plunder. William Nicoll was twice plundered, Colonel Richard Floyd, three times, and Colonel Benjamin Floyd, twice. Of the Townsends, Richard Townsend was robbed, taken prisoner, and carried to New England, while John Townsend of Oyster Bay had his house almost destroyed.[40] Elizabeth Floyd (later Cooper's mother-in-law) remembered the night she and her friend, Charlotte De Lancey, were abruptly aroused by rebel raiders. They were thrown out of their house, their possessions taken, and the building fired. One rebel tried to throw a burning curtain over Elizabeth, but the two young girls managed to escape safely into the night.[41]

These were just a few of the family legends that Cooper must have heard during his long visits with his wife's relatives. They certainly must have influenced his general attitude in *The Spy,* a novel which combines a clearly patriotic tone with a tolerant understanding of the problems of the Loyalists. The Englishmen (like Colonel Wellmere) are dull-witted, coarse-mannered, and unworthy of trust. The Colonials are rough but courageous; they lack refinement but they are thoroughly honest. The Loyalists are — at least, outwardly — the most admirable. They are gentlemen, with exquisite manners, a nice sense of hospitality, and high honor. Unfortunately, they are also a bit thick politically; they have placed their honor and allegiance in the shaky hands of George III. Cooper's portraits of these Loyalists are among his most sensitive character studies. The confusion resulting from this combination of rebel fervor and aristocratic sympathy formed the political views of the author and permeated his political and social novels.

In *The Spy,* for example, the rebel Harvey Birch is depicted admiringly; he is brave, skillful, and honest, but he is also rough and sometimes coarse. The Virginian rebel Lawton is courageous and honorable, but these qualities are somewhat marred by an impulsive cruelty and intolerance. Of the rebels, only the stranger Harper (really George Washington himself) is always courteous and always the gentleman. The leading representative of the English soldier is Colonel Wellmere. He too is brave with good manners, except in time of stress. He is, however, a liar, even to his friends, and he offers himself in marriage to Sarah, knowing full well that he has a wife back in England. In battle he is obtuse, favoring the closed marching unit of the European battle-line, and unable to adapt to the hit-and-run maneuvers of the colonists. This inability to adapt leads to the sacrifice of his men, his own capture, and defeats where there should have been victories. The other British military men follow this pattern.

The quality that Cooper most seems to dislike in them is their condescension toward, and contempt of, native Americans.

The Loyalists, including the Whartons, are depicted with sympathy. Mr. Wharton, an old weak-minded man, is gentle and kind; he opens his house to all in trouble and is always a gentleman. He loves the Mother Country and cannot disown her, but he loves, too, the land that has been his home for so many years. His son, Henry Wharton, is the finest soldier in the novel. He understands military tactics and tries to persuade the British Colonel to adapt to the rebel methods; but when his advice is refused, when the suggestion is made that he is a coward, he manfully keeps silent, takes his place in line, and takes part in a forward thrust that he knows is foolish and doomed to failure. He is gentle toward women and mindful of former friends now in the American Army. When he is captured and accused of espionage, he stoutly maintains his innocence but faces almost inevitable death with courage and honor. Cooper, one suspects, was half-Birch and half-Wharton. Birch was his adventurous side, impulsive, rebellious, and reckless, exemplified in his own life by his running away to join the Navy, by his plunge into the whaling industry, by his blunt criticism of the corruption and "false face" of European society and mores. Wharton was his aristocratic side — proud of his own and his wife's family — exemplified by his impatience with the "lower-class" who considered themselves "equals" and by his discontent with the superficiality of American society.

Just as Cooper's political attitude in *The Spy* can be traced to his own background and that of his wife, so the action and specific incidents in this story can be traced to one of Long Island's proudest achievements: the birth of the Secret Service. Cooper was thoroughly familiar with this story; he had heard it from Governor John Jay years before,[42] and he must have heard parts of it — more emotionally remembered — during his visits to the Floyds, his mother-in-law's family, who had been connected with the Long Island spy ring. The story of these early espionage agents is a fascinating one, the details of which were kept secret over 150 years until 1939 when Morton Pennypacker successfully

identified all of the agents and was able to trace their procedural
methods.

In 1778, when Washington's troops were quartered in Westchester and along the northern shore of Long Island Sound, he
needed help badly. He was cut off from New York City and
therefore from all information about British maneuvers and
projected plans. He tried first the simple, traditional method.
He asked one of his officers to find a volunteer who would go
into enemy territory to seek information. The volunteer was
Nathan Hale, and his story is known throughout this country.
Nathan Hale was not only executed; the information that he had
bought so dearly was never transmitted, so that his death truly
was in vain. This tragic incident made Washington and other
American officers aware of a real lack in American strategy: they
needed spies, men who could move about freely and relay essen-
tial data to headquarters. Sometime in 1778 (the exact date is
unknown), the Secret Service came into existence.[43] The procedural method used was almost absurdly simple. Austin Roe, a
native of Setauket, rode on horseback the fifty-five miles from
his home to New York City. Here he dropped casually into a
coffee shop frequented by Robert Townsend. Townsend, a relative
of the De Lanceys, used the code name "Culper, Jr." and —
although he was a staunch patriot — remained in loyalist New
York City from the beginning of the war until after its close.
At the coffee shop, Roe waited until Townsend saw him. Then
Townsend would leave the shop, returning to his rooms. Later,
Roe would join him there. In the quiet room, Roe turned over
to Townsend letters from Benjamin Tallmadge, code name "John
Bolton." These letters, which often contained specific requests
from General Washington, were in cipher and/or invisible ink.
While Townsend was answering the letters, using the same type
of ink, Roe would dash off to Rivington's, the printer for the
Crown, and purchase half a ream of paper. Townsend's letter
was then copied on the sixty-third sheet or the seventy-fifth
sheet, in accordance with previous instructions. Roe, carrying his
half ream of paper and other more innocuous packages, set off
on his return trip to Setauket. His first stop in Setauket, quite

naturally, was at the pasture where his cows were feeding. This field "happened" to be owned by Abraham Woodhull, another patriot. Roe deposited his precious package in a box hidden in this field, then drove his cows home. After dark, Woodhull transferred the contents of the box to a bag. Woodhull, whose code name was "Culper, Sr.," usually added additional messages at this time.

The next link in this espionage chain was Caleb Brewster, an expert with a whaleboat. There were six possible landing places at Strong's Neck, and Brewster would anchor in one of them. Nancy Strong, wife of Judge Selah Strong, cooperated by using her washing as a signal to Woodhull. A black petticoat signified that Brewster's boat had arrived; the number of handkerchiefs on the line indicated the landing place. Woodhull, noticing the signal, then sent the messages to Brewster at the indicated landing place, and Brewster ferried them across the Sound to the Connecticut shore to Tallmadge. Tallmadge took them to the nearest dragoon (Washington had three dragoons stationed every fifteen miles along the coast just for this purpose) who then rushed the messages to Washington at his headquarters. The scheme today seems amateurish and clumsy, but it worked remarkably well for several years.[44]

One reason for the success of this scheme was the "security-conscious" agents, who permitted their identity to be known only to personally-chosen friends and relatives. Almost all of the agents were from Long Island, and almost all were related. One question that bothered students for years was how the agents met in Townsend's room without arousing suspicion. Pennypacker, by zealous study of genealogies, came up with the answer. First, Townsend moved every year or so. Each time, he chose carefully. One year he rented a room in the house of Amos Underhill, a name *not* known in these circles. Investigation proved, however, that Underhill was married to Mary Woodhull, sister of Abraham Woodhull. Nothing would be easier than for Abraham Woodhull or his friend, Austin Roe, to visit Mary while in town. These visits generally "happened" just after Townsend had returned to his rented room; but it would take many such "coincidences" to arouse the suspicions of neighbors. Before such suspicions were likely to occur, Townsend was off to another rented room in the house of another safe "relative." [45]

Cooper did not use in its entirety this story of the Long Island spy ring, but he did select characters and incidents from it for use in his novel, *The Spy*. Harvey Birch has no single prototype; he is part Austin Roe, part Robert Townsend, part Abraham Woodhull, mingled with some Cooper and some pure fiction. Like Austin Roe, Birch was a countryman whose main interests apparently lay in his cattle and commerce. Roe, in New York City, would purchase necessaries for his neighbors in Setauket; Birch, with his sack over his shoulder, also peddled necessaries and small luxuries to friend and foe alike. Each used the peddling as a cover-up for his real espionage activities. Like Townsend, Birch succeeded in keeping his true political beliefs a secret. Many of the Townsends were ardent Loyalists. When Robert Townsend settled down in British-held New York City, and connected himself with Rivington, the King's printer, all concerned took for granted his Loyalist sympathies. In the novel, Harvey and his father took every opportunity to let their neighbors suspect their assumed loyalty to the British Crown. Both the fictitious Birch and the real Townsend used this apparent British sympathy as a shield for undercover work.

In April, 1779, Woodhull's home in Setauket was ransacked, and his aged father was assaulted by Colonel Simcoe and his Rangers. Simcoe and his corps of American royalists, known as the Queen's Rangers, were stationed at the fort south of Oyster Bay.[46] The assault on Mr. Woodhull and on the Woodhull home was evidently the result of rumors and suspicions pertaining to Woodhull's political activities.

It is interesting — remembering Cooper's emotional involvement — to see how he uses this story. In the novel, the house of Birch had frequently been watched with suspicion by the Americans, who hoped to catch Birch, or — at least — find evidence to prove their suspicions true. During this period, "the father of Harvey had been greatly molested, in consequence of the suspicious character of the son." But even minute scrutiny brought forth

no fact that condemned the old man, and — Cooper adds cynically — "his property was too small to keep alive the zeal of
patriots by profession."[47] Later, Harvey's father becomes ill, and
Harvey, risking his life, returns to be with his dying parent. This
time the Skinners have been watching. They suspect him of having gold gained in his peddling, and they have heard of the
reward offered by the Continental Army for his capture. They
rob him of his money and valuables, then refuse to let him return
to his father's room. Suddenly the dying man appears in the
doorway: "Around his body was thrown the sheet of the bed,
and his fixed eye and haggard face gave him the appearance of
a being from another world."[48] The Skinners, fearing it is the
spirit of the elder Birch, flee from the house, and Harvey carries
his father back to his death-bed. But the Skinners have not
finished; a few minutes calm their fear. Their leader blames
them for the panic: "From your fright, I thought a party of
De Lancey's men were upon us."[49] A day or two later, after
the father's funeral, the Skinners return, capture Birch, and set
fire to the house.

How Cooper used factual material in his fiction is here evident.
He retained much of the story of the attack on the Woodhull
home in Setauket, but he made the attackers Skinners rather
than Loyalists. The Skinners, renegade rebels who plundered and
killed under the cloak of patriotism, were the kind of unprinci-
pled men whom Cooper most detested. The figure of the dying
man in shrouds seems to be totally fictitious; its melodramatic
entrance and its arousal of superstition in the minds of the
uneducated are common elements in a Cooper novel.

Whenever Colonel Simcoe was involved in his frequent forays
on Long Island, he used as his headquarters the Townsend
homestead, Raynham Hall in Oyster Bay. Not only was it large
and comfortable, but one of its inhabitants was the lovely Sarah
Townsend, beautiful, friendly, and unwed. Simcoe courted her
diligently and at least once sent her "a Valentine and other
tokens of esteem."[50] Sarah, apparently Loyalist in her sympathies, was actually an assistant to Robert Townsend, her
brother, in his espionage activities. She accepted the Valentine

and "tokens of esteem" diplomatically, but did not return his love. Cooper used this incident briefly in the closing chapter of his novel when young Mason tells young Wharton Dunwoodie (the second generation, now involved in the War of 1812) that "Colonel Singleton offers himself to her (Aunt Sarah) every Valentine's Day..."[51]

It was the same Sarah who listened to a whispered conversation in Colonel Simcoe's room one night between the Colonel and Major John Andre. Earlier in the day, Sarah had watched Major Andre take from a seldom-used kitchen cupboard a letter addressed to James Anderson. It had been left there by a supposed Whig. Sarah might have overlooked this incident, but when Andre gave as his excuse for entering the kitchen that he had taken a dish of doughnuts still hot from the fire and hidden them, she grew suspicious. Now, eavesdropping, she heard them mention "West Point" several times. She scribbled a note and sent it to her brother Robert in New York. He sent it out to Setauket the next morning and soon Tallmadge had the puzzling message. It was this note in conjunction with a letter from General Arnold requesting an escort for James Anderson to West Point that aroused Tallmadge's suspicions and led to the capture of Andre.[52]

Cooper was fascinated by spy stories, and in his novel he compared the two executions: that of John Andre and that of Nathan Hale. The incident that triggers the comparison is the trial scene in which Henry Wharton is tried by an American military court as a British spy. He is convicted and sentenced to die within twenty-four hours. There is some criticism of the short stay of execution, and one officer replies heatedly: "The royal officers gave Hale but an hour...we have granted the usual time." In a footnote, Cooper describes Hale's capture and execution. Then he adds bitterly:

> Andre was executed amid the tears of his enemies; Hale died unpitied, and with reproaches in his ears; and yet one was the victim of ambition, and the other of devotion to his country. Posterity will do justice between them.[53]

A further parallel occurs in the closing pages of the novel. Washington, seeing Harvey Birch for the last time, dismisses him with his thanks:

> You have I trusted more than all; I early saw in you a regard to truth and principle, that, I am pleased to say, has never deceived me ... I believe you are one of the very few that I have employed who have acted faithfully to our cause ... To me, and to me only of all the world, you seem to have acted with a strong attachment to the liberties of America.[54]

In real life, Washington expressed similar high praise of Robert Townsend ("Culper, Jr.") and Abraham Woodhull ("Culper, Sr."): "Of the Culpers' fidelity and ability I entertain the highest opinion." Of Townsend especially, he had still more to say. On February 5, 1780, he wrote of "Culper, Jr.": "His accounts are intelligent, clear, and satisfactory ... " And in a letter to Congress, he wrote: "He is the person in whom I have the greatest confidence." [55]

Certainly, both the contents and the phrasing of these sentences of praise indicate that one influenced the other.

It will be remembered, in his closing words to Birch, that Washington acknowledged that while all the world considered Birch a traitor, he only knew him to be the finest patriot. The fact that Birch keeps his true achievements secret until his death has disturbed more than one critic, and has brought down upon Cooper the charge of forced contrivance and artificiality in the construction of his plots. Yet the same long secrecy existed with relation to several members of the Long Island spy ring. Whereas Tallmadge made his identity as John Bolton known shortly after the war's end, Robert Townsend steadfastly refused to admit the truth and to reap the fame and congratulations that surely would have followed. He even forfeited compensation for those years because he would not submit an itemized bill of expenses to Congress, knowing that such a bill would necessarily divulge his identity.[56] Here, too, the reason for this apparently unnecessary secrecy is unknown, and probably will remain forever unknown, but it provides a situation in real life that substantiates Cooper's "contrived plot."

A few other minor parallels exist. Austin Roe was able to make the swift journey of fifty-five miles from Setauket to New York City by the help of relay horses arranged for at strategic points. The arrangement was made with the full knowledge and approval of the British officers stationed on Long Island.[57] They evidently trusted Roe and considered him a Loyalist. In the novel, Harvey Birch is able to get information from behind the enemy lines because the British officers trust him and furnish him with passes. He too is considered a Loyalist.

In his introduction to *The Spy,* Cooper narrates part of the tale told to him by Governor Jay, whom he calls "Mr. _____." According to this story, the espionage agent was several times arrested by the local authorities and, in one case, actually condemned to the gallows. Intercession by "private orders" from a high and secret authority "alone saved him from an ignominious death."[58] This event naturally increased the trust felt in the agent by the British. This particular incident may relate to Abraham Woodhull who was looked upon with suspicion and who barely escaped arrest several times, although his threat came from the British troops. It may also relate, more probably, to James Townsend, Robert's cousin, who was sometimes employed by the ring to send on urgent messages. This James Townsend one day stopped at a house in Deansonbury. Finding there two young girls who pretended to be Tories, he became frightened, and to protect himself, convinced them he was a Tory, too. He was so convincing that their elder brother, who had overheard the whole conversation, "flew into the room and took him prisoner." He was taken to a camp, and the contents of his pockets—primarily a poem of twenty lines called "The Lady's Dress"—were forwarded to headquarters. Fortunately for Townsend, Washington himself saw these papers, discovered the poem was actually a "stain letter," and realized that the young man was in the employ of the espionage ring. The situation was highly embarrassing, but James was at last "allowed to escape" without arousing British suspicion.[59] From that time on, his value to the group was considerably enhanced since the arrest had a desirable effect on the British soldiers: it increased their trust in his loyalty to themselves. Cooper uses this also in *The Spy*. Before the story even opens, Birch had been arrested several times by the Continentals. The first time he had escaped easily, but the second time he was condemned to die. "On the morning of his intended execution, the cage was opened, but the bird had flown." [60] These first two arrests and escapes contribute to Birch's reputation among the British. Cooper, as usual, is not content to use fact only. He has Birch arrested twice more, each time escaping. He has him harassed and pursued by both the Continental Army and by the Skinners. He uses Washington's intercession, too, but uses it far more dramatically than it actually occurred. In the novel, Washington (disguised as Harper) intercedes not for Birch, but for the Loyalist, Henry Wharton, misjudged as a spy; and the intercession is not by private order, but by the use of his agent and even by his own physical intervention.

Any one of these incidents described could be attributed to mere coincidence, but when there are so many "coincidences," so many parallels, is it not logical—even necessary—to infer a direct influence of fact on fiction? When these parallels are added to our certain knowledge of Cooper's familiarity with the story of the espionage ring, it becomes evident that this long-secret chapter of Long Island history was the major force operative in the planning and writing of his second novel, *The Spy*.

Indeed, one cannot escape from the conclusion that Cooper's writing career was stimulated and sustained by his friendship with his wife's relatives in Sag Harbor and other Long Island towns. There he did his first writing; there he first became acquainted with the whaling industry which was to influence so strongly his later sea novels; and there he learned of a piece of American history that he could have acquired nowhere else at that time and that led him to the writing of *The Spy*, the first novel in America to be concerned solely with Americans and with American affairs—the novel that was to set the pattern for the development of the American novel for the next fifty years.

IV

Cooper and Bryant

When Cooper was writing *The Pathfinder* in 1840, he began chapter three with this stanza from Bryant:

> Before these fields were shorn and tilled,
> Full to the brim our rivers flowed;
> The melody of waters filled
> The fresh and boundless wood;
> And torrents dashed, and rivulets played,
> And fountains spouted in the shade.[1]

Two pages later, Cooper called the beauties of Lake Oswego and its environs "as visible to the eye as the pen of Bryant has elsewhere vividly presented them to the imagination."[2]

This was no casual compliment from one writer to his contemporary; rather, it was an admiration granted by a master of prose to a master of poetry and, at the same time, a recognition of a friendship that had already lasted sixteen years and that was to continue until the death of Cooper in 1851.

The two men met for the first time in 1824; the occasion was a meeting of the informal literary club established by Cooper just a short time before.[3] Eventually it would develop into the Bread and Cheese Club, but in 1824, both it and its members were young and relatively unknown. Cooper was thirty-five years old; Bryant was thirty. Three years earlier, each man had taken a long first step toward success: Cooper with *The Spy*, and Bryant with his first published volume of poems.

Now, in 1824, the two young writers looked at each other, liked each other, and began what was to be a life-long friendship. There would be moments of doubt before the friendship solidified. Cooper must have felt that the youth from Massachusetts was rather self-contained and austere; certainly Bryant was startled, even shocked, by the brash assertions of the novelist. Shortly after the club meeting, both men met again at the home of Robert Sedgwick at a dinner party. Bryant, at the end of a rather dizzy evening, reported drily: "Mr. Cooper engrossed the whole conversation, and seems a little giddy with the great success his works have met with."[4]

In the twenty-seven years that followed, the two men achieved a fast friendship. It was a friendship based on respect and admiration rather than on affection. They met often in New York City for long walks; they attended meetings of literary groups; but there is no indication that either one ever visited the home of the other. Cooper, who disliked all other editors, found this one editor worthy of his homage; and Bryant as editor of the *Evening Post*, whenever possible, saw that Cooper's novels received good reviews and that his legal cases were fairly reported.[5]

In 1851, James Fenimore Cooper died. Bryant, the leading literary light of his time, was asked to deliver a commemorative address. He did so on the night of February 25, 1852, at Metropolitan Hall, New York.[6] He gave a brief summary of the biography of his friend, discussed the chief novels, and predicted for them an enduring place in American fiction. His judgment of Cooper's style is as perceptive as one can find anywhere:

> He is long in getting at the interest of his narrative. The progress of the plot, at first, is like that of one of his own vessels of war, slowly, heavily, and even awkwardly working out of a harbor. We are impatient and weary, but when the vessel is once in the open sea, and feels the free breath of heaven in her full

sheets, our delight and admiration are all the greater
at the grace, the majesty, and power with which she
divides and bears down the waves, and pursues her
course at will over the great waste of waters.[7]

It is interesting that—in seeking a metaphor to aid him in
describing Cooper's style—Bryant chose the sea. Both Cooper
and Bryant had been born and had grown up in inland regions,
but, in adult life, both promptly surrendered to the smell of
salt water and the lure of heaving billows. Their oceans were
different, of course: Cooper's, on the south shore of Long Island,
was wide open and alive with the excitement of tall-masted
ships; Bryant's, off the north shore, was generally serene, its
waters rippled only by ducks and swooping sea-gulls.

PART TWO
William Cullen Bryant

V

Bryant at Cedarmere

On February 5, 1843, William Cullen Bryant sent a letter to his brother John. "Congratulate me!" he wrote. "There is a probability of my becoming a landholder in New York! I have made a bargain for about forty acres of solid earth at Hempstead Harbor, on the north side of Long Island."[1]

Before the year was over, Bryant owned the forty acres and a house; within another year or so, he had extended his holdings to include two hundred acres, the main house, a farmhouse, several cottages, some ponds, and a mill.[2]

Bryant's move to Hempstead Harbor (now Roslyn) was one that might easily have been predicted. Born in Cummington, Massachusetts, in 1794, Bryant grew up among hills and wide meadows, trees, flowers, and birds. Later, while practicing law, he spent almost ten years in Great Barrington, Massachusetts, and again he was surrounded by open land and rural landscapes. Neither law nor country living could erase his literary propensities, however, and in 1825, when opportunity beckoned, he packed up his family and headed for New York City. He spent twenty years in the City, loving its activities, its cultural advantages, and its progress, and hating its crowds, dust, and summer heat.

In 1843, Bryant was forty-nine years old. He was a successful poet and a successful editor. His financial condition was good, and his literary prestige adequate to guarantee at least a reasonable degree of security. It could have surprised no one (and least of all, his gentle wife) when, in 1843, he again packed up his family and led them east to Hempstead Harbor. This time, he kept his city house on West 14th Street, planning to use his new Long Island home only during the spring and summer months.

Hempstead Harbor, in 1843, was a small town about forty miles east of New York City. Its total population was about two hundred. Here it was that Bryant found forty acres of land with a wide frontage on Long Island Sound, with arable land, a couple of fresh-water ponds, and a great many hills that must have reminded him of his childhood days in Cummington. The homestead on the land pleased him, too. It was a large colonial house built in 1787 by Richard Kirk, a Quaker. Later it was owned by the Mudges and then by the Moultons, from whom Bryant purchased it. The fact that Joseph W. Moulton had lived there for ten years must have been satisfying to Bryant's strong sense of history, for Moulton already had a reputation as a New York State historian and as a lawyer.[3] For years he had been connected in law with Henry Clay and Daniel Webster, and these two statesmen had frequently been house guests in Hempstead Harbor.[4] The old house must have witnessed heated debates on abolition and excited planning of party maneuvers. Now, in 1843, it was to change from a political to a literary arena.

It was—and still is—a beautiful house. Situated on a high hill, the house looks down on one side on Long Island Sound, and on the other, on two small fresh-water lakes. The approach, through a gate and up a winding road, leads to a spacious house of three stories. (It was originally two stories, but Bryant added a third.) A broad veranda sweeps around three sides of the house, and the tall classic columns are covered with trailing vine. Through the front door, one enters a large hall. To the right is a dining room; to the left, a parlor.

The parlor, in Bryant's time, was a spacious room with a commanding fireplace at one end; above the mantel was a huge photograph of Guido's "Aurora."[5] Here, too, were several of

Durand's paintings, including the portrait of Bryant, and the now-famous picture of Bryant and Cole looking across the Hudson.[6] Adjoining the parlor was the library where Bryant often worked. The bookshelves, made of wood of the tulip-tree, highly varnished, held the three to four thousand volumes that made up his personal library.[7] His study had two bay-windows, in one of which his desk was situated. Sitting here, he could look out upon a terraced lawn and a cluster of pear trees. The large fireplace was surrounded by blue and white Dutch tiles, each decorated with a painted picture from Scripture.[8]

It was a fairy tale kind of house that must have appealed to the poet in Bryant; but even more exciting were the grounds. Here the beauty must be attributed to Bryant, for it was his care and supervision that made the estate a showplace in his own day. He started out as a gentleman farmer, but before long, he was doing advanced experimentation with fruit-trees and shrubs, and importing seedlings from countries all over the earth. Before the front door of the mansion was a mass of rhododendrons, with great bowls of blossoms, and to the right and left were coppices of forsythia and weigelia and mahonia. Down by the lake were feathery ferns and red cattails, and edging one pond were pink and white dogwoods.[9] In Bryant's time there were all kinds of fruits: Clarke raspberries, and strawberries (McAvoy, Triomphe, and Alpine) and gooseberries (Mountain and Houghton); but not many blackberries. He did not have much luck with them. There were pear trees, rich with fruit and blossom, and a medlar tree and a few persimmons. There were peach trees, plum trees, and fig trees. There were paw-paws and apricots. And there were grapevines everywhere — Concord, Delaware, Rogers, Isabella and Catawba.[10]

There were other trees, too. For nuts — the pecan-nut tree, the Spanish chestnut, the black-walnut, and the hard-shelled almond. There were traditionals: the weeping willows, the dark, solid pines, the red maples, the silver beeches, and the cedars that gave their name to the estate. There were the evergreens and the magnolias, the locust tree and the giant tulip-tree. There were a Deodar cedar, and a yew, and even a coffee-tree.

But inanimate life did not reign without challenge. Beneath the branches of the trees, among the heavy shrubbery, scurried bob-tailed rabbits and red foxes and muskrats; snakes slithered along the ground; the ponds were alive with families of ducks and even of occasional swans.

This was Bryant's private domain. Soon he was spending almost six months of the year here. He probably deserves the title, "Long Island's first commuter," but of this we cannot be certain. First or not, he *was* a commuter: sometimes he took the stage coach to Mineola and then a train to New York;[11] sometimes he used the water route. Years later, Mr. Harold Godwin reminisced that near the Bryant home "stood a steamboat dock.... A paddle-wheel steamboat, the *Idlewild*, sailed daily from this pier for New York City, and upon it, Mr. Bryant...was accustomed to go to and from his study at Cedarmere and the editorial office of the *Evening Post,* then on Fulton Street."[12]

To Bryant, commuting was a necessity. Cedarmere belonged to him, his family, and his muse — it had nothing to do with the *Evening Post;* the *Evening Post,* on the other hand, was connected with money and politics and had nothing to do with Cedarmere. From 1843 until 1878, he did, in effect, live two lives; and these two lives were seldom permitted to mingle. After his death John Bigelow, an associate editor of the *Post*, related an anecdote which illustrates this deliberate division:

> When the semi-centennial anniversary of the *Evening Post* was approaching, I proposed to him to prepare for its columns a sketch of its career. He cheerfully accepted the task, and in order that he might be free from interruption, I recommended him to go down to his country-home at Roslyn and remain there until it was finished, and let me send him there such of the files of the paper as he might have occasion to consult. He rejected the proposal as abruptly as if I had asked him to offer sacrifices to Apollo. He would allow no such work to follow him there. Not even the shadow of his business must fall upon the consecrated haunts

of his muse. He rarely brought or sent anything from
the country for the *Evening Post;* but if he did, it was
easy to detect in the character of the fish that they
had been caught in strange waters.[13]

    After 1843, Cedarmere was indeed the home of Bryant's muse.
Here he composed at least forty-eight poems, more than a quarter
of the poems written during his entire life. But Cedarmere was
still more: it was his passport as a citizen to participation in the
public affairs of the town. One year after his move to Cedarmere,
he was already involved in meeting with the town fathers to
discuss and select a new name for the community. The name,
Hempstead Harbor, was no longer satisfactory; its similarity to
Hempstead and North Hempstead made mail deliveries uncertain
and inaccurate. The meeting was held at the home of Augustus
W. Leggett, who chaired the discussion. Also present were Bryant,
Parke Godwin (later his biographer), Edward W. Leggett, and
H.W. Eastman.[14]   They considered many names, including Mill
Town, Thompson, and Roslyn. No official secretary was present,
and reports of the meeting are garbled. Eliza Seaman Leggett, a
descendant of Augustus W., insists that Bryant proposed the
name Mill Town, but was forced to yield to her grandpa's
suggestion, Roslyn.[15]   Augustus's son, M.A. Leggett, writing
about the event more than a half century later, claims that he
was at the meeting and agrees that it was his father who proposed the name Roslyn because two Scotch gentlemen who had
been visiting with him had said: "Should the name ever be
changed it should be called Roslyn, because it is so much like
Roslyn Castle in Scotland."[16]   Professor David J. Hill, after
some study of the problem, declared that Bryant had suggested
the name Roslyn because when the British left Long Island,
they marched out of Hempstead to the tune of "Roslyn Castle."[17]   The whole issue is further complicated by a letter written
by Ebenezer Close on September 2, 1844, in which he states that
he had submitted a list of possible names to Mr. Bryant and
Mr. Leggett for consideration, and that the name, Roslyn, was
"unanimously approved by all who were present."[18]   This letter

at least suggests that Bryant was one of the leaders of this
movement, and that he already had a reputation of a sort in the
town by 1844.

This was the initiation of the Bryant family into the affairs of
Roslyn, and the beginning of a tradition that lasts even today.
Since that event, three generations of Bryant's descendants have
been active and interested in the town and its inhabitants. In
the Civil War, Bryant played the part of any moderately wealthy
gentleman farmer, as is indicated by the following letter preserved
in manuscript form in the Grist Mill Collection of the Bryant
Library in Roslyn:

New York Dec 22d 1864.

Dear Madam

I have not forgotten your request for books to be
sent, I think, to one of the Hospitals, that at Willet's
Point — for the reading of the Soldiers. In the package
accompanying this, I send four volumes.

I am, Madam,
very respectfully yours
Miss Valentine.   Wm. C. Bryant.[19]

Years later, in 1873, he bought land on Bryant Avenue for
"The Hall."[20]   He explained his plans in a letter to Miss
Christiana Gibson:

Before you left I would show you where I am laying
the foundations of a reading-room and lecture-hall
for the village, for the people have no places to meet
in the evening save in the bar-rooms.[21]

There is an interesting note of condescension here, which Bryant
must have succeeded in keeping from his fellow-citizens, for in
the following year, 1874, when the building was completed, they
proposed calling it the "Bryant Hall." The poet refused the
honor, however, and urged them to call it simply "The Hall,"

which they did during his lifetime.[22]   In the 1940's, when the building was condemned as unsafe, the land was sold and the money returned to the Bryant heirs. They, in turn, re-presented the money to the town for the building of a new library, the present edifice on East Broadway, which is called the Bryant Library and which houses several collections of Bryant material.

Bryant's literary fame, combined with his strong interest in local affairs and local history, made him one of the first citizens of Long Island during his residence there. In 1943, Jesse Merritt, the County Historian, pointed out that Bryant had not only helped to choose Roslyn's name, but that he and his family had been active in the drive to preserve the historic Old Mill. Merritt went on to say that "in 1893, when that section of Queens destined to become Nassau, broke away from the metropolitan borough, 'Bryant' was one of the leading names suggested for it."[23]

It would be misleading not to mention that there were other Long Islanders who disapproved of Bryant. H.W. Loweree felt that Cedarmere, as it was originally built, was "a stately abode and old-fashioned but Bryant tried to modernize it and made a failure of it for it lost its antique character and look of ancient simplicity."[24]   Benjamin Thompson, an early Long Island historian, admitted that Bryant had an "exalted reputation" as a poet, but he found the poet's politics deplorable:

> It is to be regretted that he should from choice or necessity prostitute his fine talents and improved taste to the humiliating pursuit of party politics, and spend so much valuable time in the advocacy of doctrines and measures worthless in themselves and injurious in their operation and tendency to the best interests of the country.[25]

It would be interesting to know what political measures Bryant advocated that Thompson deemed "injurious" to the country, but the historian does not elaborate on his general statement of condemnation.

It is not likely that Bryant was much disturbed by either

political or architectural opposition. Bryant's life at Cedarmere
was busy and satisfying. Five days a week he commuted into
New York to work on the *Evening Post*. Week-ends and evenings
his house was full of visitors. James Grant Wilson, a long-time
friend of the poet, reported that men distinguished in art and
literature were constantly appearing in Roslyn to pay their
respects to the editor-author: "They were always welcomed and
enjoyed the purity of taste and simplicity of manner which
presided over the mansion."[26]

One frequent visitor was Mrs. Caroline Kirkland. Mrs. Kirkland spent several months in a cottage on Bryant's estate writing
A New Home.[27] In one of her books, she described Bryant
playing host to a group of visitors: "So we willingly follow Mr.
Bryant to Roslyn, see him musing on the pretty rural bridge that
spans the fish-pond; or taking the oar in his daughter's fairy
boat; or pruning his trees; or talking over farming matters with
his neighbors..."[28]

Catherine Sedgwick, author of *Redwood* and other novels, was
another frequent visitor. She and Bryant shared similar views on
the need for a truly national literature, and her common-sense
use of the American scene in her novels must have endeared her
to him. They were great friends and corresponded regularly
whenever Bryant was abroad. During one of her visits at Cedarmere, Miss Sedgwick wrote to a niece:

> Do you wonder where I am? In the guest-chamber of
> a generous, old-fashioned house, behind one of the
> massy pillars that support a piazza which surrounds
> it, in front of Hempstead Bay, a deep cut into Long
> Island from the Sound, of which and its ever passing
> home-fleets there is a distant view...[29]

After Miss Sedgwick's death, Bryant wrote an affectionate essay,
"Reminiscences of Miss Sedgwick," which was included in her
official biography.[30]

Charles Durand, the artist, was almost as fond of Cedarmere
as its owner was.[31] They spent many hours together, walking
through the woods or looking down upon the Sound. Both

believed that the purpose of art was to depict nature, and both believed that 19th century American nature was among the most beautiful and romantic in the world.

There were many other visitors of all kinds: Samuel Morse, the father of telegraphy;[32]   Edwin Booth and Sir Henry Irving, actors; Charles Dana, a fellow editor; and the writers, Margaret Fuller and Fitz-greene Halleck.[33]   Perhaps his two most famous visitors, though, were Ralph Waldo Emerson and Nathaniel Hawthorne.

Abraham Lincoln never visited at Cedarmere, but Bryant wrote in Roslyn the speech with which he introduced Lincoln at Cooper Union in 1860.[34]   The *New York Sun* of May 14, 1943, claimed that Bryant's speech of introduction could be credited with securing for Lincoln the Republican nomination for President.[35] Certainly Lincoln himself was impressed. He once said: "It is worth a visit from Springfield, Ill., to New York to make the acquaintance of such a man as William Cullen Bryant."[36]

When he was not receiving visitors, Bryant occasionally took short jaunts around Long Island, getting to know other towns. We can trace some of his traveling by requests that were made of him. In 1868, the town of Glen Cove was celebrating the two hundredth anniversary of its settlement. Town officials wrote to Bryant, asking him for some commemorative verses. He declined, pleading that he could not compose to order, then adding pleasantly: "Your charming neighborhood is well worthy of such a commemoration. When the first white man planted himself there, he could not have dreamed to what a vast number of his fellow-men he was opening a most beautiful and welcome retreat from the tumult, the dust, and the summer heats of a great town. . . ."[37]

A few years later the town of Hampton, organizing its first library, went to Bryant in distress. They had a building, a Board of Trustees, enough money to buy several thousand books — but what books were they to buy? This time Bryant was willing to help (he was always willing to help small towns organize libraries) and by the end of the year, he had advised Charles Rogers of Hampton in the selection of over three thousand volumes.[38]

Perhaps he had first become known to the people in the Hamptons in 1850 when he traveled in that area. Bryant himself left an account of this trip:

> In September ... we made an excursion to the east end of the island, visiting Easthampton, a level country of fields of heavy loam in the midst of sandy woods, inhabited by a primitive race of people much like the New Englanders. From this place we went to Montauk Point, the extreme eastern end of the island, a hilly region of hard loam, with clefts of gravel forming its shores. There are scarcely any trees on the Point, which is nine or ten miles long, and is almost all pasturage, with eight or ten Indian houses on it, and three inhabited by white people, the keepers of the herds, besides the house of the keeper of the lighthouse.[39]

The sophisticated Hamptonites of today would be either angry or amused at that reference to "a primitive race of people," but then Bryant, too, would be *both* angry and amused if he could see the results in this area of a century's progress!

Amusement is something most people do not connect with Bryant. His strongest defect, according to his detractors, was his lack of a sense of humor. This is not wholly true; at least it is not of the Bryant who lived on Long Island. Shortly after he moved to Cedarmere, he heard the story of a treasure-trove buried behind the stage-stop tavern on the site of an old farm in Roslyn. The treasure had supposedly been buried during the Revolution. One night, overhearing his farm hands gossiping about this buried treasure, Bryant encouraged them to hunt for it. He later confided to a friend that they would profit more by spending their evenings "out behind the tavern digging for money rather than in its hospitable taproom, spending it."[40]

During a trip to Cairo in 1853, Bryant grew a good-sized beard. Upon returning to Roslyn, he noticed that several of his neighbors did not recognize him. Unable to resist such a wonderful opportunity, he donned a Turkish turban and gown that he had brought back with him and went over to visit his next-door neighbor.[41] Here he appeared at the back-door and — in broken English — claimed to be a Turkish mendicant. His acting was so superb that he succeeded in getting a hand-out without being recognized![42]   He was delighted at his own success, and for years went around bragging about the time he had been mistaken for an Arabian sheik.[43]

One of several sources for the above story is Christopher Morley, who had appointed himself a committee of one to defend Bryant's wit and humor. Another story that Morley liked to tell claimed that Bryant had become a real Long Island booster and that he had written "a rather pretentious poem whose object seems to be to prove that New Jersey mosquitoes are worse than Long Island's."[44]   Unfortunately for Morley's story, the poem — "To a Mosquito" — was written in New York City in 1825.[45] It is unlikely that in 1825 Bryant had even visited Long Island. The lines in question follow:

> I call thee stranger, for the town, I ween,
>   Has not the honor of so proud a birth,
> Thou com'st from Jersey meadows, fresh and green,
>   The offspring of the gods, though born on earth...[46]

The "town" in the first line surely refers to New York City and not to Roslyn.

Beyond the accuracy of the locale, there is no question that this poem does show Bryant in a playful mood. The mosquito to whom the verse is addressed is complaining: he has come to the city in quest of fairer diet, but is near sick from rouge, and China bloom, and Rowland's Kalydor (evidently 19th century cosmetics). The poet warns the insect to leave the fair ones alone — "And well might sudden vengeance light on such / As dared, like thee, most impiously to bite." It should leave poets alone, too: their blood is too scant and too meager. If it really wants a banquet, it should search out some plump alderman who had fed on oyster and green turtle, washed down with red vintage, and who will be too sleepy even to brush its wings!

If the mosquitoes did not bother Bryant in Roslyn, the bad weather sometimes did. On October 5, 1863, he invited the Rev.

Dr. Dewey to Cedarmere, but warned him to come soon before
the weather took a turn for the worse. On the reverse side of
the letter, he wrote the following verses to substantiate his
warning:

> The season wears an aspect glum and glummer;
> The icy north wind, an unwelcome comer,
> Frighting from garden-walks each pretty hummer,
> Whose murmuring music lulled the noons of summer,
> Roars in the woods, with grummer voice and grummer,
> And thunders in the forest like a drummer.
> Dumb are the birds — they could not well be dumber;
> The winter-cold, life's pitiless benumber,
> Bursts water-pipes, and makes us call the plumber.
> Now, by the fireside, toils the patient thumber
> Of ancient books, and no less patient summer
> Of long accounts, while topers fill the rummer,
> The maiden thinks what furs will best become her,
> And on the stage-boards shouts the gibing mummer.
> Shut in by storms, the dull piano-strummer
> Murders old tunes — there's nothing wearisomer.[47]

This bit of doggerel by itself should effectively bury for all time
the obvious slander that Bryant had no sense of humor!

There is also a story that Bryant himself liked to tell. In the
1870's, Lord Houghton was a house-guest at Cedarmere. With
him, of course, was his valet. One evening the English noble-
man's valet and Bryant's servant were chatting in the kitchen.
The valet announced arrogantly: "My master is a lord, and the
finest poet in England." Bryant's servant thought for a moment,
then not to be outdone, retorted, with a bit of a brogue: "Our
man is better nor a lord, and the greatest poet in the world!"[48]
Bryant was amused at this "downstairs" hyperbole, but he was
impressed, too, at the American servant's disdain of the word
master.

It was the human quality in Bryant that enabled him to
appreciate his servant's attitude that also made him popular with
his Long Island neighbors. Eliza Seaman Leggett remembered
fondly a visit that Bryant and his wife made to her family's

home. The celebrated couple had been out walking and had just "looked in." They were urged to stop for tea and did. Old Dorcas (a sort of combination cook-and-maid) held back the commonplace apple pie when she saw the famous visitors and substituted in its place the household's best preserves. Bryant evidently heard someone mention the pie, for he insisted she bring it back. Old Dorcas put the pie on the table, feeling all the while it was a mistake. She "was clear lifted off of her feet" when Bryant asked if she had another one that he could take home. "La! For goodness sake!" she exclaimed, "for the quality to like my apple pie!"[49]

Bryant was a politician, a citizen, a humorist, and an understanding human being, but he was, above all, a literary man. One of his joys in owning Cedarmere was that he could surround himself with flowers and trees that reminded him of other great writers. One favorite was a cactus plant which the Wilsons had brought him from the tomb of Virgil at Naples. Bryant wrote to thank them: "It has taken its place in the greenhouse here, where it will be tenderly cared for, on account of the old Roman poet."[50] Another flower, the *mirabilis* (called, in Spain, the Don Pedro), he treasured because it had been given to him by the artist Cole who had brought it back from Sicily.[51]

Tree or flower-planting, however, was just an alternate occupation to his literary labors, and there was never any doubt as to which was more important. Years after the poet's death, James Grant Wilson remembered that one day in Roslyn, Bryant brought to the breakfast table some pages in manuscript. It was his morning's work on Homer. "Like Scott," commented Wilson, "he was always an early riser, and by that excellent habit he gained some hours each day."[52]

VI

Landscapes and Seascapes

The poet's eye, sensitive and ever-curious, notes the crested wave, the fallen feather of a bird, the broken petal. From the Roman Horace to the youngest contemporary bard, each poet detects the most minute variation in nature, absorbs it into his poetic consciousness, and uses the result to give his work sensual appeal and universality. William Cullen Bryant was no exception.

During his lifetime Bryant moved from Cummington, to Great Barrington, to New York City, to Roslyn. Each change brought changes in his natural environment — changes in flowers and trees, in insects, birds, and animals. Nature remained a constant factor in his poetry, but the *details* of nature changed with each change of residence. For example, his Cummington poems include references to brier-roses and violets, ferns and maize, gourds, beans, and rye. A few years later, in Great Barrington, he had switched to watercress and primroses, clover and barley. His move to New York City in 1825 brought with it a change to more exotic flowers: anemones and the Orchis plant, the pomegranate and the jessamine, papaya and mistletoe, and a dozen others mentioned only once. After 1843, in Roslyn, his poems indicate a new interest in water-lilies (they were before his eyes all day, on his fresh-water ponds), in daffodils and dandelions and crocuses, all of which grew on the grounds at Cedarmere. Here, reflecting his new interest in fruit, are references for the first time to plums, apricots, nectarines, oranges (which he tried

74

to grow), and apples. The only flowers mentioned liberally in the works of all periods were violets and roses.

A similar pattern occurs in his references to trees. In the early poems there are beeches, hemlocks, maples, larches, birches, hazels, and alders. In the New York poems there is a sudden switch to less-known trees: the cocoa, aspen, sycamore, myrtle, cypress, and butternut. After he settled in Roslyn, his references to trees reflect those on his own property: oaks, pines, willows, apples, black-walnuts, cedars, and pears.

The pattern recurs too often to be accidental. In the early poems there are few references to birds; those few include the mountain-bird, the ringdove, the kingfisher, the ground-bird, and the oriole. The New York poems include the redbird, the prairie fowl, the wood-bird, the petrel, the grouse, and the whippoorwill. After 1843, in Roslyn, the bird most frequently cited is the common sparrow, important to any gardener; also mentioned are the robin, the bluebird, the wood thrush, and the hummingbird. As for animals and insects — the early poems use the otter, jackal, grasshopper, cricket, wildcat, and raccoon. The New York poems, again turning to the unusual, use the locust, cod, lion, snake, ostrich, seal, ox, cock, cougar, and panther. The Roslyn poems reflect two influences: the suburban farmer's experience with the army worm, Hessian fly, fruit moth, slug, canker worm, and moths; and a slight sea influence with the mention of the whale and dolphin. Bees and butterflies are used almost equally in all periods.

The conclusion that can be drawn from the above examples is perhaps obvious. Bryant's poems, for the most part, reflected his immediate environment, with the exception of the New York period. The probable explanation for the sudden flare-up of exotic names in this period seems to be that his separation from nature led him to books and to the imagery gleaned from reading rather than from his surroundings. Certainly, the poems after 1843 prove that Bryant's imagery was affected by Cedarmere and the wild-life with which he was in daily contact. Realization of this influence leads directly to another question: How exactly did Bryant use nature in the poetry of this period?

He himself once said, in a general study of nature's influence:

> The earliest occupation of man, we are told — his task
> in a state of innocence — was to tend and dress the
> garden in which his Maker placed him. I cannot say
> that as men addict themselves to the same pursuit they
> are raised nearer to the state of innocence; but this
> I will say, that few pursuits so agreeably interest with-
> out ever disturbing the mind, and that he who gives
> himself to it sets up one barrier more against evil
> thoughts and unhallowed wishes. The love of plants
> is a natural and wholesome instinct. Through that,
> perhaps, quite as much as through any other tendency
> of our natures, the sense of beauty, the grateful per-
> ception of harmony of color and of grace, and fair
> proportion of shape, enter the mind and wean it from
> grosser and more sensual tastes.[1]

This quotation allies Bryant with Wordsworth and most of the
poets of the romantic school in 19th century England and America. Like them, this sophisticated child of Rousseau turned his
eyes upon his natural surroundings not only to enjoy their
beauties, but also to learn from them the moral lessons that they
taught. This was true even in his earliest poems, which he wrote
in Cummington, Massachusetts; it continued to be true throughout the forty-three years he lived in Roslyn. His grandson,
Harold Godwin, recognized this aspect of the poet's mind in a
letter to *The Roslyn News* on November 20, 1930, concerning
the recently-established Bryant Park:

> Mr. Bryant was a great lover of wild life, and when
> he settled in Roslyn, I feel sure that the rustic character
> of the place appealed to him most deeply. It would, I
> think, have touched a tender spot in his nature if he
> could have foreseen the surroundings of his home here
> kept as a natural beauty spot and a home or shelter
> for the "wild fowl" that symbolized to him in his
> poem a deeply religious reverence for the beauties of
> Nature still manifest in our surroundings.[2]

At Cedarmere, Bryant was almost submerged in nature. Around

him were all varieties of trees and flowers, of birds and animals. Above him was a sky of clouds and stars, and under his feet were hills and plains. There was the fresh water of the lakes and springs, and the salt water of the bays and Sound.

*   *   *   *   *   *

Long Island Sound and Inland Lakes

Water of any kind had for Bryant the significance it has had for most poets: it gave life; it even, at times, merged with life. "The Stream of Life,"[3] the first poem he wrote at Cedarmere, is a short, two-stanza piece. The first stanza simply describes a stream in a field; the second stanza, beginning with the cry — "Oh Stream of Life!" sees the stream pulling away from its sources until "dust alone remains." Thus a single stream and a single life are equated.

A more practical preoccupation with water resulted in the poem "A Rain-Dream."[4] Bryant, as farmer and gardener, was acutely aware of the importance of rain and felt the horror of drought. In 1851 he wrote to Charles Sedgwick that " . . . the later summer heats parch and wither the verdure of an island."[5] At another time he wrote — in prose that is more poetical than some of his poetry — "The sky over our heads is not brass, quite, nor the earth under our feet ashes, but Roslyn suffers for want of rain."[6] Those last words form an understatement, as anyone familiar with a Long Island drought knows. Certainly it was experiences like these that inspired "A Rain-Dream." This poem, written in blank verse, begins as a storm begins, and the poet urges the reader to leave the city streets and watch the approaching storm "from the shelter of our rural home." The attitude at first is almost reverent:

> Who is not awed that listens to the Rain,
> Sending his voice before him? Mighty Rain!

A description follows, rich in detail and thoroughly practical: "every leaf in all the woods / Is struck, and quivers"; hill-tops

slake their thirst; arid fields and gardens are refreshed; rivulets
start to flow again. And the earth drinks in the rain—for her
cottage wells, her woodland brooks, the springing trout, and the
brooding bird, for her tender flowers and tall oaks. Squirrels and
marmots, butterflies and insects scamper for shelter from the
storm's violence. Then the poet turns from the practical and
indulges for a moment in fantastic reverie:

> I shut my eyes, and see, as in a dream,
> The friendly clouds drop down spring violets
> And summer columbines, and all the flowers
> That tuft the woodland floor, or overarch
> The streamlet . . .

The imagery is felicitous, for the rain does, of course, in one
sense, drop down violets and columbines. The next day all nature
is fresh, as from a rebirth: the water-lily proudly "rides the
brimming pool" and "gay troops of butterflies . . . light to drink/
At the replenished hollows of the rock."

The phrasing sometimes is that of a city man, but the details
belong to the country; only he who has lived there will notice
the difference in the bearing of a water-lily before and after a
rain, or the way in which birds and butterflies will drink from
pools of water left in the hollows of a rock.

"Sella,"[7] a long narrative poem written in 1862, owes its
existence to water in its many forms. Sella is a beautiful young
maiden who has turned from earthly love and has chosen to bestow her love, instead, on streams and rivers. She knows each
rill and lakelet near her home and is familiar with the rushes on
the stream's edge and with the wild vines that hang over it.
From her small shallop she dips her oars into the waters and
rows from shore to shore. Her one dream is that she "might
go forth alone, to trace/ The mighty rivers downward to the
sea . . ." One day she finds a pair of white slippers on the river's
bank. Warned against them, she cannot resist trying them on; they
are magic slippers, and carry her swiftly to the water's edge where
a sea-nymph awaits her. They travel down the stream until it

becomes a wide river, then continue on until they reach the ocean itself. Here they dip beneath the billows into a new undersea world of coral and dulse, of sea-thong and sea-lace. Dolphins roll past them, and huge whales, and hideous hammersharks. They dine at a sea-banquet "culled from the ocean's meadows" and admire groves of coral loftier than earth's mighty cedars. In the very hollow of the abyss, they spy

> The skeletons of sharks, the long white spines
> Of narwhal and of dolphin, bones of men
> Shipwrecked, and mighty ribs of foundered barks.

(One wonders if Bryant had been reading Cooper's whaling stories or listening to Long Island legends of ships wrecked at sea.) Sella returns home. Soon her mother dies, and her journeys in the white slippers become more frequent. An older brother, fearing for her life's safety, casts the slippers into the sea. Sella broods for a while, then finds peace in prayer. Now, instead of traveling in the sea, she spends her time in teaching men all crafts related to water. She teaches them to find water beneath the earth, to bring river waters to town, to build fountains. She teaches them to make water wheels to do their work for them. And she herself gathers the rain waters into pools as reservoirs, and then, in times of drought, leads them forth "in glimmering rivulets" to refresh the fields. She lives one hundred years, as counted by the openings of the water-lily; and when she dies, the flowers that love the stream caress her grave.

It is a charming legend, but its interest here lies in what it reveals about Bryant's love for the sea. When Cooper became fascinated by the sea, he signed on board a merchant-vessel as a seaman or bought a whaler. Bryant, a less active and adventurous man, sought his outlet in reading and writing about the sea. "Sella," as well as many of his other poems, shows some knowledge of sea-life, both plant and animal. It shows still more his philosophical interest in the sea: his visualization of the common knowledge that every stream eventually seeks out its mother-source, the ocean; and his corresponding awareness that the ocean is the source not only of all streams, but also of all life.

Life on Long Island was eventually to teach Bryant another aspect of the sea. Before 1843, his knowledge of the ocean was primarily literary. He saw it as an awe-inspiring mass of water, but it seldom possessed the vitality, the paradoxical combination of terror and joy that it holds for those who know it well. From his high hill at Cedarmere, he watched the Sound day after day. He saw it serene, and he saw it angry. He must have seen its surface torn and ravaged by autumn hurricanes and by winter storms. Slowly, a sea-change takes place in his writing. It is there already in 1845 in "The Unknown Way,"[8] but still in muted tones:

> I hear a solemn murmur,
>   And, listening to the sound,
> I know the voice of the mighty Sea,
>   Beating his pebbly bound.
>
> Dost thou, oh path of the woodland!
>   End where those waters roar,
> Like human life, on a trackless beach,
>   With a boundless Sea before?

Fifteen years later, in 1860, in "The Tides,"[9] Bryant is able to reap some of the rewards of his closer association with the ocean. The poem is concerned primarily with the attraction between the moon and the sea. The waves stretch and leap in a mad desire to reach the moon. They fail, of course, but — Bryant adds serenely — through the agency of the sun they will eventually be changed to "cloudy trains" that will "rise above the hills of earth, and shine/ In a serener sphere." The poem is too artificial, too deliberately didactic, to be very good poetry, but there are lines and phrases that are good and that show his dawning awareness of the ocean's power.

> But ever heaves and moans the restless Deep;
>   His rising tides I hear,

Afar I see the glimmering billows leap;
I see them breaking near.

There are other examples: "...the Deep/ Recalls his brood of waves"; "...they shall rush...with noise and tumult"; and, again—"O restless Sea, that, in thy prison here/ Dost struggle and complain."

As "The Stream of Life," one of Bryant's first Long Island poems, equated a stream with a man's life, so one of his last, "The Flood of Years"[10] in 1876, equated the ocean with the life of the human race. This is not the tinkering pseudo-philosophy of "The Tides," but a mature return to the great theme that the poet first broached in "Thanatopsis." There is a difference: the ocean is here in much of its true force, controlled by the sure hand of one who knows both content and form.

The Present there
Tosses and foams, and fills the air with roar
Of mingled noises.

Here are an action and brute strength lacking in the earlier poems. The woodman, the artisan, and the student are seen for a moment on the mounting billow, then "the flood sweeps over them and they are gone." Groups of revelers "ride the topmost swell awhile," until they too "are whirled beneath the waves and disappear." A loud-voiced orator is choked by the waters and "all is still." A kneeling crowd is swallowed by an engulfing wave. "The torrent wrests" a babe from the arms of its mother; and two lovers are flung apart by the rushing flood.

Lo! wider grows the stream—a sea-like flood
Saps earth's walled cities; massive palaces
Crumble before it; fortresses and towers
Dissolve in the swift waters; populous realms
Swept by the torrent see their ancient tribes
Engulfed and lost; their very languages
Stifled, and never to be uttered more.

This was Time Present; the poet, looking back, sees "the silent

ocean of the Past, a waste / of waters weltering over graves..."
Now, instead of tumult and action, the reader senses only a
stagnancy, a barrenness. Ahead, "where yet/ The Flood must
pass" is Time Future, with the people and events that are yet
to happen. What lies beyond, beyond even the Future? The poet,
who in "Thanatopsis" saw only union with the earth, now sees
something akin to a final Judgment Day, when all who were or
are good

> ...are raised and borne
> By that great current in its onward sweep,
> Wandering and rippling with caressing waves
> Around green islands...

In "The Flood of Years," Bryant has used the ocean to provide
structure and metaphor. His handling shows artistic skill and
emotional richness controlled with dignity. The result is one of
the most successful poems of his last decade.

*   *   *   *   *   *

Trees

Along the edges of the lakes at Cedarmere were pink and
white dogwoods. Around the homestead were dark, solid pines.
Trees were everywhere, trees of all kinds. Some were there long
before Bryant purchased the land. Others, he imported from dis-
tant lands and planted there. Among the latter were some beech
and cedar and elm, Sophora from Japan, and box hedges and
ivy from Kenilworth, England.[11]   One day in June he wrote to
a friend: "It is now the holiday of the year, and the country
around me is beautiful: the trees, most of them, full-leaved, and
noisy with birds."[12]
The oaks were his favorites. They appear in many of his
poems, not on special occasions, but whenever he wanted to
mention a tree, any tree. The only exception to this is in "Among
the Trees,"[13] in which he devotes a sixteen-line stanza to an
old oak that stands on the hillside. Even here, the old oak
becomes a symbol for the universal tree:

> An unremembered Past
> Broods, like a presence, mid the long gray boughs
> Of this old tree, which has outlived so long
> The flitting generations of mankind.

The most "alive" oak tree occurs not in his poetry but in one of his letters. He wrote once that Pedro d'Alcantara had sent him an oak leaf and acorn from Smyrna, a town loved by Homer; Bryant planted the acorn, but—he added wistfully—he did not know if the acorn took root.[14] Another "famous" tree on the Bryant property was a mulberry, planted from a root that he himself had brought to Long Island from the garden of John Milton.[15]

The most famous tree of all was a black-walnut tree which Adam Smith had planted and which made its first appearance above ground in 1713. According to James Grant Wilson, a friend, by the time Bryant bought Cedarmere, the tree had already attained a girth of twenty-five feet and had an immense spread of branches. "It was," says Mr. Wilson, "the comfortable home of a small army of squirrels, and every year strewed the ground around its gigantic stem with an abundance of 'heavy fruit.'"[16] The black-walnut was a favorite with the whole neighborhood and had a small kind of fame (probably unjustified) for being the biggest and oldest black-walnut on Long Island. Bryant's pride in this tree is illustrated in "The Third of November, 1861":[17]

> On my cornice linger the ripe black grapes ungathered;
>   Children fill the groves with the echoes of their glee,
> Gathering tawny chestnuts, and shouting when beside
>   them
>   Drops the heavy fruit of the tall black-walnut tree.

The chestnut is mentioned in the above stanza also, another favorite tree. James Grant Wilson tells of taking a walk with Bryant when the poet was seventy-six years old. As they approached a Spanish chestnut tree, his host suddenly jumped up, caught an open burr from a branch, and gave the two chestnuts inside it to his city guest.[18]

He admired the black-walnuts and the chestnuts and the oaks; but he reserved most of his love and experimentation for the trees that produce—the fruit trees. In an address delivered before the New York Horticultural Society on September 26, 1856,[19] he spoke not as a poet, but as a naturalist and orchard-owner. He urged the cultivation of the native crab apple and the native wild plum, believing that with care and experimentation they could become as delicious as any fruits grown in this country. He reminded his listeners that in China lamps are lighted by oil pressed from the fruit of a tree. He reminded them, too, that by 1856 our supply of whale oil had been seriously depleted. Whalers now had to chase their game into ever more remote areas. Journeys took years, and the returning whalers had such small cargoes of oil that the financial return barely covered expenses. Why could we not obtain our oil from some fruit or vegetable?

One long section of the address was devoted to the peach tree, a perennial source of frustration to Bryant. Year after year he had planted peach trees on his Roslyn estate, and the result was always the same. For two or three years the trees bore fruit unmatched anywhere else in the world; then the trees died. There seemed no cause, no explanation. Then he added:

> On Long Island in the hedge-rows, or among heaps of stones, in neglected spots never turned by the spade or torn by the plough, you may see peach trees, self-planted, which flourish in full vigor, with leaves of the darkest and glossiest green, bearing fruit every year, and surviving generation after generation of their brethren of the gardens. In the soil and situation of these places exist the qualities which are necessary to the health of the peach tree. What are they? Can the practical gardener determine? Can the chemist? The question is worthy of long and most careful research.[20]

Bryant's interest in fruit trees can be traced back to his childhood days in Cummington, Massachusetts. There, under his mother's direction, he and his brothers had planted several apple trees near the family homestead. The trees survived for decades.[21] This act must have given Bryant a small taste of immortality, and a few years after buying Cedarmere, he was repeating the action in his new home. In a letter to Mr. Dewey, on November 17, 1846, he explained both what he was doing and why he was doing it:

> I have been, and am, at my place on Long Island, planting and transplanting trees, in the mist: sixty or seventy: some for shade; most for fruit. Hereafter, men, whose existence is at present merely possible, will gather pears from the trees which I have set in the ground, and wonder what old *covey* — for in those days the slang terms of the present time, by the or-dinary process of change in languages, will have become classical — what old *covey* of past ages planted them? Or they will walk in the shade of the mulberry, apricot, and cherry trees that I have set in a row beside a green lane, and think, if they think at all about the matter — for who can tell what the great-grandchildren of ours will think about — that they sprang up of themselves by the way.[22]

Both the act of planting the fruit trees and the significance of the act must have lain in the poet's subconscious mind for the next three years. Then, in 1849, came "The Planting of the Apple-Tree,"[23] a poem that combined the memories of the childhood planting with the more recent memories at Cedarmere. It begins with the actual planting: making a hollow bed, laying in the roots, sifting the dark mould. Then he asks — "What plant we in this apple-tree?" The question is asked three times, and the answers are many and various: a shade, a shelter, a home for the thrush; blossoms for the bees, flowers for a sick girl, a sprig of bloom for an infant; most of all, fruit — red and sweet — for the children who gather round the tree in Sep-tember. Then his horizon grows, and he sees the apples trans-ported to foreign lands where they will act as silent ambassadors

between nations. Finally this apple tree will act as a marker of
Time; first it will mark the time that will close his life until he
lies quietly beneath the earth and the wind still sighs in its
boughs. Then it will mark its own time, as it too grows old
and wasted. And when it is old, the poet asks, turning his eyes
for a moment to the country's enslaved, "Shall fraud and force
and iron will / Oppress the weak and helpless still?" the final
stanza returns again to this specific apple tree, this specific poet,
and his grandchildren, and to the immortality that he had tasted
first in those childhood days in Cummington:

>"Who planted this old apple-tree?"
>The children of that distant day
>Thus to some aged man shall say;
>And, gazing on its mossy stem,
>The gray-haired man shall answer them:
>   "A poet of the land was he,
>Born in the rude but good old times;
>'Tis said he made some quaint old rhymes,
>   On planting the apple-tree."

The poem is fairly successful; one wishes it had been written
six years later when a touch of humor might have mingled a
tart taste with its sweetness. It was in 1855 that Bryant found
a recipe for making beer from fermented apples. Nothing fermented could be bought or sold at the time, and everyone
therefore had to make his own. Bryant noted drily: "The ferment
will, I suppose, cause the planting of large apple orchards again,
and we shall hear the creak of the cider-mill with the return of
the autumnal frosts..." It was the same "creak of the cider-
mill" and its delightful product which was to enchant Christopher
Morley almost a century later when he too lived in Roslyn.
Meanwhile, Bryant resigned himself, with a surprising cheerful-
ness, to the fact that "the beer-tub — shall I call it vat, for
dignity's sake? — must take its old place among household
furniture."[24]

Second only to the apple tree in Bryant's favor was the pear
tree. Several of them stood just outside of Bryant's study win-

dow;[25] often, while he was working at his desk, he must have
looked out at them and gained sustenance — spiritual from their
delicate blossoms in spring, and physical from their tangy fruit
in late summer. His interest in them, half literary and half
technical, is illustrated in a letter that he wrote in 1863: "I came
down to Roslyn last night, and, instead of the 'grandia poma',
the big apples Tibullus speaks of, found some pears, the kind
called Osband's Summer, just ripened for me on their dwarf
trees, and very handsome, with their orange skin and scarlet
cheek."[26] In his poem, "Among the Trees,"[27] Bryant spends
a stanza on his beloved pear trees "that with spring-time burst/
Into such breadth of bloom." One has a scar made by a stroke
of lightning, but it still lives on and still bears blossoms. The
stanza ends with the philosophizing so common in Bryant's
poetry: he is grateful to the tree not only for its own beauty
but for the birds and bees that it attracts and for the shouts of
joy "from children gathering up the fruit/ Shaken in August
from the willing boughs."

This poem closes in much the same way as does "The Planting
of an Apple-Tree":

> Ye that my hands have planted, or have spared,
> Beside the way, or in the orchard-ground,
> Or in the open meadow, ye whose boughs
> With every summer spread a wider shade,
> Whose herd in coming years shall lie at rest
> Beneath your noontide shelter? who shall pluck
> Your ripened fruit?

His fruit trees, to Bryant, meant many things: present beauty
and joy, fine fruit for his friends, an attraction for laughing
children; but they also, like his poems, acted as a link with the
future. Later generations would eat his fruit as they would read
his poems, and in each act he would continue to live and the
stream of life would be uninterrupted.

Bryant's interest extended to other fruits. At Cedarmere he
grew great beds of strawberries; and the highlight of each spring,
for the children of the neighborhood as well as Bryant, was the

strawberry festival. The youngsters waited eagerly for this special
day; when it finally arrived, the whole school packed up and
moved to Cedarmere. For that one day the school-children had
the run of the estate. They picked strawberries, crushing the sweet
juices into their eager mouths. They ran up and down the steep
grass terraces and paddled about on the smooth lake.[28]   It was
a day rich in memories both for the children and for the poet.
Poem after poem of this period includes a warm reference to
children gathering fruit — grapes and pears, strawberries and
apples, black-walnuts, and pecans — and to their joyous laughter
ringing in the air. Surely these references must have been triggered not only by his own children, but by his memories of that
one hectic, noisy day each spring when sedate Cedarmere became
a glorious playground.

One day he took the two-year-old child of a neighbor to see
the pigs and chickens. When the boy demanded nourishment,
Bryant climbed a tree and brought down cherries for him.
Bryant was fifty-six at the time, and you can almost hear him
chuckle as he tells the story to his friend, R.H. Dana, and urges
him to come to Roslyn for the "first of the raspberries and the
last of the strawberries..."[29]

*   *   *   *   *   *

Birds and Flowers

Bryant's interest in fruit plants and fruit trees led naturally to
an interest in certain birds. One of his less-known poems, "The
Old-World Sparrow,"[30]   reflects this interest. The English sparrow, considered a pest in its native land, was brought to this
country deliberately in an attempt to control the insects that
were ravaging the nation's fruits and vegetables. I quote this
poem in its entirety, because it does not appear in most editions
of Bryant's poetry and because it reflects Bryant's knowledge of
the fruit and insect world of Long Island:

"The Old-World Sparrow"

We hear the note of a stranger bird

That ne'er till now in our land was heard;
A winged settler has taken his place
With Teutons and men of the Celtic race;
He has followed their path to our hemisphere —
The Old-World sparrow at last is here.

He meets not here, as beyond the main,
The fowler's snare and the poisoned grain,
But snug-built homes on the friendly tree;
And crumbs for his chirping family
Are strewn when the winter fields are drear,
For the Old-World sparrow is welcome here.

The insect legions that sting our fruit
And strip the leaves from the growing shoot —
A swarming, skulking, ravenous tribe,
Which Harris and Flint[31]   so well describe
But cannot destroy — may quail with fear,
For the Old-World sparrow, their bane, is here.

The apricot, in the summer ray,
May ripen now on the loaded spray,
And the nectarine, by the garden walk,
Keep firm its hold on the parent stalk,
And the plum its fragrant fruitage rear,
For the Old-World sparrow, their friend, is here.

That pest of gardens, the little Turk
Who signs, with the crescent, his wicked work,
And causes the half-grown fruit to fall,
Shall be seized and swallowed, in spite of all
His sly devices of cunning and fear,
For the Old-World sparrow, his foe, is here.

And the army-worm, and the Hessian fly,
And the dreaded canker-worm shall die;
And the thrip and slug and fruit-moth seek,
In vain, to escape that busy beak,
And fairer harvests shall crown the year,
For the Old-World sparrow at last is here.
(Roslyn, 1859)

Bryant had reason to be grateful to the sparrow. He had been
fighting the battle of the insects for years. In 1869, he had tried
sawdust saturated with coal-tar in a vain effort to curb the

curculio (a snout-beetle) that was destroying his plums. When that did not work, he planted plum trees on a ridge of land near the bay-shore so that the larger share of the plums were directly over the water. This seemed somewhat more successful. The curculio were equally fatal to the apricots.[32]

He wrote a poem to the song sparrow in 1861, and other birds — the robin, the jay, the wood thrush and the hermit thrush, the hummingbird and the bluebird — appear in his poems during these Roslyn years. It was not the beauty of the birds that fascinated him most, nor even their practical assistance. It was their song. His letters of these years indicate this. To Dana he wrote that "the fire bird and the song sparrow have been singing all day among my locusts and horse chestnuts";[33] to Miss Gibson he praised the "song-sparrow twittering on the sprays, and the hermit thrush making the arches of the neighboring wood resound with his sweet and mellow note..."[34] In another letter he mentions two swans, a gift from a neighboring gentleman, which "are moving about with lifted wings as proudly as if they were the sole proprietors of the place,"[35] and in still another, he refers to the American quail in the fields calling out his plaintive "Bob White."[36]

Birds play a similar role in his poems. In "An Invitation to the Country,"[37] a sparrow sings and a bluebird chants; in "The Little People of the Snow,"[38] the swallows twitter, and in "Among the Trees,"[39] the song-sparrow warbles, the hermit thrush pipes, and the robin carols. Bird *sounds* never ceased to arouse his interest. There is a story, treasured in Roslyn, which shows this almost extraordinary sympathy. He and a friend were walking one day among his shade trees. They came to a low, overhanging bough which had been almost sawed from the tree but which was held in place by ropes interlaced among the other branches. The visitor was curious, and Bryant admitted that some time before he had come upon his gardener in the very act of sawing the limb from the tree. Nearby, two song birds cried their distress; they had been rearing their babies in a nest high up in the limb. Bryant at once ordered the gardener to stop, and the two men tied the branch securely in place. Several weeks later, the baby birds were strong enough to fly and the nest was deserted. Then the branch could be untied, and the work of sawing off the limb completed.[40]

Especially satisfying to Bryant's sensitive ear was the call of the bob-o-link, and he devoted a complete poem to this "Robert of Lincoln."[41] It begins with the merry little fellow, dressed in sparkling black and white, singing gaily. Then he takes a wife, a plain brown-winged Quaker who promptly lays six white eggs, flecked with purple. Robert of Lincoln is still singing merrily, but soon the little ones break out of the shell and there are six wide mouths waiting to be fed. Now Robert must bestir himself; soon he is "sober with work, and silent with care." By the time the children have grown, Robert is a "humdrum crone" and everyone is glad to see him go. He'll not be welcomed back until he can "pipe that merry old strain" again!

The poem has a sparkling lilt unusual in Bryant's poetry. The bird's gay song has infected the poet who temporarily forgets his moralizing and just sings along with Robert:

> Modest and shy as a nun is she;
>   One weak chirp is her only note.
> Braggart and prince of braggarts is he,
>   Pouring boasts from his little throat:
>   Bob-o'-link, bob-o'-link,
>   Spink, spank, spink;
> Never was I afraid of man;
> Catch me, cowardly knaves, if you can!
>   Chee, chee, chee.

Flowers appealed to Bryant, too, and at Cedarmere he had great gardens full of them. He sprinkled their names, almost carelessly, throughout his Roslyn poetry: periwinkles, ground laurel, squirrel cups, and daffodils; dandelions, crocuses, golden-rod, and columbine; brier-roses, asters, pansies, and jessamine. But the flowers seldom seem real, and the names seem tags. One feels that if one shuffled the tags, it would make little difference to the poems. The only flowers he definitely favored were the violets and the roses. The violets were old friends, and his allegiance to them can be traced back to his early years in Cummington. The roses he was interested in, at least partly, because of the way they had changed in his lifetime. He pointed out at one time that an earlier poet had spoken ironically of roses in December, implying exaggeration, but that in the intervening years this had become literal truth. He added that he had gathered roses in his Long Island garden on the twentieth of December; then added: "It is curious to see the plant go on putting forth its flowers and rearing its clusters of buds as if without any presentiment of approaching winter, till, in the midst of its bloom, it is surprised by a frost nipping all its young and tender shoots at once, like a sudden failure overtaking one of our men of commerce in the midst of his many projects."[42]

VII

The Changing Seasons

The city-dweller may scarcely notice the passing of one season and the advent of another, but the countryman *must* notice. There are leaves to be gathered and burned in October, walks to be cleared of snow in January, flowers to be planted in April, and lawns to be mowed and pampered in July. William Cullen Bryant, as poet and as estate owner, noticed the changing seasons, and the four seasons bore poems as well as produce.

Bryant seldom wrote about summer, probably because it seemed a comfortable and satisfied time; winter he wrote about occasionally. In "The Snow-Shower,"[1] for example, he describes a rather typical snowfall. The loveliest lines are the refrain— "Flake after flake/ Dissolved in the dark and silent lake." Perhaps he was standing at a window of his home at Cedarmere, looking down upon his own lake, watching the snow fall and disappear into it. Even this slight poem must bear a message: the snowflakes are people, the lake is death. The narrative poem, "The Little People of the Snow,"[2] handles winter more imaginatively. Here the oaks, the cedars, even the roses seem made of stainless alabaster. There are frost-wreaths, and tufts of silvery rime...like blades and blossoms. There are windows of pellucid ice, and walls of snow, ice-cymbals to make music, and ice-cups from which to drink. But it is a work of almost pure fantasy; and though its inspiration may have come from his own ice-sheathed oaks or snow-topped firs, it may just as well have come from his reading or daydreams.

93

*   *   *   *   *   *

Autumn

The two transitional seasons, autumn and spring, interested
him far more. "The Voice of Autumn,"[3] one of his earlier Long
Island poems, describes the first approach of fall: the falling
leaves, the autumn breeze, the sedgy brook, the last pale flowers.
It attains a breath of life for a moment, when it contrasts two
aspects of the autumn wind:

> O'er shouting children flies
>   That light October wind,
> And, kissing cheeks and eyes,
> He leaves their merry cries
>   Far behind,
>
> And wanders on to make
>   That soft uneasy sound
> By distant wood and lake,
> Where distant fountains break
>   From the ground.

November is an unusually beautiful month on Long Island. Days
of sharp cold alternate with days of summer warmth. Maple
leaves and oak leaves are parti-colored; and flowers, perhaps
because of their scarcity, appear brighter and more full of hope
then did the summer multitudes. Bryant experienced many such
Novembers, and wrote about one of them in "The Third of
November, 1861."[4] In this poem, he talks of the west wind, the
golden haze, the woods in "their latest gold and crimson." Then:

> Tenderly the season has spared the grassy meadows,
>   Spared the petted flowers that the old world gave the new,
> Spared the autumn-rose and the garden's group of pansies,
>   Late-blown dandelions and periwinkles blue.

In the last few stanzas he compares the season of the year to
his own time of life: "Past is manhood's summer, the frosty
months are here."

Far different is another autumn poem, written three years later, "My Autumn Walk."⁵ It is the most heart-breaking year of the Civil War, and Bryant, forgetting himself, remembers only the sorrow of his countrymen. It starts with a traditional seasonal stanza, a note of conventional sadness:

> On woodlands ruddy with autumn
> The amber sunshine lies;
> I look on the beauty round me,
> And tears come into my eyes.

But now when the poet looks around him, he looks with a longer view. The breeze blowing over his goldenrod and purple aster is "a breath from the land of graves"; and the leaves are falling from the trees as fast as "our brethren fall in death." He gazes down at the sleeping village, with its peaceful dwellings, its crofts and gardens and orchards; and he thinks of the meadows of the Chattahoochee with its "night-sky red with flames." He turns for comfort to his woodlands but the mock-grape's "blood-red banner" has a new and dreadful significance; and the banks of the serene Long Island Sound evoke only the wasted banks of the James. Bryant has found new power in this poem, and the symbols of autumn have become symbols of the slaughter of '64.

* * * * * *

Spring

In those years, spring as well as autumn came in terror. In "The Return of the Birds,"⁶ Bryant looked at the still-brown meadows and thickets alive with birds, and asked — "Oh choir of spring, why come so soon?" It is only March; frost is still in the air, and there may still be snow. But as the poet asks the question, he knows the answer. The birds have been frightened from their winter homes by the bugle-blast and the booming gun. Their orchards and groves in the South are filled with pitched camps and soldiers burying their dead. The birds are right: the storm-clouds and the wintry winds are not so bad as the battle-clouds and the dust tossed up by marching armies.

"The Return of the Birds" is not as effective or forceful as "My Autumn Walk," but there is the same attempt to make a natural event stand for and express the emotions evoked by a man-made event. It is an attempt to express the inexpressible, and to this extent, it is a primitive effort to use the objective correlative, which T.S. Eliot, almost a century later, was to use so effectively.

In other years, before and after the war, spring had a more joyous meaning for Bryant. "An Invitation to the Country,"[7] is just that — a poetic invitation to his daughter Julia, extended in May of 1855, to come to Cedarmere. It is a delightful poem, bursting with the excitement of spring. It is full of sparrows and bluebirds, elms and willows, violets and daffodils. It grows urgent:

> Come, daughter mine, from the gloomy city,
>   Before those lays from the elm have ceased...

Then it emphasizes the freedom of the country:

> No lays so joyous as these are warbled
>   From wiry prison in maiden's bower;
> No pampered bloom of the green-house chamber
>   Has half the charm of the lawn's first flower.

Julia is reminded that all these fair sights and sunny days are waiting for her, that the joys of spring are not (as Emerson would have claimed) in themselves, but in the human eyes that behold them. He ends with a personal stanza, a private epistle:

> Come, Julia dear, for the sprouting willows,
>   The opening flowers, and the gleaming brooks,
> And hollows, green in the sun, are waiting
>   Their dower of beauty from thy glad looks.

* * * * * *

Frances Fairchild Bryant

Spring was beautiful for still another reason to Bryant; for
with the spring came Mrs. Bryant's birthday. To Bryant, his
wife was always the lovely Frances Fairchild, whom he had
married in 1821. They were a happily-suited couple, and their
life together seemed one of constant serenity and mutual affection.
In 1855 Bryant wrote "The Twenty-Seventh of March,"[8]   a
birthday greeting to his wife. Perhaps, he begins, other poets
would prefer June for the birthday of a loved one, June with its
newly-blown rose and the longest, brightest day in all the year.
But he does not; he finds March, as it softens into April, the
most fitting season for her birth.

                    Then we have
      The delicatest and most welcome flowers,
      And yet they take least heed of bitter wind
      And lowering sky. The periwinkle then,
      In an hour's sunshine, lifts her azure blooms
      Beside the cottage-door; within the woods
      Tufts of ground-laurel, creeping underneath
      The leaves of the last summer, send their sweets
      Up to the chilly air, and, by the oak,
      The squirrel-cups, a graceful company,
      Hide in their bells, a soft aerial blue —
      Sweet flowers, that nestle in the humblest nooks,
      And yet within whose smallest bud is wrapped
      A world of promise!

Before we can appreciate the sincerity of this poem, we must
understand the relationship between this man and his wife, and
between the two of them and their home at Cedarmere. To
him, Frances Fairchild Bryant was always a bud in which "a
world of promises" waited. They had met in Great Barrington;
she had come to New York City with him; and together, in
1843, they had felt a need for fresh air and living things and
had turned with hope to Cedarmere. In those first years in
Roslyn, they had worked together, with their own hands building
paths in the woods where no paths had ever been before. There

is a special satisfaction in leaving one's mark on hitherto virgin
territory, and this satisfaction the Bryants must have shared.
Years later, when she was often ill and could no longer wander
with him through the woods, he wrote "The Path."[9] The first
stanza reflects that early experience:

> The path we planned beneath October's sky,
>   Along the hillside, through the woodland shade,
> Is finished; thanks to thee, whose kindly eye
>   Has watched me, as I plied the busy spade;
> Else had I wearied, ere this path of ours
> Had pierced the woodland to its inner bowers.

Later in the poem, Bryant considers the effect of a path: where
it wanders, grim rocks become familiar, swamps become gardens,
and savage nooks become friendly havens. Paths indicate human
presence and link one human being to another. He catalogues
the people who walk a rural path, and includes whimsically:
"There he who cons a speech, and he who hums/ His yet
unfinished verses, musing walk . . . "

Frances Fairchild Bryant died on July 27, 1866. She was buried
in the cemetery in Roslyn, and her grave was shaded by a tall
silver beech. Bryant grieved in silence for a few months; then he
wrote "October, 1866,"[10] a last poem to the woman he loved.
He looks back to that summer day on which they carried her
to her grave, and he remembers how they all walked softly and
spoke softly:

> Feared they to break thy slumber? As we threw
>   A look on that bright bay and glorious shore,
> Our hearts were wrung with anguish, for we knew
>   Those sleeping eyes would look on them no more.

That day passed, and summer passed, and now it is autumn
once again. He "tells over" the lingering flowers, the purple
oak leaf, the birchen bough.

> And gorgeous as the morn, a tall array
>   Of woodland shelters the smooth fields around;

And guarded by its headlands, far away
Sail-spotted, blue and lake-like, sleeps the sound.

I gaze in sadness; it delights me not
To look on beauty which thou canst not see;
And, wert thou by my side, the dreariest spot,
Were, oh, how far more beautiful to me!

The mood of the above stanza was to remain with him throughout the rest of his life. He could not bear to be in Roslyn, nor
could he bear to be away from it. He tried traveling. From
Seville, in January, 1867, he wrote: "I cannot keep the thought
of Roslyn out of my mind; and, the sadder its memories are, the
more I cling to them."[11]   Two months later, from Rome: "I
have often wished that somebody were in my place whose curiosity had a sharper edge than mine, and that I were back at
Roslyn."[12]   A month and a half later, from Paris: "I cannot
help thinking of a place several thousand miles off, now more
than ever dear to me, and at the same time saying to myself,
How glad I shall be when I get back to it again!"[13]   And three
months later still, in Leam, he was counting the days, and even
the hours, that separated him from Roslyn.[14]   At last, back in
Cedarmere, in October, he wrote to a friend:

I confess that all this while my heart turned toward
Roslyn, and that I was glad to get back to it, after
a not very favorable passage of eleven days across
the Atlantic. I find the place very beautiful; the changes
please me, but there is a sadness in all this beauty,
since the eye for which these changes were originally
designed can look on them no more. It is now a
more beautiful October day; the maples, at the end of
our little lakelet, are glowing with the hues of autumn,
and over all lies the sweet golden sunshine. I look out
upon the landscape from the bay-window while I
write...[15]

The few poems that he wrote during his remaining years carry
the same tone of loss. "May Evening,"[16]   a song to spring,

cannot rise to the joy and new life usually connected with that
season.

> Yet there is sadness in thy soft caress,
>   Wind of the blooming year!
> The gentle presence, that was wont to bless
>   Thy coming, is not here.

"A Lifetime,"[17]   a poem written during a visit to Cummington
in 1876, reviewed his whole life from boyhood on. It is a long
poem, almost five pages, and the last two pages concern his
Long Island residence. His Roslyn home was still dear to him,
and he still spent most of his time there, but more and more
his thoughts of Cedarmere were being re-focused and telescoped,
until they settled on one small plot of ground:

> A grave is scooped on the hillside
>   Where often, at eve or morn,
> He lays the blooms of the garden —
>   He, and his youngest born.

He could not readjust. Perhaps he was too old; perhaps with
his wife's death, life really had lost its meaning. He tried once
more, in January, 1873, to empty himself of his grief by writing.
Sitting alone at Cedarmere, he started —

> The morn hath not the glory that it wore,
>   Nor doth the day so beautifully die,
> Since I can call thee to my side no more,
>   To gaze upon the sky.
>
> For thy dear hand, with each return of Spring,
>   I sought in sunny nooks the flowers she gave,
> I seek them still, and sorrowfully bring
>   The choicest to thy grave.
>
> Here, where I sit alone, is sometimes heard,
>   From the great world, a whisper of my name,
> Joined, haply, to some kind, commending word,
>   By those whose praise is fame.
>
> And then, as if I thought thou still wert nigh,

I turn me, half forgetting thou art dead,
To read the gentle gladness in thine eye,
    That once I might have read.

I turn, but see thee not; before my eyes
    The image of a hillside mound appears,
Where all of thee that passed not to the skies
    Was laid with bitter tears.

And I, whose thoughts go back to happier days,
    That fled with thee, would gladly now resign
All that the world can give of fame and praise,
    For one sweet look of thine.

Thus, ever, when I read of generous deeds,
    Such words as thou didst once delight to hear,
My heart is wrung with anguish as it bleeds
    To think thou art not near.

And now that I can talk no more with thee
    Of ancient friends and days too fair to last,
A bitterness blends with the memory
    Of all that happy past.

Oh, when I _____ [18]

It was never finished.

*   *   *   *

Bryant's Death

Once, many years before, when he was a very young man, he had hoped that he would die in June. In 1866, when he had stood by his wife's grave, he had reserved the place by her side for himself. In 1878, he no longer feared death; rather it seemed to him the fruition of this life, and the opportunity for a reunion with those he loved in a still better life.

On a Sunday shortly before his death, Bryant went to church as usual. Later he dined with Dr. John Ordonaux, an old friend who occupied a cottage on the Roslyn estate. After dinner, the two men walked along Bryant's favorite path by the shore of the

bay. They returned to the big house together and talked, and
their talk was of the wonders of nature.[19]

A few days later, after delivering a speech in Central Park,
Bryant returned to his New York residence. On the steps he
fell, striking his head. Fourteen days later, on June 12th, 1878,
he died. Two days later a special train left Hunter's Point at
one P.M., carrying the poet's body back to Roslyn. His friend,
James Grant Wilson, described the ceremony that afternoon:

> It was indeed a glorious day, and the daisies were
> dancing and glimmering over the fields as the poet's
> family, a few old friends, and the villagers saw him
> laid in his last resting-place at Roslyn, after a few
> words fitly spoken by his pastor, and beheld his coffin
> covered with roses and other summer flowers by a little
> band of country children, who gently dropped them as
> they circled round the poet's grave. This act completed,
> we left the aged minstrel amid the melody dearest of
> all to him in life — the music of the gentle June breezes
> murmuring through the tree-tops, from whence also
> came the songs of summer birds.[20]

Today, the poet's body lies in rest, next to his wife's, in the
cemetery in Roslyn. A modest monument marks his grave, but
in this small Long Island town, this poet needs no monument.
Through the middle of the town runs Bryant Avenue, named in
his honor. In the center of the town is Bryant Park, and the
intellectual hub of the town is the Bryant Library.

But what would have pleased him most is that his great-
granddaughter, Miss Frances Bryant Godwin, preserves his cher-
ished Cedarmere. Most of the surrounding acres have been sold,
but the homestead stands today, almost unchanged, as it once
stood in the poet's lifetime. One can almost see him today,
standing on the hill looking down on the Sound, as his friend,
Dr. Ordonaux, described him many years ago:

> I turned and saw him standing bareheaded, with his
> face toward the sparkling waters of the bay, his white
> locks and beard just moved by the passing breeze, and

he looking like one of the Bards of the Bible in the
rapture of devotion, or, better still, as the imperson-
ation of Homer himself listening to the murmuring
waves of his own blue Aegean.[21]

VIII

Bryant and Whitman

We have called Bryant one of the best poets in the
world! This smacks so much of the exaggerated that we
are half a mind to alter it, true as we sincerely believe
it to be. But we will let it stand.[1]

With these words, Walt Whitman paid tribute to the elder
poet, William Cullen Bryant. It was a tribute made with affection
as well as with admiration. Rough, rowdy Walt succumbed in
almost every way (but not artistically) to his polished predecessor.
Bryant, the older by twenty-five years, was everything that the
younger Whitman hoped to be: a respected and successful editor
and an established national poet.

The two men must have met for the first time in the early
1840's. There is no record of that first meeting; but the meeting
itself was inevitable since both were involved in the political and
journalistic life of the city. When Whitman made a speech at a
Democratic rally in 1840 or '41, the *Post*, under Bryant's editorship, gave him generous coverage.[2] In 1845, Bryant took a
"firm but reasonable stand" regarding the conflict between the
United States and England over the Oregon boundary, and
Whitman echoed his agreement.[3] Both men believed that the
expansion of the United States was "natural and inevitable," and
to both of them this "was both a political and a religious con-
viction."[4] Such political unanimity provided a good foundation

for friendship, and it is not surprising that when Whitman was "released" from the *Daily Eagle* in 1848 because of his political views, Bryant wrote about the incident, adding shrewdly that Whitman the "Barnburner" had to leave to make way for the "Old Hunkers."[5]

By this time the two men knew each other well. In 1846, Whitman described Bryant as "a plainly-dressed man of middling size, considerably beyond the younger age of life, with rather bloodless complexion, sparse white hair, and expressive quiet grey eyes."[6] They often met and talked. Many years later, when he was writing *Specimen Days,* Whitman recalled that they had often come together in the middle of the afternoon to take "rambles miles long, till dark..."[7] During these rambles, Bryant talked at length about his travels abroad and about the art, customs, and appearance of European cities; Whitman, younger and untraveled, listened with a kind of awe. After the first edition of *Leaves of Grass* was published in 1855, Bryant made a special trip on the Brooklyn ferry to meet with Whitman and to talk about the poems. He could not give Whitman his full approval, but "each poet respected the other as a democrat and a lover of nature."[8]

In spite of Bryant's conditional praise, Whitman continued his praise of Bryant unstintingly. He had begun quoting the older poet in *Franklin Evans*; chapter two begins with a stanza from "The Ages," and chapter nineteen, with four lines from an unidentified poem by Bryant. In 1851 in "Art and Artists," he quoted several lines from Bryant's "Forest Hymn";[9] and in "My Tribute to Four Poets," he spoke of Bryant's "pulsing the first interior verse-throbs of a mighty world — bard of the river and the wood, ever conveying a taste of open air, with scents as from hayfields, grapes, birch borders..." In the same essay Whitman compared Bryant's chants of death with those of Aeschylus, "as grim and eternal, if not as stormy and fateful..."[10] Later, in *Goodbye My Fancy*, his praise grew still more fulsome. He granted Bryant lyrical genius, and asked who could seek anything more magnificent than "The Battle-Field" and "A Forest Hymn." Then he eulogized:

> Bryant, unrolling, prairie-like, notwithstanding his
> mountains and lakes — moral enough (yet worldly and
> conventional) — a naturalist, pedestrian, gardener and
> fruiter — well aware of books, but mixing to the last
> in cities and society. I am not sure but his name ought
> to lead the list of American bards.[11]

If such praise from the exuberant Whitman for the carefully
restrained Bryant seems anomalous today, it is well to remember
the circumstances and times. Bryant had an international reputation; Whitman was a stumbling beginner. Bryant had initiated,
with his emphasis on an American nature and a national literature, the causes that Whitman would later espouse and carry to
their fruition. For the older poet, Whitman felt a sort of reverence, even a kind of hero-worship that lingered until Bryant's
death. Writing about his friend's funeral, Whitman described
"the good, stainless, noble old citizen and poet..." The scene
was simple but impressive; and the phrases Whitman used — "the
finely rendered anthem"..."the church, dim even now at approaching noon"..."the mellow-stained windows"..."the pro-
nounced eulogy"...[12]   seem more appropriate to the poet
written-about than to the poet writing.

In addition to the political and literary ties that Bryant and
Whitman shared, there were human links that connected the two
men. Bryant knew the Brooklyn artist, Charles L. Heyde, who
later married Whitman's sister Hannah, and, at least once, with
Heyde, he visited the Whitmans.[13] Bryant knew another friend
of Whitman's, Henry Kirke Brown, the artist responsible for the
bronze statue of Washington in Union Square. Indeed, Bryant's
admiration for Brown's work and his subsequent recommendation
of him for election to the National Academy of Design may have
stimulated Whitman's articles about Brooklyn artists later published in the New York *Post*.[14] Both men also knew well Eliza
Seaman Leggett of Long Island. This was the same Eliza whose
family Bryant and his wife had visited one summer day, partaking
of the "commonplace apple pie" with great relish. Many years
later, Eliza, a comfortably married woman living in Detroit,

corresponded with Whitman. In 1880, just two years after Bryant's death, she wrote reminiscently:

> I feel lonely in October since William Cullen Bryant died... I remember the sweet October days in Roslyn, when he and his wife would come over to Hillside... he would climb up the hill and get into the woods, always stopping upon the brow of the hill back of the barn, just under a famous great butternut tree, and, turning, take a look upon the harbor and far away Long Island Sound, the Red Mill hid among the willows, the lake under the close Harbor hill, and the busy village. Bryant always loved just this view of the bay.[15]

The nostalgia for her own childhood days on Long Island must have evoked a corresponding nostalgia in Whitman, for he too was of Long Island, born and bred.

Because he was *born* there, Whitman's memories of Long Island were far different from Cooper's or Bryant's. Cooper knew Sag Harbor, the great whaling era, the excitement and adventure. Bryant knew Cedarmere and the quiet village of Roslyn. But Whitman knew and embraced all of it, from its ocean-shrouded eastern tip to the great city that marks its western limit. Consequently, the influence exerted by the Island on these three men as authors differed too. On Cooper and Bryant it was a clear but erratic influence, an "acquired" influence, mixed with memories of Cooperstown or Cummington and Great Barrington. On Whitman, it was a continuing influence, beginning with birth, enduring till his death; for he not only lived on Long Island — he was *of* Long Island — and that made all the difference.

PART THREE
Walt Whitman

IX

Whitman: A Son of Long Island

Walt Whitman's Origin

About fifty miles east of the giant city of New York is West Hills, in Whitman's time as in our own, part of Huntington Township. West Hills, in 1819, when Whitman was born, was a small village of large farms, inhabited by rugged, independent farmers. It was by no means a new settlement, having been founded in 1653 when three Englishmen purchased the whole area from the Matinecock Indians for a few coats and shirts, some agricultural implements, and "six fathoms of wampum." Almost immediately, it was named Huntington, after "Huntingdon," the birthplace of Oliver Cromwell.[1] This was the first of the many small ironies that surround Walt Whitman on Long Island — that the poet who was to liberate his countrymen from the puritanical yoke was born in the township named in honor of the greatest English Puritan.

Joseph Whitman was the first of the poet's family to settle on Long Island. Born in England, in 1640 he traveled first to Stratford, Connecticut, and then in 1660 crossed the Sound to Huntington. Here he married Sarah Ketchum, a native of Southold.[2] This was no traditional marriage. Like his famous descendant, this first Whitman attracted anger, accusations, and court scenes. Sarah's stepfather, Henry Whitney, found Joseph unworthy of his daughter. He even brought formal accusation

111

against Joseph for stealing his daughter's affections and for
refusing to recognize a parent's right to withhold consent. The
would-be groom ·met the accusation with spirit and, fortunately
for him, the court decided to postpone the case until Sarah
herself could be questioned.[3] What exactly happened will probably never be known, for no further records are available; but
Sarah either refused to be questioned, or else battled successfully
with her accusers. At any rate, a few months later Sarah and
Joseph were married.

This is the only instance recorded in which Joseph appeared
reckless or self-willed. The little more that we know about him
indicates an independent, intelligent man who early won and
retained the respect of his neighbors, for in that small colonial
community he was elected or appointed to several responsible
posts. In 1672, he acted as emissary between the towns of
Huntington and Smithtown in a border dispute. In 1686, with
two other men, he was active in defining the boundary of Lloyd's
Neck. In the 1680's, he served as Constable, Grand Juryman,
Commissioner, and "leather sealer."[4] In 1690, again with two
other men, he was appointed Commissioner for the ensuing year
"to take care of all afairs Rellaitting to ye Publicke good of the
towne."[5] Nor did his civic duties limit his material success.
During these same years, he acquired a large valley between
Huntington and Smithtown that soon came to be known as
"Joseph Whitman's Great Hollow" — and that today is Com-
mack.[6] In 1694, he "took up" 170 acres of land on the south
side of town at a place known as "gorges spring."[7] He must
have owned most of "east necke," since there are deeds extant
showing sales by Joseph and Sarah of one land tract in east
necke in 1688,[8] and of another in the same area in 1692.[9]
Three years later, he made his will in the form of a deed,
dividing his land among his sons, Joseph, John, Nathan, and
Samuel.[10] The making of the will, however, did not indicate
a cessation of activity, for in 1698, Joseph Whitman was again
buying — this time a good piece of land called Baiting Place
Purchase (now Lower Melville).[11] In 1688, his estate had been
assessed at 118 pounds.[12] This would seem to place Joseph

Whitman among the more prosperous men of this young community. This was Walt Whitman's earliest Island-ancestor: a man proud, independent, stubborn, perhaps ruthless in attaining his goals.

Recent genealogical studies indicate that Joseph's son, John, is probably next in line leading down to Walt.[13]   John must have been a rather quiet individual, by his father's standards, but he too was evidently respected by his neighbors as he was appointed Town Trustee for at least one year, and Town Assessor for at least four years.[14]   Little else is known about John Whitman.

The story grows more exciting, however, when we come to John's son, Nehemiah Whitman. This grandson of Joseph, this great-grandfather of Walt, chose a strong-minded, strong-bodied girl, Phoebe (Sarah) White, whom he married in December, 1740, in the First Presbyterian Church in Huntington.[15]   Walt wrote about his great-grandmother, remembering stories of her longevity (she lived to be ninety years of age), her swearing, chewing tobacco, using opium, and managing a farm more efficiently than a man.[16]   In 1799, it had been ruled that children born of slaves in New York were born free. In the next few years there were two instances in which Phoebe Whitman declared officially that a slave of hers had had a child, said child to be free. There is ironical (though accidental) foreshadowing of Walt's reputation in the name of one such slave – Freelove.[17]

It is easy to let Phoebe overwhelm her husband's memory, but Nehemiah was a strong character, too. Those were the years of the Revolutionary War, and Nehemiah, like the other Long Island Whitmans, was true to the rebel cause. Like most Long Islanders, he took the oath of loyalty before Governor Tryon, but this evidently was merely a formality which no one took seriously.[18]   There is a record, too, of five bushels of oats that Nehemiah was forced to "sell" to the British Army for the use of the Second Battalion Jersey Volunteers stationed in Jericho – value, 1 pound, 15 shillings – and there is also recorded that this sum was never paid.[19]   Nehemiah Whitman, a good businessman, must have been more sure than ever of his patriotic leanings. For Nehemiah was a good businessman. He had extended his land-holdings until he held at least five hundred acres of good farm land in the West Hills area.[20] In 1782, at the close of the war, the town assessed his property at 244 pounds,[21] an appreciable increase over his grandfather's holdings less than one hundred years earlier. When he died, he left his son Jesse the meadow called Little Neck, and a large share of his other property.[22]

Jesse Whitman, son of Nehemiah and grandfather of Walt, was a conservative Whitman. He managed to hold most of his land together, but added little to it. In his will, he divided it among his children and was thus instrumental in ending the 150-year-old Whitman holdings. Never again was one of this Whitman line to own much property or prosper materially. We know little about Jesse; he probably supported the rebels, though records show that he assisted the British in the building of the fort at Lloyd's Neck [23] and in the establishment of Fort Golgotha in Huntington.[24] However, it is possible that men and materials for these fortifications were drafted by the British who controlled Long Island at that time. Certainly, his townsmen held no animosity toward Jesse for his actions since they appointed him, in 1780, Town Constable and Collector.[25] Jesse is not a very colorful character, and is easily over-shadowed by Hannah Brush, his wife. Hannah lived thirty-one years longer than Jesse, until young Walt was fifteen years of age. Many times Walt listened to exciting stories from her lips about the Revolutionary War and about early Long Island.

Their son Walter was the last link in this family chain—and a weak link at that. He not only could not add to the family land-holdings; he could not even hold on to those he inherited. He was constantly unlucky in financial moves, and was certainly the main cause for the family poverty in Walt's early years. Walt Whitman may have inherited some of his father's restlessness—but that was the whole legacy. His initiative, his determination, his eternal questing spirit—those he received from Joseph, from Nehemiah, from Jesse, and certainly from Phoebe. Beyond these, one must turn to the Van Velsor line, his mother's family.

WHITMAN—A SON OF LONG ISLAND

Louisa Van Velsor's ancestors were a fascinating lot. There was Grandfather Van Velsor, the Major, who made weekly trips into Brooklyn for over forty years to sell his farm produce.[26] (Walt loved those early trips taken in a stage and market wagon, and years later remembered still the ghastly smells of lampblack and oil from the canvas covering.) There was "Amy" (really Naomi Williams Van Velsor), Walt's grandmother, a mild, gentle, sweet-tempered woman whom Walt loved and admired. There was Amy's gallant and exciting father, Captain John Williams, master of a ship engaged in the West Indies trade — a man who may have served under John Paul Jones in 1779, and whose stories (told by Amy) stimulated Walt's boyish imagination.[27] There was the Major's mother, Mary Kossabone, wife of Garrett Van Velsor and granddaughter of Old Salt Kossabone. Old Salt lived to be ninety; he was an old sailor who spent his last years watching the bay from the piazza of the Van Velsor Cold Spring home.[28] Walt heard many stories about him, too, from Grandmother Van Velsor.

These were the ancestors of Walt Whitman — important as background for the poet's mind and knowledge; important because they provided the little security that the poet ever found; important because they provided grist for the poet's mill. Whitman himself, with his mind, believed that environment is more important than heredity in the formation of character,[29] but his heart told him a different story. In "Song of Myself," he wrote clearly and surely:

> My tongue, every atom of my blood, form'd from
>   this soil, this air,
> Born here of parents born here from parents the
>   same, and their parents the same . . .[30]

Little more is needed to prove Whitman's firm belief in both heredity and environment.

* * * * * *

Ancestral Legends and Local History

As a child, Whitman delighted in family stories; as a man, he incorporated his ancestors into his poems. In "Song of Myself," he dedicated two sections to his great-grandfather, Captain John Williams.

> Would you hear of an old-time sea-fight?
> Would you learn who won by the light of the moon
>   and stars?
> List to the yarn, as my grandmother's father the
>   sailor told it to me.[31]

Whitman was probably using poetic license when he claimed that he had heard this story from his "grandmother's father." Captain Williams was the owner or part-owner of a merchant ship that traveled between New York and Florida, but, as Holloway pointed out, there is no evidence that he witnessed the fight between the *Bon Homme Richard* and the *Serapis.* Yet the poem unquestionably describes this particular sea-fight. Where, then, did Whitman get his facts? The answer seems to lie in a two-volume history, *Washington and His Generals,* written by J.T. Headley, published in 1847, and described by Whitman in a review in the Brooklyn *Eagle* in 1847.[32] A line-by-line comparison of the two versions of this sea-battle indicates strongly that Headley was Whitman's source.

Both versions state that the battle began at sunset and continued into the night. Headley writes: "...the full round moon pushed its broad disc above the horizon, and shed a flood of light over the tranquil waters."[33] Whitman writes: "...and by the light of the moon and stars..." and later, "...the full moon well up." Both agree that eighteen-pound shots were exchanged, that the *Richard* had only three guns, two of which "burst at the first fire."[34] Both agree that the lower deck ports had to be closed because of the explosion, and the fight carried on from the top deck only. In both versions the English captain is described as courageous (Headley: "Never did a man struggle braver than the English commander"; Whitman: "His was the surly English pluck, and there is no tougher or truer.") and in both, he calls on the *Richard* to surrender. The answers differ slightly: Headley uses the long-famous version: "I have not yet begun to fight," while Whitman changes it to "We have just begun our part of the fighting."

Jones, realizing the fight was going against him, ordered his ship to be pulled alongside the *Serapis;* then, according to Headley, he ordered them to be lashed together and "in his eagerness to secure them, helped with his own hands to tie the lashings." Whitman says: "My captain lash'd fast with his own hands." The ships were now so close that "the guns touched muzzles" (in Whitman: "the cannon touch'd"). The *Bon Homme Richard* was in such peril that the master-at-arms released the prisoners confined in the hold (this appears in both versions). Headley adds that "both vessels looked like wrecks, and both were on fire." Whitman said, "The two great hul's motionless on the breast of the darkness." The *Richard*'s pumps were not working properly, and the hold was filled with water (according to Headley, six feet; Whitman, five feet). The *Serapis* surrendered, and Paul Jones ordered his men to leave the *Richard* and board the conquered ship. Both versions agree that the *Richard* was "riddled" and sinking slowly, and that, when it went down, its decks were covered with stacks of dead bodies.

There are a few minor discrepancies: Headly reports six feet of water in the hold to Whitman's five, and Headley places the *Serapis'* surrender at 10:30 P.M. while Whitman places it at midnight. But the similarities are startling, with several identical phrases and many other phrases that vary only slightly. It seems clear, then, that Whitman did use Headley as his source; the *way* in which he used it suggests a recurring pattern of technique. He used the details which seemed to him most striking, varied them when it seemed necessary,[35] and (because "Song of Myself" is a personal poem) attributed the story to an ancestor who, as a seafaring man, might have witnessed the event.

"Old Salt Kossabone" is the story of another ancestor, almost prosaically told. The Old Salt (Whitman's great-great-grandfather) is almost ninety years old, too old to do much except to sit on the piazza and look out over the bay. One day, sitting there, he watches an outbound brig struggling throughout many hours. At nightfall, the breeze changes and the brig shakes free and rounds the cape. " 'She's free — she's on her destination' — these the last words — when Jenny came, he sat there dead."

Still another ancestor, Nehemiah Whitman (not the great-grandfather) fought in the Revolutionary War, was promoted to a lieutenant, and was killed in the Battle of Brooklyn. Reincarnated, he is probably the main figure in the long poem, "The Centenarian's Story." The old soldier is watching the volunteers drill in Washington Park, Brooklyn. He tells of an earlier time, when a battle raged in earnest over this same ground — a battle in which he played a part. Here, too, there is gallantry, yet more than gallantry:

> It sickens me yet, that slaughter!
> I saw the moisture gather in drops on the face of
>   the General.
> I saw how he wrung his hands in anguish.

With the tragedy is blended hope:

> But when my General pass'd me,
> As he stood in his boat and look'd toward the coming
>   sun,
> I saw something different from capitulation.

How skillfully the poet takes the family story for action and color, adds a touch of irony (for the volunteers the old veteran is watching are only drilling; pretense, not reality), brings the past up to the present by analogy, then closes with "this land" — these "hills and slopes of Brooklyn." One thinks of John of Gaunt's "this England" — and feels the poet's passionate love for his land, for both America and his own special Long Island earth.

Whitman actually saw the volunteers drilling at Fort Hamilton, and described the experience in some detail in August, 1847.[36] When he wrote "The Centenarian's Story" fourteen years later, he changed the setting from Fort Hamilton to Washington Park, later renamed Fort Greene Park. This change cannot be attributed to accident or forgetfulness. Whitman had a strong and lasting affection for Fort Greene, the scene of the tactically-important Battle of Brooklyn. One or two of his ancestors had actually fought in this battle. It was the major battle fought on Long Island during the entire war; perhaps most important of all, it was the scene not only of a battle but also of the masterly retreat of Washington and his raw troops across the river to the island of Manhattan and safety. Historically, there is no question about the importance of this retreat. If it had not succeeded, the core of the young army and its most intelligent commander would have been destroyed or captured, effectively ending the fight for independence.[37]

All three of these factors must have influenced Whitman. He was certainly aware of Fort Greene's military importance. Writing in 1862 a series of articles surveying the history of Brooklyn, he reminded his readers that in 1775, the Fort Greene site "offered almost as desert and bleak an appearance as the untenanted wilds on the east end of Long Island do at this day."[38] He then described the part it had played in the Revolutionary War:

> ...it was in this very neighborhood that the lines of fortified posts and entrenchments were made, reaching from Wallabout to Red Hook, that formed the American lines, in the battle of Long Island, in the early part of the Revolutionary War. It was this line of rude fortifications that stopped the progress of the enemy, and secured the safety of the American troops — till Washington made his masterly retreat over to New York Island, which saved the revolutionary cause.[39]

Whitman's intense interest in Fort Greene was accentuated by a movement in 1846 to raze the fort to make way for some projected buildings. In July of that year he retorted angrily: "More room, we want, do we?" and then added that if more room is needed, there is a stretch of "some hundred and twenty miles to grow out upon, at our leisure..." [40] He was referring, of course, to the 120-mile-long Long Island.

Probably more effective as propaganda was the ode that he wrote to be sung at Fort Greene on the Fourth of July, 1846. He specified that it was to be sung to the tune of "The Star Spangled Banner." It is not a very good poem, tending toward over-sentimentality and archaic language; but one stanza is worth quoting here because it emphasizes the aspects of the Battle of Brooklyn that most interested and appealed to Whitman:

> Say! sons of Long-Island! in legend or song,
>   Keep ye aught of its record, that day dark and
>   cheerless —
> That cruel of days — when, hope weak, the foe strong,
>   Was seen the Serene One — still faithful, still fearless,
> Defending the worth, of the sanctified earth
> We are standing on now. Lo! the slopes of its girth
> Where the martyrs were buried: nor prayers, tears,
>   or stones,
> Mark their crumbled-in coffins, their white, holy
>   bones! [41]

These eight lines stress the setting (sons of Long Island), the weakness of the rebel army, the strength of the foe, and the apotheosis of Washington (the Serene One) — all items of special interest to Whitman.

The four-stanza ode was listed as the seventh event on the program for the celebration, and it was immediately followed by Benediction.[42]   The setting, the tune, and its place on the program must have surrounded it with an almost sacred aura which is certainly lacking when one merely reads the words.

The ode was the strongest, but not the last shot fired in Whitman's private war to save Fort Greene from the construction trade. He continued writing articles, editorials, and brief notes to support his petition. He became skillful in the art of innuendo. In a sketch entitled "Last Evening upon Fort Greene," he described a delayed Fourth of July celebration. There were thirty thousand people present, but they were quiet, subdued by the beauties of nature, not noisy as they would have been in the city. He concluded, almost ecstatically, "Ah, God *did* make the country indeed; and cities — man's work — can't compare with His!" [43]

This private war ended in 1847 when the Legislature authorized the creation of Fort Greene Park. Whitman acknowledged his victory, then immediately opened fire again, starting a new battle. This time he wanted a monument erected to the prisoners who had died in the Revolution in "the British hulks, at the Wallabout." This battle, too, he would win; but the victory would not come until years after his death.[44] In 1888 he still remembered the old cause and wrote "The Wallabout Martyrs," a five-line memorial poem. The explanation that precedes the poem is longer than the poem itself. In it, Whitman notes bitterly that "in an old vault, mark'd by no special recognition, lie huddled at this moment the undoubtedly authentic remains of the stanchest and earliest revolutionary patriots from the British prison ships and prisons of the times of 1776-83 . . . " In the poem Whitman points out that the memory of those unknown soldiers is more important, more meaningful to the world than the memory of Achilles or Ulysses or Alexander, because these men became "the stepping stones to thee to-day and here, America."

These two crusades remained vivid in Whitman's memory throughout the rest of his life. In a letter to Charles M. Skinner in 1885, he declared that the preservation of old Fort Greene which he had championed thirty-five years earlier was a "feather in his wings" that he hoped always to preserve.[45]

Whitman's interest in the Revolutionary War embraced more than Fort Greene and the Wallabout prison ship. He was traditionally against war and the agony it caused to the human beings involved, but this particular war was different. *This* war won freedom for the nation he so loved, and it began (as far as Whitman was concerned) on land in which he felt a proprietary interest. Whitman was no historian. Lexington and Concord barely existed for him; "the first active movement in behalf of the American cause against the government of Great

Britain, began here on Long Island early in the spring of '76.''[46]
Bunker Hill, Saratoga, even Yorktown faded into insignificance,
but "upon the Battle of Long Island turned more momentous
results than upon any battle fought elsewhere upon the American
continent.'' Whitman was a local patriot, and to him this
battle and the men who fought in it formed a microcosm of the
war as a whole. This is true of his approach to this subject in
his poetry as well as in his editorials. "The Dying Veteran" is
carefully sub-titled "A Long Island incident — early part of the
present century." It describes a "queer, old savage man," a
native of Long Island, who fought under Washington, and who —
now on his deathbed — recalls the glory of that old "wild battle-
life."[48]

This rather limited view of the Revolutionary War was not the
nostalgic tendency of an old man; it began in his youth with
the short story, "The Last Loyalist," written in 1842. This story,
set "on a large and fertile neck of land that juts out in the
Sound," concerns Vanhome, owner of an old-fashioned residence.
In the War for Independence, Vanhome, fearing that if the
British won he would lose his estate, turned Loyalist. When the
colonists won, his estate was confiscated and he himself was
despised and condemned by his patriotic neighbors. Years later,
he returns as a stranger to spend the night in his old residence,
but his sleep is bedeviled by the plaintive ghost of a child. Then
all comes clear; this is indeed the fiend Vanhome who not only
played traitor to his country but who had, still earlier, tormented
his innocent child-nephew to his death.[49] This story, written
when Whitman was twenty-three years old, is baroque with
melodrama and blind patriotism. It equates Loyalist and fiend;
and in doing so, suggests a possible source for Whitman's local
partisanship. Long Island was the scene of violent conflicts during
the war between the Loyalists and Patriots, and in the decades
following, this enmity was not forgotten. Like Cooper, Whitman
lived on the Island in the first half of the 19th century, at a time
when many of the former combatants were still alive and still
voluble about the happenings of an earlier day. The tales that
Cooper heard about the Loyalists were softened in the retelling

by the author's innate aristocratic tendency; the tales that Whitman heard were not. The Whitmans were solidly middle-class, and their rebel sympathy was outraged equally by British oppression and Loyalist betrayal. It is not surprising that in such an environment even the peace-loving Whitman learned contempt for the enemy and fierce pride in the martial exploits of his fellow Islanders.

*   *   *   *

Family and Friends

Not all of Whitman's family had been involved in the adventures of war; most of them were peaceful people, occupied with peaceful pursuits. These, too, interested and influenced the poet. His family was a closely-knit unit whose members cared about each other. Whitman himself provided for his mother until her death, kept a brotherly eye on his sister Hannah's unhappy marriage, and was patiently tender with the mentally-handicapped Eddy. Though he himself escaped early from the family home, he visited it often; one of the earliest-developed tenets of his philosophy was a profound respect and belief in the family group as a foundation for a free and healthy America. The family provided first a background: "Before I was born out of my mother generations guided me."[50] It provided next a love-filled security of "precious ever-lingering memories (of you my mother dear — you, father — you, brothers, sisters, friends)."[51] Perhaps most important of all, it provided permanency, a place to which one could return — "to lay in port for good — to settle...no spot will do but this."[52] To Whitman, the restless wanderer, it was vitally necessary to have some permanency underlying the constant change and growth of this nation. This was the role of the family, in his life and in the lives of all Americans.

His mother was the most important person in the family. She was the "perfect mother," sublime, constant, understanding, even in his earliest writings. Archie Dean accepts the burden of school-teaching in order to support his mother, and as quickly as possible returns to her.[53]   Tim Barker was getting food for his widowed mother when he was accused of stealing.[54]   Wild Frank, after running off to sea, yearns to see his "loving mother" once again; after he is killed by Black Nell, he is dragged "batter'd, and cut, and bloody" to the very feet of that mother.[55]   Whitman's unusually strong attachment to his mother accounts for her frequent appearance in his poetry and prose, in her own person and in the ocean, the world-mother. His eulogy culminates in the poem meant to immortalize her life and death, "As at Thy Portals Also Death." He sits by the coffin and kisses convulsively "the sweet old lips, the cheeks, the closed eyes," then writes these lines — as a monument — "to her, the ideal woman, practical, spiritual, of all of earth, life, love, to me the best ... "

His father fared less well in Whitman's works. Even in "Wild Frank's Return," the father is stern, sometimes harsh, occasionally unjust, and he is the cause of his son's running away.[56] Tolerance and a little sympathy for his father grew as Whitman matured, and in 1855, shortly before his father's death, Whitman took the old man down to West Hills for a last visit.[57]   Together, father and son shared once more the land of their origin. Later, when he writes, he parallels his mother with the ocean and his father with the island of Paumanok.[58]   For his father, this is a Janus-type compliment; for the poet loves this land — he throws himself upon it, clings to it, seeks its touch; but at the same time he notes that the land (unlike the ocean) is the receiver of drift and debris.

His brothers and sisters are mentioned only casually and infrequently, but there is a special warmth and defensive sympathy for Eddy, the younger brother who was feeble-minded, paralytic, and epileptic.[59]   That Whitman was the only member of the family who could be counted upon to help Eddy is made clear by a letter written by their mother: "They none of them want edd, Walter and they would soon get tired of paying his board and we aint much expense to any but you walter dear ... "[60] Whitman's spontaneous sympathy for the sick and the weak must have kept poor Eddy constantly in his mind. He described once

an epileptic in the middle of a seizure, and the phrases — the
wordless tongue, the distended neck, the rolling eyes, "the palms
of the hands...cut by the turn'd-in nails" — are so vivid, so
obviously the result of personal observation and involvement, that
they call forth an answering sympathy in the reader.[61]

For Jesse, the older brother who spent the last six years of
his life in the Kings County Lunatic Asylum,[62]   Whitman felt
sharp pity:

> The lunatic is carried at last to the asylum a confirm'd
> case,
> (He will never sleep any more as he did in the cot
> in his mother's bed-room...) [63]

Unfortunates like Jesse and Eddy need understanding and acceptance. Whitman demanded it for them in the poem, "Faces,"
section 3:

> I saw the face of the most smear'd and slobbering
> idiot they had at the asylum,
> And I knew for my consolation what they knew not,
> I knew of the agents that emptied and broke my
> brother,
> The same wait to clear the rubbish from the fallen
> tenement,
> And I shall look again in a score or two of ages,
> And I shall meet the real landlord perfect and un-
> harm'd, every inch as good as myself.

*   *   *   *   *

Quaker Influence

One of the strongest influences on Walt Whitman in his youth
was the Quaker religion. His mother's mother, Amy Williams,
was a Quaker,[64]   "a woman of sweet, sensible character, house-
wifely proclivities, and deeply intuitive and spiritual."[65]   His
mother Louisa and his father Walter were not Quakers, but they
were attracted to the religion and sometimes attended meetings,
especially when Elias Hicks was scheduled to speak. Like the

Whitmans and the Van Velsors, Hicks too was a native Long
Islander, born near the town of Jericho on March 18, 1748. His
boyhood was like Whitman's; it included fowling and fishing,
horseback riding, some singing and dancing. He also liked
sleighing, and Whitman's great-grandfather remembered that they
had often taken sleigh rides together over "the plains."[66]   Hicks
was already an old man when Whitman first heard him speak at
a meeting held on Long Island. Years later Whitman tried to
recall what had been said. He remembered a discussion of the
inner light, which he interpreted as a sort of religious conscience,
capable of eventually molding a National Morality.[67]   Certainly
it was this aspect of the Quaker religion, along with the peace
and serenity, that seemed to appeal to him. In his old age he
wrote an essay, "Elias Hicks," discussing Hicks himself and his
teaching. The following prefatory note preceded the essay:

> As myself a little boy hearing so much of E.H., at that
> time, long ago, in Suffolk and Queens and Kings
> Counties—and more than once personally seeing the
> old man—and my dear, dear father and mother faith-
> ful listeners to him at the meetings—I remember how
> I dream'd to write perhaps a piece about E.H. and his
> look and discourses, however long afterward—for my
> parents' sake—and the dear Friends too![68]

He once told Horace Traubel that when he was a "young feller
up on the Long Island shore" he had seriously considered becoming a Quaker.[69]   There is no indication that he ever did more
than consider it. Even the Quakers would eventually have seemed
too institutionalized and too formal for the free-roving poet. But
this association with Hicks and with Quaker belief did influence
the poet in two ways: by providing direct references and by
helping to develop Whitman's personal philosophy.

The direct references are relatively unimportant. In "Song of
Myself," there is a casual mention of a Quakeress putting off her
bonnet and talking melodiously;[70]   in several poems there are
references to the "First Month" or the "Fifth Month" instead
of to January or May, in accordance with Quaker custom; but

the most important direct reference occurs in the poem, "Faces." This poem describes all kinds of faces: good and bad, ugly and beautiful, sacred and bestial; then culminates in a description of the ultimate face—"the old face of the mother of many children." As he depicts this face, two influences are apparent: his respect for the Quakers and his admiration and affection for his mother and grandmother:

> Behold a woman!
> She looks out from her quaker cap, her face is
>   clearer and more beautiful than the sky.
>
> She sits in an armchair under the shaded porch of
>   the farmhouse,
> The sun just shines on her old white head.
>
> Her ample gown is of cream-hued linen,
> Her grandsons raised the flax, and her grand-
>   daughters spun it with the distaff and the wheel.
>
> The melodious character of the earth,
> The finish beyond which philosophy cannot go
>   and does not wish to go,
> The justified mother of men.[71]

In this conclusion Whitman has used the Quaker reference to amplify and extend by association the serenity and fruitfulness of the scene. He is speaking here not as a member of a particular sect, but as an artist utilizing implication to gain emotional intensity.

This leads directly to Whitman's philosophy and how it was affected by his acquaintance with the Quakers. He referred once to Elias Hicks as "this Personality." [72] At another time he admitted that people who had known Hicks personally considered him ambitious and proud, desirous of establishing a sect that would reflect his own name and ideas.[73] Whitman could see nothing wrong in this. All strong men with strong convictions used such means to achieve anything definite.[74] He, too, was ambitious and proud; he too considered himself a Personality— single, unique, yet all-embracing; he too wished to establish a "sect" whose main tenet would be that each man must develop his own Personality.

This love of the "Personality" pervades his poetry. It is the driving force in "Song of Myself," in "Salut au Monde!" and in "Song of the Open Road." Did Hicks actually help to mold this prime concept of Whitman's, or did Whitman in his later life simply admire in Hicks some of his own ideas? Probably a modified yes is the only possible answer to both questions.

*   *   *   *

A Horseman's Joys

Another interest of the Van Velsors in Cold Spring was fine horses, which the men of the family "bred and train'd from blooded stock."[75]   Whitman's mother had been a skilled horse-woman in her youth, with a daily ride part of her regular routine. Whitman as a boy learned to know and love horses on the Van Velsor farm. On Saturdays and during the summer months he took long rides, most often alone, across the hills and plains on the north shore of Long Island. He loved the stage-coach horses, too, that pulled his grandfather's wagon from Cold Spring to Brooklyn and back again. It was a boyhood fascination that never lessened. When he was teaching in Smith-town, he sometimes accompanied Joseph Hull Conklin who drove the stage from Orient Point to Brooklyn during a seven-year period. They were quite good friends and almost of the same age, for Whitman was eighteen and Hull, twenty-two. It must have been a delightful trip for the young teacher. The stage left Orient Point at four A.M., stopped at Riverhead to add two horses, then went on to Smithtown where it stopped for the night. Hallock's Inn (where Whitman boarded) provided over-night quarters for travelers. Then, early the next morning, the stage was again on its way, destination Brooklyn.[76]

After he left Smithtown, Whitman moved to Huntington to establish the *Long-Islander*. He enjoyed this experience thorough-ly, especially the weekly jaunts around Long Island to deliver his newspaper. Each week he would fill a wagon with copies of the *Long-Islander,* harness up a horse or two, and take off for a leisurely ride.[77]

As Whitman began writing fiction a year or two later, he used these experiences many times. "Wild Frank's Return" pivots on a handsome, blooded horse, Black Nell. When she is taken away from him, Frank leaves home. When he returns, he rides the horse proudly, but before the ride is over, thunder frightens Black Nell and she drags him to his death. In the temperance novel, Franklin Evans is tensely aware of the stage-coach horses as they take him from his safe rural home to the city full of temptations and wickedness. Archie Dean, the young school-teacher in "The Shadow and the Light of a Young Man's Soul," is a fop and a discontented loafer when he moves out to Long Island; there, the brisk country air and the horseback rides every Saturday sweeten his disposition and infuse him with fresh vitality.

Later, when he was writing poetry, Whitman remembered with delight "the saddle, the gallop, the pressure upon the seat, the cool gurgling by the ears and hair," and he cried ecstatically, "O the horseman's and horsewoman's joys!"[78] In "Song of Myself" (section 32), Whitman explains why he likes animals: they do not whine, or weep for their sins, or discuss their duty to God; they are not dissatisfied, do not kneel to one of their number, are neither respectable nor unhappy. As he turns to a specific animal to illustrate natural nobility and independence, he chooses the horse:

> A gigantic beauty of a stallion, fresh and responsive
>   to my caresses,
> Head high in the forehead, wide between the ears,
> Limbs glossy and supple, tail dusting the ground,
> Eyes full of sparkling wickedness, ears finely cut,
>   flexibly moving.
>
> His nostrils dilate as my heels embrace him,
> His well-built limbs tremble with pleasure as we race
>   around and return.

The lines resound, both in rhythm and diction, with Whitman's knowledge of and love for a fine horse. Some of the description could have come from books or from observation, but the phrase, "my heels embrace him" and the reference to the horse's well-built limbs trembling with pleasure are the direct result of years of affectionate association with fine horses.

When Whitman saw John Jacob Astor, he was impressed not by the stout old man wrapped in furs, but by the splendid team of horses that drew his sleigh. He added, parenthetically, to the impudent young: "You needn't think all the best animals are brought up nowadays; never was such horseflesh as fifty years ago on Long Island...folks look'd for spirit and mettle in a nag, not tame speed merely." [79]

References to horseflesh and to riding are not frequent in Whitman's poetry, but when they do appear, they inject a warmth and a vivid detail that highlight the surrounding lines. It is a traditional writing technique. Whitman could have written about life on the moon, familiarly and well, if he had placed there a ferry, a brace of horses, a Quaker mother, and a country creek. These objects, bred of his bone and blood, bursting with their own reality, would have lent an aura of realism to such unfamiliar objects as moon craters and moon-men.

This technique worked well for Whitman throughout his long life. He exploited his early acquaintances and experiences to the fullest possible degree. His first writings abound in faintly-veiled descriptions of family members, Long Island veterans, fine horses, and Quaker tenets; they are used, in a blatant and rather moralizing way, as the subject-matter of his works. His later writings, intent on conveying his now-developed philosophy, used them differently. They have been "purified." In the still of Whitman's mind, their essence or universal quality has been extracted, perceived, and clearly defined. In *Leaves of Grass,* they continue to appear, no longer important in themselves, but vitally important as concrete correlatives of emotions and ideas that he was endeavoring to express.

The first twenty years of Whitman's life, then, and the experiences that occurred during this period, have a three-fold importance: (1) they provide information pertinent to an understanding of the poet as man; (2) they provided subject-matter for the young apprentice-poet; and (3) they acted (from 1850 on) as concrete and vividly-outlined "anchors" that held down Whitman's philosophizing and oracular prophesying, and thus prevented his poetry from becoming too cold, too impersonal, or too detached from human life.

X

Whitman the Schoolmaster

Whitman once said: "I don't value the poetry in what I have written so much as the teaching; the poetry is only a horse for the other to ride."[1] Posterity has, to some extent, reversed that self-evaluation; but it should not be overlooked. Whitman *was* a teacher first, and a poet second. Teaching was a part of his youth and was to become a part of his personality. He remained to the end of his life not a poet only, but a poet-prophet whose intent was to teach, guide, and inspire his countrymen in the quest for the good life.

Teaching on Long Island

He began teaching in Norwich in June, 1836.[2] He apparently became a schoolmaster because he was unable to find suitable work in the city and because "getting a school" on Long Island was fairly simple. Trained teachers were scarce, especially in rural areas, and school boards must have been pleasantly impressed by this young man with confidence and verbal fluency.[3] The candidate himself was evidently less impressed by the school board and by the notion of teaching. In "The Shadow and the Light of a Young Man's Soul," written twelve years later in 1848, Whitman described the fears and distaste with which Archibald Dean set forth on a teaching career. Because he had been unable to find work, Archie was leaving the city that he loved for the country, where he was to take charge of a little district school. He was a fashionable young man who liked nice clothes and disliked menial work, and he dreaded the prospect of keeping a country school for "poor pay and coarse fare."[4] Necessity forced the change, however, and Archie began teaching in early spring. His first letter to his widowed mother was full of despair: "Mother, my throat chokes, and my blood almost stops, when I see around me so many people who appear to be born into the world merely to eat and sleep, and run the same dull monotonous round..."[5]

If Whitman felt similar apprehensions as he began his duties in Norwich in 1836, he must have been in a rebellious and rather bitter mood, but the bitterness quickly evaporated both for Whitman and young Archie Dean. The author interrupts Archie's story to discourse rather pompously on the unexpected advantages of country living:

> There is surely, too, a refreshing influence in open-air nature, and in natural scenery, with occasional leisure to enjoy it, which begets in a man's mind truer and heartier reflections, analyzes and balances his decisions, and clarifies them if they are wrong, so that he sees his mistakes... Whether this suggestion be warranted or not, there was no doubt that the discontented young teacher's spirits were eventually raised and sweetened by his country life, by his long walks over the hills, by his rides on horseback every Saturday, his morning rambles and his evening saunters; by his coarse living, even, and the untainted air and water...[6]

Archie began teaching in 1835, Whitman in 1836; Archie's love for his mother parallels Whitman's devotion to his "perfect mother"; and Archie's "moody pride and frustrated ambition suggest the self-revelations of Whitman's own early verse."[7] This short story is almost definitely autobiographical, and the author's interpolation concerning the effect of nature on Archie Dean is, in all probability, based on his own experience. Certainly Whitman's attitude toward teaching changed sufficiently to induce him to continue as a schoolmaster for the next few years.

From 1836 to 1841 he taught single or double terms in Babylon, Long Swamp, Smithtown, Woodbury, Little Bayside, Whitestone, Dix Hills, and Triming Square.[8] Detailed records exist only for the two terms he taught in Smithtown in the autumn and winter of 1837-1838, but the situation there was certainly similar to those he encountered in the other towns and therefore suggests the type of experience to which Whitman was submitted during this five-year period.

Twenty years later Whitman wrote an article, "Long Island Schools and Schooling," in which he described the typical school building and curriculum:

> There are still left some old-fashioned country school-houses down through Long Island, especially in Suffolk County. The representative building is generally a primitive, unpainted edifice with a batten door, fastened by a padlock, and up above, a small chimney peering out at one end of the eaves. The "studies" pursued in this temple, are spelling, reading, writing, and the commoner rules of arithmetic, with now and then geography and "speaking," and perhaps in more ambitious cases, in addition to these branches, a little grammar, surveying, algebra, and even Latin or French.

The description of the school building closely parallels the description of the Smithtown schoolhouse as it is given in Katherine Molinoff's monograph.[10] The interior of the building was no more edifying than the exterior. It was cold and unattractive, heated only by one large fireplace at the west end of the room. It was the teacher's task to keep the room in order; usually he assigned several girls to do the sweeping and some boys to do the cutting and bringing in of the fire wood. The children sat on hard benches facing the north, east, and south walls, with their backs to the center of the room and the teacher.[11]

In the Smithtown school, Whitman taught eighty-five pupils, most of them between five and fifteen years of age. The curriculum for that year called for the teaching of reading, writing, arithmetic, spelling, grammar, and geography. His compensation for teaching under those conditions for rather more than five months was $72.20.[12]   Normally he would also have been "boarded round" by the parents of his scholars, but available records indicate that in Smithtown he boarded himself, probably at Hallock's Inn. Local legend remembers still that Walt had to go to bed while his single shirt was being laundered by Thankfull Udall, niece of Thomas Hallock, owner of the inn.[13]   In addition to the tasks already mentioned, Whitman as a teacher was expected to rule foolscap paper for the children's use, to sharpen their goose quills, and to sit up with any existent corpses. Since school was in session six days a week (with Saturday afternoon off every other week) and since there were no holidays, Whitman must have spent a busy five months in Smithtown.[14]

Whitman's teaching methods were unique, both for his time and place. He understood the psychology of indirection and sometimes shamed the guilty and averted additional wrongdoing by telling his students stories about children who did bad things and suffered for their misdeeds. He taught mental arithmetic to stimulate quick thinking, and played the "Twenty Questions" game with them for the same purpose. He often had them memorize poetry, sometimes his own.[15]   Charles A. Roe, a student of his at Little Bay Side, remembered that Whitman had had him memorize a poem called "The Fallen Angel." Years later he recited it to Horace Traubel, who recognized the poem, with minor variations, as Whitman's "The Punishment of Pride."[16]   The poem evidently was written while Whitman was teaching and just before Roe memorized it, but it was not published until two years later in the New World. "The Punishment of Pride" is an excessively sentimental bit of verse about an angel who felt pride and contempt for men and was subsequently punished by being sent to earth. There he tasted guilt, sickness, and fear for the first time, and this new experience taught him to avoid pride and embrace humility.[17]   The poem shows little of the power, force, and love of living that were to be later Whitman trademarks.

Whitman was also one of the first American educators to emphasize the importance to the child of cooperation between parents and teacher. He urged parents to remember that "it is a sure death-blow to a teacher's influence over any child, when that child is taught at home to find fault with or think contemptuously of his teacher." [18] Such an attitude, Whitman continued, would seriously undermine the confidence of a child in his master and consequently hamper the child's education.

One aspect of teaching that angered Whitman throughout his life was flogging. The Smithtown school (before Whitman's time) was equipped with a cat-o-nine tails to correct unruly students. [19] Most teachers were content with a birch rod or a few feet of supple twig snapped from a tree outside the schoolroom door. Whitman dispensed with flogging altogether, [20] believing that children learn better when happy than when frightened. Years later, after reviewing a new public school in Brooklyn, he announced triumphantly in an editorial that in this school no children were whipped, and that the young scholars seemed brighter and more willing to work because of this. [21] His own early dramatic concern with flogging is depicted vividly in the short story, "Death in the School-Room," published and probably written in 1841. The setting is a village school. Lugare, the schoolmaster, is a cruel and brutal man. He accuses poor Tim, a half-starved innocent, of stealing. Tim denies the charge, and Lugare gives him an hour to reconsider and to retract his denial. An hour later Lugare goes to Tim's desk. The boy seems asleep, and Lugare, enraged, flogs him for several minutes. Suddenly the boy's body slumps sideways and the schoolmaster realizes he has been flogging a dead child! The story is wildly melodramatic and is filled with angry asides about birch rods, child-torture, and teaching by brutality. The ultimate touch, of course, is that the child was actually innocent of any wrong-doing. [22] The story, like the earlier "Punishment of Pride," is naive, overly-moralistic, and totally without subtlety. It ends with this gentle sentence: "Death was in the school-room, and Lugare had been flogging a CORPSE."

The part of his teaching career that Whitman himself considered especially important was the "boarding round" whereby a teacher, as part of his salary, received room and meals for several nights or a week from the families of his students. It was excellent training for a would-be writer, as Whitman soon realized:

> This "boarding round" gives a first-rate opportunity for the study of human nature. You go from place to place, from the rich to the poor, from the pious to the atheistical, from where there are good kind-hearted women to places where there are _____ . . . [23]

Years later, while writing *Specimen Days,* he re-evaluated this experience and emphasized still more its ultimate value to him: "This latter (boarding round) I consider one of the best experiences and deepest lessons in human nature behind the scenes, and in the masses." [24]

This experience of living with many families paid still another kind of dividend: it taught Whitman to look more deeply into the minds and hearts of the common people. At first, like Archie Dean, he had found them dull and monotonous; later, again like Archie, he "found something to admire in the character and customs of the unpolished country folk; their sterling sense on most practical subjects, their hospitality, and their industry." [25] As he grew to know them better, he respected them still more. Time and again he reminded the city-readers of the Brooklyn *Daily Eagle* that the farmers of Suffolk County were, indeed, the "country's pride" — that though the city might look with contempt upon them, "a more generally intelligent race of men and women exists nowhere . . . " [26] He reminded them, too, that while the farmers were not as superficially glib as the city people, they were well-informed, clear in their political views, and often profound. [27]

Certainly this awareness in the young Whitman exerted an incalculable influence on his general development and on the development of the basic ideas that eventually resulted in *Leaves of Grass.* Without this appreciation for country people, Whitman might have been merely an early Sandburg; with it, plus his knowledge of city dwellers, he was able to become truly a poet of the masses.

He remained always proud of his schoolteaching experiences.
The *Sun-Down Papers,* a series of articles printed in the *Long
Island Farmer,* were sub-titled "From the Desk of a Schoolmaster." When he was editor of the Brooklyn *Daily Eagle,* the
Brooklyn *Advertiser,* his chief journalistic adversary, "frequently
taunted him with being a 'school-master.' "[28] Evidently the *Star*
tried the same tactics, for in September, 1847, Whitman retorted
with this editorial volley:

> The *Star* seems to think it demolishes us skin and bone
> by calling us "country schoolmaster." We are rather
> pleased with the title, if given sincerely; a proper
> schoolmaster is one who is an honor and a benefit to
> his race — and many a more famous man don't do half
> as much good. Our ancient neighbor also talks of the
> "true scurrility" of our character as a schoolmaster;
> by which we are to suppose, not only that teachers are
> generally scurrilous persons, but that there is also such
> a thing as false scurrility . . . [29]

That last sentence suggests that Whitman had not stopped being
a schoolteacher; it is a masterly "rapping of the knuckles" for
careless writing.

*   *   *   *   *   *

Teaching in His Poetry

As he turned away from teaching and toward the writing of
poetry, his years as a schoolmaster continued to yield rich benefits. Such a verse as "The teaching is to the teacher, and comes
back most to him,"[30] is meaningful to the professional, but
would hardly have occurred to one who had never stood in front
of a classroom full of youngsters. The words are steeped in truth
for the man who is truly a teacher, and the fact that they were
significant to Whitman suggests that he could have been a local
Bronson Alcott if he had continued in the field of education.
More important, as we consider the poet, is that the thought

itself may have triggered or at least dramatized for Whitman the allied thoughts that precede and follow the line in question:

> The song is to the singer, and comes back most to
>   him,
> The teaching is to the teacher, and comes back most
>   to him,
> The murder is to the murderer, and comes back most
>   to him,
> The theft is to the thief, and comes back most to him,
> The love is to the lover, and comes back most to him,
> The gift is to the giver, and comes back most to
>   him . . .

Whitman had had no experience in several of the areas mentioned in the poem, but he had seen the "rule" in action in his own teaching, and his poet's mind was able to universalize the rule and make it applicable in other fields.

Another truth that the good teacher learns early in his career is that he is honored most by the student who outstrips him. He is disgraced by the student who, coming too strongly under his influence, is unable to free himself to strike out along new paths. Whitman learned this lesson well. In "Song of Myself," he sang perceptively:

> I am the teacher of athletes,
> He that by me spreads a wider breast than my own
>   proves the width of my own,
> He most honors my style who learns under it to
>   destroy the teacher.[31]

Here is no pedagogical timidity, but a full understanding of the purpose of teaching. A little later he develops this idea still further: "I teach straying from me, yet who can stray from me?"[32]   Here again the meaning is clear in terms of teaching: the student who does break away and develops his own independence is at the same time proving his truest allegiance to his former teacher, for his independence is the fulfillment of the teacher's purpose. However, in both the illustrations given, the

references are not to teaching in the formal sense, in the classroom, but to the teaching of life, everywhere, all of the time.
The poet makes this clear in these lines:

> No shutter'd room or school can commune with me,
> But roughs and little children better than they.[33]

Almost the same cry is echoed in "Song of the Open Road"
when the poet urges, desperately, that his comrades set out with
him: "the road is before us!" Papers may remain unwritten,
books unopened, and "Let the school stand! mind not the cry
of the teachers!"[34]   Here "teachers" are those in the classroom,
too often (in Whitman's mind) standing between the students and
the true object of learning. It is the same message, repeated in
greater detail, in "When I Heard the Learn'd Astronomer." The
professor in the lecture room can produce charts and diagrams, he
can calculate light-years and list proofs, he can anatomize and
particularize; but he cannot convey to his students the mystical
quality and wonder of the night's stars. The individual can learn
this only by going to the greatest teacher, nature, by wandering
off by himself, and by looking up "in perfect silence at the
stars."
To be a human being is not automatically to be a student of
Whitman's or nature's. One must approach with reverence and
with love. For " . . . if blood like mine circle not in your veins. . .
Of what use is it that you seek to become eleve of mine?"[35]
He speaks not of ancestral blood, of course, but of the blood
that links comrades, that relates one man to another. In "The
Base of all Metaphysics," Whitman teaches this lesson once more:

> And now gentlemen,
> A word I give to remain in your memories and mind,
> As base and finale too for all metaphysics.
>
> (So to the students the old professor,
> At the close of his crowded course.)

After this prim attempt at pedanticism, the poet casts off his academic coat and plunges recklessly into a lush catalogue of philosophical names and systems. He cites the Greek and Germanic systems, Kant, Fichte, Schelling, Hegel, Socrates, Christ — but underneath all, he sees love, the true base of metaphysics:

> The dear love of man for his comrade. the attraction
>   of friend to friend,
> Of the well-married husband and wife, of children
>   and parents,
> Of city for city and land for land.

Here Whitman's teaching grows more narrow, and at the same time more intense. There is only one thing worth teaching, and that cannot really be taught: love — love for all men and for all things. Even wisdom, allied to love, cannot be taught. Wisdom cannot be tested in the schools, he says; it cannot be given from one to another; it is not susceptible of proof. He concludes that "something there is in the float of the sight of things that provokes it (wisdom) out of the soul."[36]

Leaves of Grass is an epical lesson. It is the great primer for adults. Whitman the teacher denied the possibility of teaching, a conclusion shared by most good teachers; but also, like most good teachers, Whitman was unable to resist that attempt at teaching. He simply exchanged his spelling and geography books for lessons on love and living. Instead of a classroom of children, he had a world-room of readers. He addressed not the individual reader as most writers do, but his readers *en masse:* "List close my scholars dear..."[37] Throughout *Leaves of Grass* he was a teacher first, teaching all who were willing to learn. His curriculum was orthodox. He taught history: the founding of America,[38] the Revolutionary War,[39] the Civil War,[40] abolitionism,[41] the plight of the aborigines,[42] the pioneer movement,[43] the office of the Presidency,[44] and the value of popular elections.[45] He taught geography: local,[46] national,[47] and international.[48] He taught the science of sociology of the cities [49] and of rural areas.[50] He taught philosophy,[51] and natural history,[52] and anatomy.[53] He taught man still other things: to use his eyes to see,[54] his ears to hear,[55] his fingers and his body to touch.[56]   He taught man how to achieve. In "The Pupil" he asks — "Is reform needed? is it through you?" Then he answers his own question: "The greater the reform needed, the greater the Personality you need to accomplish it." The rest of the poem is devoted to the methodology involved in the creating of a Personality.

Later in life, when a new public school opened in Camden, New Jersey, Whitman wrote a poem to commemorate its inauguration. His attitude toward the formal school and the formal classroom situation had mellowed considerably; his reverence for youth and true learning remained consistent. He begins with a nostalgic tone:

> An old man's thought of school,
> An old man gathering youthful memories and blooms
>   that youth itself cannot.

This seems a bit forced since Whitman was only fifty-five years old at the time, but his illness may have made him feel older than he was. He then talks of the children:

> And these I see, these sparkling eyes,
> These stores of mystic meaning, these young lives,
> Building, equipping like a fleet of ships, immortal
>   ships,
> Soon to sail out over the measureless seas,
> On the soul's voyage.

His feeling here parallels his own earlier feelings when in the late 1830's he faced just such "sparkling eyes" and "young lives." They are not just "a lot of boys and girls" engaged in spelling, writing, and ciphering; they are (and he echoes the Quaker, George Fox) the "living souls," the men and women of tomorrow.[57]

Leaves of Grass is no pedant's handbook, but it does illustrate the considerable influence exerted on his poetry by his years as a schoolmaster and by his close acquaintance with young people and with the learning process. His educational philosophy — that one must teach the whole child or the whole man — is as old as

Plato and as modern as John Dewey. He taught both child and man, and ultimately he did, indeed, prove "that the teaching is to the teacher, and comes back most to him."

*   *   *   *   *   *

Debating Experience

Another aspect of Whitman's teaching experience deserves separate consideration. This was his participation in the art of the debate. He himself claimed that he began debating when he was sixteen years old,[58] but the only records available in this area begin in 1837. In the fall and winter of 1837-38, while Whitman was schoolmaster of the district school in Smithtown, he became interested in the town's debating group. It had been in existence since the 18th century, but was in a rather moribund condition. Whitman's interest helped to spark its revival; and between December 7, 1837, and March 28, 1838, it held seventeen active meetings. Whitman was the secretary of the organization during most of this period, and the minutes he recorded provide an interesting index to the topics in which he was interested and to his point of view concerning these topics.[59]

If Whitman needed a whetting-stone for the sharpening of his own thoughts in this period, he could not have chosen a more satisfactory group of men than the members of this debating group. They were politically active, mentally keen, and eminently practical. Later in life, two became judges, one a congressman, and one a state assemblyman; one was a blacksmith who later became a dentist, two became doctors, one, a minister, and two became justices of the peace; one was successful in New York in business and eight were (and remained) farmers.[60] Their varied backgrounds and interests provided Whitman with a small cross-section of the country's population with whom he could match wits and on whom he could test theories.

Whitman was actually slated for participation in only three debates, but he joined in, in eight others, either as a substitute for an absentee or simply because he felt strongly about the subject.[61]   It is tempting to claim that Whitman's participation in these debates first stimulated his interest in the subjects discussed, but such a claim would be presumptuous and quite without foundation. It is more likely that Whitman chose to uphold the affirmative or negative in each debate in accordance with views already held and partly formulated. However, argument and opposition do force one to clarify one's views and to sharpen one's reasoning, and these benefits undoubtedly accrued to the young schoolmaster during these five months of discussion.

The first scheduled debate in which he took part propounded the question: "Is the system of slavery, as it exists in the South, right?" Whitman spoke for the negative, and the decision at the end of the evening went to the negative, so his first formal attempt was successful.[62]   It must have been a satisfying success for Whitman, for it was a subject on which he held strong views. As a child, he had been familiar with slavery in its mildest form. His grandfather and great-grandfather at West Hills had owned Negro slaves who had performed most of the hard labor on the farm. Years later he remembered a dozen or more "pickaninnies" squatting in a circle on the kitchen floor, "eating their supper of pudding (Indian corn mush) and milk." [63]   He remembered, too, "old Mose," a liberated West Hills slave — "genial, correct, manly, and cute, and a great friend of my childhood." [64]   By 1838 (this debate was held on January 3 of that year), Whitman must have heard and read a good deal about the sufferings of slaves in the South. Revulsion at these stories and memories of Old Mose eventually merged with one of the basic tenets of Whitman's slowly evolving philosophy: that all men are created equal. In the years that followed, he handled this theme time and again. In the early "Song of Myself," he described the day a runaway slave arrived at his house, seeking frightened refuge in the woodpile. Through the half-opened kitchen door, he saw him, "limpsy and weak," and he brought him water and clothing, and gave him a bed. At the end of a week, the slave was strong enough to be passed along to the North and freedom.[65]   Later in the same poem, as he identifies himself

with all men and all men with himself, he gives his most vivid
description of the slave's fate:

> I am the hounded slave, I wince at the bite of the
>   dogs.
> Hell and despair are upon me, crack and again crack
>   the marksmen,
> I clutch the rails of the fence, my gore dribs, thinn'd
>   with the ooze of my skin,
> I fall on the weeds and stones,
> The riders spur their unwilling horses, haul close,
> Taunt my dizzy ears and beat me violently over the
>   head with whip-stocks.[66]

It was a theme he would return to many times — in "I Sing the
Body Electric," in "Salut au Monde!" and in "Ethiopia Saluting
the Colors" especially. Perhaps some of his enthusiasm and
assurance in this crusade derived from the firm stand he advocated in Smithtown Branch in 1838.

The next scheduled debate in which Whitman elected to take
part asked: "Are the original settlers of this country justifiable
for their conduct toward the aborigines?" Again Whitman took
the negative, and again the negative was granted the decision.[67]
This topic was also close to Whitman's heart. He knew much
about the Indian problem in this country, both from his knowledge of Long Island history and from an acquaintance in childhood and youth with Indians in several Island towns; but this
topic will be studied in more detail later. It suffices now to
indicate that an early interest influenced his stand in this debate,
and that the debate, in turn, probably re-enforced and refocused
this interest.

The third debate for Walt Whitman was the twelfth debate
of the season. The topic was one that was later to be of special
interest to Whitman: "Have the arts and sciences flourished more
under a Republican form of government than any other?" Whitman defended the affirmative and again won the decision.[68]   One
can accept with equanimity and a degree of confidence the
probability that Whitman had had a prior interst and commit-

ment on the subjects of slavery and Indian welfare, but it is
more difficult to believe that a twenty-year-old country school-
teacher had established any clear views concerning the condition
of the arts and sciences under any particular form of government.
Surely this challenge was one of the earliest stimulants leading
to the formulation of this portion of his philosophy.

His final theory regarding the relationship of the arts and
government seems to have been arrived at through a two-step
process: (1) the mutual interpenetration of poet and country,
e.g., "The proof of a poet shall be sternly deferr'd till his country absorbs him as affectionately as he has absorb'd it;"[69]   and
(2) the awareness on the part of the poet that he must sing for
all and not for one class or one part of one class.[70]   Whitman
insisted that the time had come for a readjustment of the theory
and nature of poetry. He asked: "Does not the best thought of
our day and Republic conceive of a birth and spirit of song
superior to anything past or present?"[71]   The American experi-
ment had already culminated in one new ideal — "the great pride
of man in himself."[72]   Whitman admitted that this was more or
less the motif of all of his poems, and that the great poet of
the future (necessarily an American) would develop it as it had
never been developed before. This could happen only under a
Republican form of government in which each man was equal
to each other man.

It is certain that this theory, expounded in the closing years
of Whitman's life, did not exist, full-blown, in the mind of the
young Whitman of 1838; but it is also certain that the early
debate on this subject must have sent the young man home with
his mind racing with startling new concepts and possibilities.
Within months of this debate, he gave up schoolteaching for a
time and established the *Long-Islander,* his own newspaper, an
independent organ for this new voice in America. This could,
of course, be coincidence; but there is a feeling of sequence,
almost of inevitability, about it that suggests deliberate action,
not accident.

Whitman's participation in the other eight debates was the
result of chance. He had not been scheduled as a speaker in

any of them; yet the topics themselves and his argument in each case indicate the major reforms that he would advocate eight years later when he was writing editorials for the Brooklyn *Daily Eagle*. The January 10th debate discussed the emigration of foreigners to this country, which he supported; the January 17th debate urged that capital punishment be abolished. This too he supported. The February 11th debate asked if the law abolishing imprisonment for debt should be repealed; Whitman, with his constant sensitivity for the impoverished, argued against such repeal. The final debate on March 28th asked if the right of suffrage should be based on the possession of property. Again Whitman took the negative.[73]

The topics, Whitman's affirmed views, and even the decisions granted depict the probable spirit of the young schoolteacher and of the leading intellectuals of Smithtown in 1838. The activities of this group acted as a fine incubator for Whitman the editor, and as a moderately good one for Whitman the poet. The effect of this period on the ideas later developed in *Leaves of Grass* cannot be actually proved, but it is inconceivable that a young man of Whitman's calibre could have been exposed to sharp mental activity (probably for the first time in his life) and not have reaped lasting advantage from it.

XI

Whitman and the Ocean

As I ebb'd with the ocean of life,
As I wended the shores I know,
As I walk'd where the ripples continually wash you
  Paumanok,
Where they rustle up hoarse and sibilant,
Where the fierce old mother endlessly cries for her
  castaways,
I musing late in the autumn day, gazing off southward,
Held by this electric self out of the pride of which
  I utter poems,
Was seiz'd by the spirit that trails in the lines under-
  foot,
The rim, the sediment that stands for all the water
  and all the land of the globe.[1]

To Whitman, the ocean was part of childhood, youth, and maturity. A native of West Hills, he could stand on the highest hill in that area and see to the south the broad expanse of the Atlantic; then, by merely turning his head, he could look to the north on the blue waters of Long Island Sound. Like his Paumanok, he too was surrounded by water. "As I Ebb'd with the Ocean of Life" indicates that sometimes the power of the ocean held him back from uttering poems; more often, the ocean stimulated and acted as the source of his poetry.

When he was a little boy in the family home at West Hills, he could lie in bed on a summer evening or on the grass in the

garden and listen to the roar of the surf only a few miles away.²
It was one of his earliest memories and one of his most vivid.
It was his first great teacher; even as a youngster, he must have
been absorbing the great rhythm of the ocean, its ebb and flow,
its uncanny calmness on a summer's day or its majestic fury in
a winter storm. From it, he learned to reject the restricting
limitations of iambs and trochees, and to use, instead, the fine,
free, flowing line that so well suited his personality and philosophy. From it, he learned the magnificence of Nature and the
insignificance of Man until Man learned to merge with this
illustrious predecessor. From it, he may have learned his dearest
poetic technique — cataloging — with incident following incident
or description following description, as wave follows wave until
they tumble together on a sandy shore.

Consider for a moment "A Song of Joys." (One could substitute almost any other poem he wrote, except the very short
ones.) This poem begins with a brief but exuberant line: "O
to make the most jubilant song!" — similar to the quick gasp
when one first sees the ocean. The two lines that follow are
serene and complete: "Full of music — full of manhood, woman-
hood, infancy!/ Full of common employments — full of grain and
trees." These lines are reminiscent of the ocean beyond the
breakers, that great expanse of still water where tiny, nearly
invisible ripples conceal deceptively an almost incredible, nascent
power. Then the poem proper follows — more than thirty stanzas
of varying lengths rushing pell-mell toward the shore. Each
stanza, like a breaker, heaves itself up from the still waters,
explodes into birth by violence, then flings itself shore-ward. The
concluding stanza breaks into short clipped phrases: "To dance,
clap hands, exult, shout, skip, leap, roll on, float on!" just as
the breakers, hitting the sand, disintegrate into minor rills and
small pools. The last three lines represent that moment of time
after the wave has receded, leaving the sand moist and glistening,
finished with the one, waiting for the next. That time between
two breakers is a time of rare completion, of a near-satiety:

To be a sailor of the world bound for all ports,

A ship itself, (see indeed these sails I spread to the
   sun and air,)
A swift and swelling ship full of rich words, full of
   joys.

The language, too, is appropriate. Through most of the poem, he
uses series of infinitives and a scattering of participles to suggest
constant motion. In the concluding stanza he stretches the intro-
ductory infinitive into three long lines that convey simultaneously
a sense of continuance and of folding back on itself. This tone
of completion is accentuated by his choice of words: "bound,"
"spread," "swelling," "rich," "full" — each associated with birth
and fruition.

The *form* of the poem, then, parallels the *form* of the ocean,
even when the ocean is not the subject-matter of the poem. That
this is neither accidental nor coincidental is indicated by some
notes Whitman wrote in *Specimen Days:*

> Even as a boy, I had the fancy, the wish, to write a
> piece, perhaps a poem, about the seashore — that sug-
> gesting, dividing line, contact, junction, the solid mar-
> rying the liquid — that curious, lurking something, (as
> doubtless every objective form finally becomes to the
> subjective spirit,) which means far more than its mere
> first sight, grand as that is — blending the real and
> ideal, and each made portion of the other. Hours,
> days, in my Long Island youth and early manhood, I
> haunted the shores of Rockaway or Coney Island, or
> away east to the Hamptons or Montauk. Once, at the
> latter place, (by the old lighthouse, nothing but sea-
> tossings in sight in every direction as far as the eye
> could reach,) I remember well, I felt that I must one
> day write a book expressing this liquid, mystic theme.
> Afterward, I recollect, how it came to me that instead
> of any special lyrical or epical or literary attempt, the
> sea-shore should be an invisible *influence,* a pervading
> gauge and tally for me, in my composition. (Let me
> give a hint here to young writers. I am not sure but
> I have unwittingly follow'd out the same rule with
> other powers besides sea and shores — avoiding them,
> in the way of any dead set at poetizing them, as too

big for formal handling—quite satisfied if I could
indirectly show that we have met and fused, even if
only once, but enough—that we have really absorb'd
each other, and understand each other.)[3]

This explains clearly and without any possibility of misinterpreta-
tion the influence of the ocean on him, his fusion with it, and
his attempts to express it. It is the same technique that he used
in his best poems when dealing with his family, the Quakers, or
teaching. It is writing not *about* something, but *through* it. It is
using the ocean not only as subject-matter, but also as association, as connotation, as symbol, and as flavor.

However, it is important to remember that Whitman did use
the ocean as subject-matter at times—that it was an entity to
him as well as an intangible. For years he had a recurring dream:

> There is a dream, a picture, that for years at inter-
> vals...has come noiselessly up before me, and I really
> believe, fiction as it is, has enter'd largely into my
> practical life—certainly into my writings, and shaped
> and colored them. It is nothing more or less than a
> stretch of interminable white-brown sand, hard and
> smooth and broad, with the ocean perpetually, grand-
> ly, rolling in upon it, with slow-measured sweep, with
> rustle and hiss and foam, and many a thump as of
> low bass drums. This scene, this picture, I say, has
> risen before me at times for years. Sometimes I wake
> at night and can hear and see it plainly.[4]

It is obvious that the sea was one of the greatest influences
exerted on Whitman. It influenced his style and his subject-
matter, his thinking and his emotions. But to appreciate fully
this influence, one must first study it in its separate parts.

*   *   *   *

The Sea and His Style

It has already been seen that the sea influenced the structure
of Whitman's poems, as it influenced the rhythm, the flow, and

the freedom of his lines. But it influenced his style in still other
ways: in the vocabulary, in the figures of speech, and in the
prophetical and oratorical quality of his verse.

Whitman's choice of words startlingly illustrates this influence.
There is, first of all, basic sea terminology: "sea cabbage,"
"ooze," "sea-gluten," "sea-scum," "spawn," "surf," "salt
hay," "sea rushes," "salt-perfume,"[5] as well as the constantly-
recurring "ocean," "billows," "breakers," "waves," "tides,"
etc. The last five words suggest an acquaintance with the sea,
and may be found in the works of Bryant and Cooper as well
as in the works of such well-known poets of the sea as Mase-
field and Longfellow; but the first group of words indicate far
more than an acquaintance; they indicate a close familiarity, a
day-by-day knowledge of the sea and of the flora and fauna
indigenous to it. They appear frequently and casually throughout
Leaves of Grass.

The second type of sea terminology used by Whitman is less
specific. This group includes words associated with the ocean:
words like "heave," "flow," "float," "ebb," and "surge."
They are used not only to describe the ocean, but also as meta-
phors applied to a city street, a human body, a crowd, or the
current of history. They are used surely, unconsciously, welling
up to the surface from Whitman's inmost memories and emotions.
They contribute to the easy flow and melodious fluency that are
so characteristic of much of Whitman's poetry.

When this sea terminology was utilized in conventional figures
of speech, Whitman achieved some of his most successful results.
The sea-metaphor has been popular, of course, since the time of
Homer. Centuries later it was exploited successfully by the Anglo-
Saxon poets. In Whitman's poetry it is ubiquitous, occurring
unexpectedly and yet appropriately in poem after poem. In
"Recorders Ages Hence," the friend has a "measureless ocean
of love within him" which he freely pours forth; in "Whispers
of Heavenly Death," death approaches as "ripples of unseen
rivers, tides of a current flowing"; in "Election Day, November,
1884," the ballots cast are "stormy gusts and winds that waft
precious ships" and that once "swell'd Washington's, Jefferson's,

Lincoln's sails." "Passage to India" is especially rich in this respect: the desire for union is a rivulet running down the slopes of history, "sinking now, and now again to the surface rising"; the world is a vast Rondure, "swimming in space"; the past is a "teeming gulf," bibles and legends are "deep diving," and the soul prays to "bathe" in God.

The sea-metaphor is effective, but still more effective is the homeric simile based on the ocean's greatness. Homer's "wine-dark sea," so appropriate for the Mediterranean, gives way to Whitman's wondrous but wild Atlantic. The poem, "Rise O Days from Your Fathomless Deeps," is one long, splendid simile. This poem, which chants the rise of democracy, begins with the pregnant line: "Rise O days from your fathomless deeps, till you loftier, fiercer sweep..." The fathomless political and human deeps from which democracy emerges is likened to the fathomless deeps of the ocean. A discussion follows of a storm at sea, of the "threatening maws of the waves," of white combs, of the wind piping and black clouds, of thunder and of lightning. Then the whole is compared to the coming of democracy: the waves become torrents of men; the billows, cities; the thunder, a herald; and the lightning, a torch. The excitement tapers off in the third section to a feeling of quiet completion: "I am fully satisfied, I am glutted." The poet no longer has to roam the mountain or sail the stormy sea; the simile, along with the violence of birth, is over. Warlike America and the common man have risen together.

A third trope, personification, is another Whitman favorite, with a strong emphasis on the personification of the ocean as a mother. The sea is a "fierce old mother incessantly moaning," "a savage old mother incessantly crying," or an "old crone rocking the cradle, swathed in sweet garments, bending aside..."[6] Again it is an "old mother" crying for her castaways[7] or swaying to and fro "singing her husky song."[8] It is an old husky nurse who culls the race of men and unites nations.[9] Sometimes it has an "ample, smiling face, dash'd with the sparkling dimples of the sun," but at other times it bears a "brooding scowl and murk — thy. unloosed hurricanes."[10] Not always does the mother-image prevail; occasionally the personification turns in a different direction. Then the breakers become "white-maned racers"[11]   and once, in a sportive mood, the water "sports and sings!"[12]

Another "Whitmanesque" characteristic is the oracular mood that is so often present in his poems. This was partly the result of his personality, but it had its roots also in a habit that he developed during his adolescent years. He once told Traubel:

> I was to be an orator—to go about the country spouting my pieces, proclaiming my faith. I trained for all that—spouted in the woods, down by the shore, in the noise of Broadway where nobody could hear me; spouted, eternally spouted, and spouted again. I thought I had something to say—I was afraid I would get no chance to say it through books; so I was to lecture and get myself delivered that way.[13]

At Far Rockaway he stood on the shore and looked out over the breakers, raising his voice above their din, shouting to them Jupiter's menaces against the gods; his bible at that time was Pope's *Homer.*[14]   At Montauk Point, he and some companions ran over the hills and scampered along the shore, jumping from rock to rock. His bible now was Shakespeare; and as they ran, they "declaimed all the violent appeals and defiances we could remember, commencing with 'Celestial states, immortal powers, give ear!' away on to the ending which announced that Richard had almost lost his wind by dint of calling Richmond to arms. I doubt whether these astonished echoes ever before vibrated with such terrible ado." Then they wrestled for a while, and finally turned to the girls who were with them and made love "in the divine words of Shakespeare and other poets."[15]

It is not surprising that—with this background—Whitman sometimes turned prophet-poet. The opening lines of "Song of Myself" might well be shouted above the breakers. Their strong, firm rhythm reflects echoes of Homer and the surf:

> I celebrate myself, and sing myself,
> And what I assume you shall assume,

> For every atom belonging to me as good belongs
>   to you.

The same is true of most of "Starting from Paumanok," and
especially of section three which begins "Americanos! conquerors!
marches humanitarian!" and continues with a series of lines,
each starting with the ringing word, "chant." Not only does the
ocean provide a rhythmical background for such writing; it also
provides a spiritual background. Any human being, standing at
the water's edge and looking across that infinite expanse of
ocean, would find it easy to imagine that another nation or
another race lay just beyond the horizon, that the ocean was a
great bridge connecting all peoples. This, too, was necessary to
Whitman, the poet, and to his all-embracing, all-loving heart.

*   *   *   *

The Sea as Subject-Matter

The ocean was many things to Walt Whitman, but it was —
first of all — a playground. Years later he remembered his childhood and wrote: "The shores of this bay, winter and summer,
and my doings there in early life, are woven all through *Leaves
of Grass*." There was much to do in those simple days, if you
were a boy on the Long Island shore. A boy could spear eels
through the ice, or gather sea-gull's eggs, or talk with blue-
fishers and sea-bass takers.[16]   A boy could roll up his trousers
and dig for clams in the shallow water, where he was surrounded
by both saline smell and the perfume of nearby sedge-meadows.
He could take part in chowder and fishing excursions.[17]   He
could swim, or shout at the breakers, or let himself be pounded
by the surf. When the boy became a youth, he could continue
most of these activities and add still others.

One of Whitman's favorite pastimes as a youth was eeling.
Many a winter morning he and his friends equipped themselves
with eel-basket and eel-spear and axe and set forth for a few
hours' sport. The axe was used to chop a hole in the ice. Then
the spear was poised lightly over the water, waiting for a vic-

tim.[18]   It was great fun; just as important, the eels, fried in deep fat to a toasted-brown, provided fine fare either for a picnic lunch or a family dinner. Eels were so much a part of Whitman's daily life that when, in 1846, the *Tribune* asked how many Long Island eels one could buy for a shilling, he wrote a brief answer under the derogatory title, "More Hottentot Ignorance." He said succinctly: "Every body that 'knows eels' at all (which not to know argues one a noodle,) is well enough aware that from Shewango neck to Hog Inlet, twelve and a half cents is equivalent to a *mess* of that savory edible..."[19]

In the spring one could go lobstering. A day or two before, one sank the lobster-pots, weighed down with heavy stones. Then, on a sweet May morning, before sunrise, one went out on the water and pulled up the wicker pots: "the dark green lobsters are desperate with their claws as I take them out, I insert wooden pegs in the joints of their pincers..."[20]   Later, one rowed back to shore and dropped the lobsters into a huge kettle of boiling water until their color turned scarlet and their meat succulent.

There were other kinds of fishing, too. One could fish for mackerel, "voracious, mad for the hook";[21]   or for blackfish, using fiddlers for bait;[22] or for bluefish off Paumanok.[23]   Whitman remembered once that he "cut up divers clams into small bits, and thrust the said bits upon fish-hooks, and let down the said hooks by long lines into the water, and then sat patiently holding the lines, in the vain hope of nabbing some stray members of the finny tribe."[24]   Indeed, there were few fish worthy of a fisherman's skill that could not be found in the Long Island waters of that day. Whitman called the south shore, and especially the Great South Bay area, an "inexhaustible sea-mine, full of treasures, that are really worth as much as the mines of California."[25]

There's an old saying—"Scratch a Long Islander and you'll find a clam-digger." (It refers, of course, to the pre-1940 Long Islander, i.e., the pre-housing development era.) Clamming was a vocation, an avocation, almost a way of life, especially in the shore villages. Whitman was an old hand with the clam-rake and spade.[26]   He liked, too, the "briny and damp smell, the shore, the salt weeds exposed at low water"[27]   that form a necessary part of clam-digging. And he liked the aftermath: clams roasted "in the old Indian style, in beds covered with brush and chips, and thus cooked in their own broth."[28]

Clams have a way of appearing suddenly in a Whitman poem. Sometimes they are simply a reminder of a way of life:

> The boatmen and clam-diggers arose early and stopt
>   for me,
> I tuck'd my trouser-ends in my boots and went and
>   had a good time;
> You should have been with us that day round the
>   chowder-kettle.[29]

Sometimes the clam appears as a kind of symbol. In a discussion of existence, of evolution, and of human development, Whitman asserts that if nothing else were developed, the "quahaug in its callous shell" were quite enough. But that statement made (and accepted), he instantly adds a condition, proudly declaring, "Mine is no callous shell,/ I have instant conductors all over me whether I pass or stop."[30] Years later, when he was an old man, he revised this part of the poem: "if there were nothing more developed, the clam in its callous shell in the sand were august enough."[31]   The revisions are interesting; after decades of being away from clam-digging, Whitman reverts to the general term "clam" in place of the specific "quahaug." He also adds the adjective "august," which lends extra weight and dignity to the humble clam. The contrasting statement, "Mine is no callous shell," changes to "I am not in any callous shell," which seems less egotistical, less flauntingly superior than the first version. In this instance, at least, distance has made the clam more worthy.

The eel, the lobster, and the clam all have a secure niche in Long Island life, but they do not even begin to compete with the whale. Even today, the Long Island school child thrills with tales of whaling ships out of Sag Harbor and Greenport and Southold. How much more true this must have been of Walt

Whitman the boy. In 1819, the year of Whitman's birth, James Fenimore Cooper was outfitting the first stock-company whaling expedition out of Sag Harbor. That ship made fourteen profitable voyages, bringing home $350,000 worth of oil and bone. Long Island homes, Whitman's among them, must have echoed with reports and legends of these expeditions. Whitman himself was permeated with whaling lore and adventure. He and his friends even had a "Spouting Club"; anyone who could entertain them with "some highly exquisite specimens of Shakespearian eloquence" could become a member and thereby earn the title, "whaler."[32] The facetious use of "spouting" and "whaler" indicates that by this time (1841), whaling as a Long Island industry had already started to decline, but that its memories were still fresh in the minds of the young.

In his poetry, Whitman treated whaling with respect. The whaler, like the farmer, represents manhood, sturdy, alert, courageous: "The mate stands braced in the whale-boat, lance and harpoon are ready."[33] He refers to the whale-crews of the south Pacific and the north Atlantic in "Salut au Monde!" (section eight) and in "Song of the Broad-Axe" (section nine). He displays a knowledge of whales when he declares that "the she-whale swims with her calf and never forsakes it,"[34] and again when, describing the ocean-world, he mentions the sperm-whale at the surface "blowing air and spray, or disporting with his flukes."[35] An interesting use of this knowledge appears in "Song of Myself," section forty-three, in which he is speaking not of whales, but of doubters and skeptics. To illustrate the sea of torment in which such people live, Whitman says vividly: "How the flukes splash!/ How they contort rapid as lightning, with spasms and spouts of blood!" He then adds gently: "Be at peace bloody flukes of doubters and sullen mopers." The imagery is so effective, the parallel between the dying whale and the tortured doubter so felicitous that one wishes Whitman had used his whaling knowledge more often in this indirect fashion.

Whitman's most memorable use of whaling occurs in "A Song of Joys." Here, in thirteen vivid lines, he depicts the chase, the kill, and the death. It begins exuberantly:

> O the whaleman's joys! O I cruise my old cruise
>   again!
> I feel the ship's motion under me, I feel the Atlantic
>   breezes fanning me,
> I hear the cry again sent down from the mast-head—
>   *There—she blows!*

There—she blows!—that wild cry of the whaling era, that nostalgic cry of the post-whaling era. Did Whitman first hear it from an old whaleman in Sag Harbor or at Montauk?[36] Or did he learn it from *The Pilot* or one of Cooper's other sea novels? An affirmative answer to either question is possible. Whitman loved to talk to the old-timers in Long Island villages; he also read Cooper's novels with great interest and admiration.

The poem goes on to describe the lowering of the boat, the pursuit, the harpooner standing up, the weapon darting from his vigorous arm, and then the wild, frantic, life-seeking flight of the wounded whale. He ends with the death itself:

> ...the life is leaving him fast,
> As he rises he spouts blood, I see him swim in circles,
>   narrower and narrower, swiftly cutting the water—
>   I see him die,
> He gives one convulsive leap in the centre of the circle,
>   and then falls flat and still in the bloody foam.

It is beautifully told, in many respects paralleling Long Tom's pursuit and harpooning of the whale in *The Pilot*. The sharp details, the excitement, indicate a familiarity, a first-hand experience that we cannot account for by present available records.

Any boy who has ever lived near the ocean has dreamed of shipwrecks. He may dream of finding a treasure from a wreck, of being a hero during a wreck, or of going down with a ship. For this reason it is surprising that Whitman so rarely mentioned shipwrecks in his prose writings. He does, in *Specimen Days*, mention two wrecks: the ship *Mexico*, in 1840, off Hempstead Beach, and the ship *Elizabeth*, a few years later, at Hampton.[37] The latter wreck interested him because in it Margaret Fuller, writer and critic, was lost. However, it was the wreck of the

Mexico that most impressed him and that he wrote about in "The Sleepers," section four:

> The beach is cut by the razory ice-wind, the wreck-
> guns sound,
> The tempest lulls, the moon comes floundering through
> the drifts.
>
> I look where the ship helplessly heads end on, I hear
> the burst as she strikes, I hear the howls of dismay,
> they grow fainter and fainter ...
>
> I search with the crowd, not one of the company is
> wash'd to us alive,
> In the morning I help pick up the dead and lay them
> in rows in a barn.

The above lines certainly suggest that Whitman was on the Hempstead shore the night the *Mexico* went down, but his own reference to it is unusually evasive: "As a youngster," he wrote, "I was in the atmosphere and traditions of many of these wrecks — of one or two *almost* an observer."[38] If he did not actually observe any wrecks, the memories he retained from stories he must have heard certainly affected him. He used wreck-imagery again and again in his poems.

He used it to show man's responsibility for and love of his fellow man. In "Song of Myself" (section thirty-three), he describes a skipper who saw "the crowded and rudderless wreck of the steam-ship, and Death chasing it up and down the storm." For three days and nights, he follows them closely, offering them hope, once holding up a board on which large letters were chalked: "Be of good cheer, we will not desert you." At last the storm quiets, and he is able to pull his ship alongside the sinking vessel and transfer to safety the men, women, and children. The poet tasted both the suffering and the saving; he comments: "I am the man, I suffer'd, I was there."

Sometimes he used it to depict a mystery he could not understand. In the middle of a great feast, a thought would come to his mind ("whence it comes I know not," he cried in confusion) of a wreck at sea, of certain ships that sail from port with hope

and are never heard from again, of the death of the President, of
the disappearance of the steamship *Arctic,* of women drowning.[39]
Evidently then, a shipwreck could be two things simultaneously:
a tragedy in itself, and a symbol representing a tragedy shrouded
in mystery.

Often it was just a scrap of a memory that he inserted into
a poem, a scrap designed to evoke pathos or a surge of sympathy. It might be the dirge chanted by "the voices of men and
women wreck'd";[40]   it might be the shore strewn with wrecks
after the "night's fierce drifts";[41]   it might be the bell by the
sea-reefs ringing "to warn the ship from its wreck-place."[42]   At
other times he used the image of the wreck to illustrate some
intangible concept that he was trying to express. In discussing
the spirit of man — of how man, in seeking to preserve his body,
may avoid death at the cost of his spirit — he points a finger of
revelation at those who stand steady and aloof on wrecks, in
self-denial yielding their seats in the boats to others. Such a
man, though he dies, preserves body *and* soul.[43]   A similar feeling pervades the poem, "Assurances"; though Life does not
provide answers for all life's incidents, "Heavenly Death" will
provide an answer and an accounting, even for "wrecks at sea,
no matter what the horrors of them, no matter whose wife,
child, husband, father, lover, has gone down..."

Occasionally, the shipwreck is important not for itself, but for
its use as a simile. In "O Star of France," it provides the
framework for the first stanza:

> O Star of France,
> The brightness of thy hope and strength and fame,
> Like some proud ship that led the fleet so long,
> Beseems to-day a wreck driven by the gale, a mastless
>   hulk,
> And 'mid its teeming madden'd half-drown'd crowds,
> Nor helm nor helmsman.

It is an effective simile: France, the leader of Europe, paralleled
to the leader of a fleet; the catastrophe of 1870 paralleled to a
great storm; broken France paralleled to a dismasted and broken

ship. Unfortunately, this single simile does not satisfy Whitman, and within another two stanzas, he is erecting a second simile, this time comparing France to the Star crucified. During the rest of the poem he juggles the two similes, alternating them. Although he tries to draw a distinction between the ship (or country) and the star (or spirit), the strived-for and partly-attained effect never quite compensates for the clashing similes. Perhaps the two similes (like two shades of a certain color) are too much alike for contrast, and too different for harmony.

*   *   *   *

Swimming: Act and Symbol

Bathing in this clear, pure, salt water, twice every day, is one of my best pleasures. Generally the water is so clear that you can see to a considerable depth. I must have the bump of "aquativeness" large; dear to me is a souse in the waves. Dear, oh, dear to me is Coney Island! Rockaway, too, and many other parts of sea-girt Paumanok.[44]

Whitman was vacationing at Greenport, Long Island, when he wrote the above words. Bathing, or swimming, was not a new delight; he had been enjoying it hugely for years. Indeed, it was a kind of ritual with him. He derived strong sensuous pleasure from stripping at the ocean's edge, running along the warm-gray shore-sands, and then plunging into the pounding surf.[45] It was also a health measure. Years later, when he was writing for the Brooklyn *Daily Times,* he urged the city-fathers to build immense public baths where people could bathe free of charge. The boys of the city could learn to swim there; after they had become proficient swimmers, they could bathe in the nearby ocean waters.[46]

Much as Whitman loved swimming, he was always concerned with the danger it presented to the inexperienced. He dramatized this fear in "A Fact-Romance of Long Island," a short story published in 1845. The setting of this short story is the south

shore of the Island near Huntington. There, near the road
called Gunnetaug, was a spot where the creek met the bay.
According to tradition, this piece of water was so deep that no
lines had ever sounded its bottom. It was here that a group of
young people met one day for a beach party. They had pro-
visions for a picnic lunch, and they made the water-part of their
journey in small boats. Suddenly one boat turned over, tipping
a young man, his sister, and his fiancée into the deep waters of
the creek. Most Long Islanders can swim, Whitman noted, but
the two girls could not, and the young man was torn between
saving his sister or his fiancée. He chose his fiancée, but the
ghostly memory of his young sister haunted him for the rest of
his life. He was never again heard to laugh. Ever after, this
piece of deep water was known as "Drowning Creek."[47] The
story is typically melodramatic and sentimental, but it does help
to explain why Whitman so wanted a place where young people
could learn to swim in safety.

Public baths built in Brooklyn would not only provide a safe
place for people to learn to swim; they would actually benefit
everybody. Both adults and children, Whitman insisted, would
benefit from regular exercise; and bathing (at least twice a week)
would help prevent the "multitude of undeveloped, dyspeptic,
stunted, cadaverous, bad-countenanced, bad-actioned, hardly-
ever-well persons . . ."[48]

Swimming, good health, and happiness are almost synonymous
in many of Whitman's poems. In "Song of Myself," section
forty-six, he tutors the timid:

> Long have you timidly waded holding a plank by the
>   shore,
> Now I will you to be a bold swimmer,
> To jump off in the midst of the sea, rise again, nod to
>   me, shout, and laughingly dash with your hair.

The same mood of exultancy appears in "A Song of Joys": "O
to bathe in the swimming-bath, or in a good place along shore,/
To splash the water! to walk ankle-deep, or race naked along the
shore." There is a vibrancy in both excerpts that shows Whit-

man's laughing delight in the ocean-playground. At other times his happiness is less exuberant, more meditative: "When I. wander'd alone over the beach, and undressing bathed, laughing with the cool waters, and saw the sun rise..."[49] Here the ocean is the scene of a rendezvous, and the love of friend and of sea unite to form a still happiness. A similar softness of mood exists in "I Sing the Body Electric," section two, in which the swimmer is seen through the semi-opaque waters:

> The swimmer naked in the swimming-bath, seen as
> he swims through the transparent green-shine, or lies
> with his face up and rolls silently to and fro in the
> heave of the water...

Whitman defined a more exact significance for the ocean and for bathing in section eleven of "Song of Myself." These are the well-known lines beginning: "Twenty-eight young men bathe by the shore,/ Twenty-eight young men and all so friendly..." Here the act of swimming and the act of sexual intercourse become confusedly mingled. There is an additional element of confusion when one remembers that Whitman constantly referred to the sea as his "mother." Does this mean that Whitman had a hidden desire for his mother? That he was treading on the brink of incest? It might, or course, but a different interpretation is possible. To Whitman, all *real* women possessed the embracing quality, the softness, and the sympathy that he connected with both his mother and the ocean. To him, the purpose of women (though he supported their equality) was to act as insulation for men, a sort of buffer state for man's sharp edges. Taken in this sense, the ocean could be mother, sister, wife, or even daughter — any woman who answered Whitman's definition of "Woman." In this selection, then, the ocean would be wife or lover, not mother.

Still another aspect of the ocean to the swimmer is portrayed in "The Sleepers," section three. Anyone who has ever fought the breakers on Long Island's south shore knows the almost masochistic joy of being overpowered and tossed about by a force overwhelmingly suprahuman. The fact that the force is detached

and inanimate and that it cannot be trusted adds, perhaps per-
versely, to the swimmer's delight. Whitman, long accustomed to
ocean swimming, must have experienced this joy many times. He
describes it lovingly, and yet brutally:

> I see a beautiful gigantic swimmer swimming naked
>   through the eddies of the sea,
> His brown hair lies close and even to his head, he
>   strikes out with courageous arms, he urges himself
>   with his legs,
> I see his white body, I see his undaunted eyes,
> I hate the swift-running eddies that would dash him
>   head-foremost on the rocks.

Then comes a personification of the opponent:

> What are you doing you ruffianly red-trickled waves?
> Will you kill the courageous giant? will you kill him
>   in the prime of his middle age?

The swimmer continues to struggle, though he is aware of his
eventual defeat:

> Steady and long he struggles,
> He is baffled, bang'd, bruis'd, he holds out while
>   his strength holds out,
> The slapping eddies are spotted with his blood, they
>   bear him away, they roll him, swing him, turn him,
> His beautiful body is borne in the circling eddies,
>   it is continually bruis'd on rocks,
> Swiftly and out of sight is borne the brave corpse.

Eulogies to the ocean may be written by land-bound poets who
have seen the ocean once or twice and dabbled their toes in an
expiring breaker, but only a poet who has *lived* with the ocean
over the years could sketch so affectionately this cruelty that
lures and destroys.

*   *   *   *

The Sea as a Molder of Philosophy

The last and most complex aspect of the sea remains to be
discussed. This is the sea as the molder of Whitman's philosophy,
as the shaper of his personality. It appears in its most succinct
form in "Song of Myself," section twenty-two. The poet, standing on the beach, is certain that the ocean will "cushion me
soft, rock me in billowy drowse." He then describes the sea, in
four lines covering almost every aspect of its meaning to man:

> Sea of stretch'd ground-swells,
> Sea breathing broad and convulsive breaths,
> Sea of the brine of life and of unshovell'd yet always-
>   ready graves,
> Howler and scooper of storms, capricious and dainty
>   sea,
> I am integral with you, I too am of one phase and of
>   all phases.

The fifth line sums up man's capitulation and merging, his identification, permanent and binding, with all phases of the ocean's
personality.

The ocean has many phases in Whitman's poetry. It is, first,
the embodiment of love: "Out of the rolling ocean the crowd
came a drop gently to me, Whispering *I love you*..."[50] There
is a meeting, and therefore safety. The "irresistible sea" is di-
visive and yet cohesive. But the ocean is also love in a more
general sense. Walking along the shores of Paumanok, the poet
hears the voices of the living and the dead, feels union with his
mother and father, sympathizes with all men everywhere. He
even experiences, momentarily, a relationship (though one beyond
understanding) between man and God:

> We, capricious, brought hither we know not whence,
>   spread out before you,
> You up there walking or sitting,
> Whoever you are, we too lie in drifts at your feet.[51]

The ocean is also adventure. It is pathless and wild seas—

"We will go where winds blow, waves dash, and the Yankee clipper speeds by under full sail."[52] It is an "unbounded" sea, on which a ship starts forth with spreading sails and flying pennant on its chartless voyage.[53] It is the home of wild storms, with "the sea high running," with "shouts of demoniac laughter," and with the savage trinity: waves, air, and midnight.[54]

Beyond love and adventure, the ocean is a span, a bridge, that unites the world and the world's peoples. It is a "vast similitude" which encloses all living bodies, all distances of place and of time, all spheres, all nations and races, all lives and deaths, the past, present, and future.[55] It bears on its bosom the ships of all nations, each flaunting its separate flag, yet it reserves one flag for itself and "for the soul of man": "a spiritual woven signal for all nations."[56] This one flag, "a pennant universal," waves for all men of all times and all seas. The ocean spans also the ages of the earth. It teaches man the evolutionary change from ocean-life to life in the open air, and it teaches also the anticipated change from life on this earth to life in other, more ethereal spheres.[57]

Finally, and most important, the ocean is love, and life and death, and song—all irretrievably mixed. In "Out of the Cradle Endlessly Rocking," both the expression and the conclusion are complex. It begins with the love of two birds, "two feather'd guests from Alabama," the love of a boy watching the birds, and the love of a man who, through memory, watches the boy. The boy, listening to the song of the one bird left alone, looks out over the ocean. The breakers seem to have white arms (again the woman, comforting). The boy grows intent:

I, with bare feet, a child, the wind wafting my hair,
Listen'd long and long.

The bird-song continues, singing of the ocean: "Close on its wave soothes the wave behind"; but the embracing quality of the waves serves only to emphasize the bird's own loss: "my love soothes not me." The loss is permanent; but the poet suddenly raises the poem's meaning to a higher dimension. The bird's lost love and the ocean's embracing love combine to awaken in the listening child a new awareness, a maturity of yearning. "The boy ecstatic, with his bare feet the waves, with his hair the atmosphere dallying," feels the love in his heart burst forth and feels his tongue from sleeping, wake. He knows now the purpose of his life: it is to sing — to sing the song of unsatisfied love that the bird has taught him mingled with the song the sea now whispers in his ear — "death, death." The tempo of the poem decreases, and Whitman, in his own person, states quietly: "My own songs awaked from that hour."

Seldom in literature has a writer outlined so clearly the origin of his genius, for the ocean not only influenced Whitman's personality and his writings, but literally gave birth to the poet in him. Born inland, or on the coast of the serene Pacific, would Whitman have been the same poet? Or a poet at all? The answer, almost definitely, is "no." The Atlantic, turbulent and treacherous, loving and gentle, cruel and ruthless, was the very core of his existence. It penetrated his infant mind at West Hills when he lay still, listening to the far-off roar of the surf; it teased his defenceless toes when, a few years later, he waded in the shallow waters at the ocean's edge; and it provided him, in his maturity, with mother, wife, and daughter; with love, adventure, and danger; with an insight into life and an understanding and acceptance of death. It provided the origin of his genius and the techniques of his style. What more could one factor in a man's life do? Without the Atlantic Ocean, there would have been a Walter Whitman — but not a Walt Whitman.

XII

Whitman and Paumanok

> Of all the streams of influence which flowed later into
> the wide channel of his poetry, his boyhood experience
> of Long Island was, in his own later view, the deepest
> and most dynamic. He felt sometimes, he said in old
> age, as if he had incorporated the Island.[1]

Walt Whitman never had any doubt about the vital part Long
Island had played in his formation both as man and as writer.
Indeed, even more than with most authors, in Whitman, the
man and writer were intertwined. Richard Bucke who knew him
well said of him: "His body, his outward life, his inward spiritual
existence and poetry, were all one; in every respect each tallied
with the other, and anyone of them could always be inferred
from the other."[2] That Whitman himself was aware of the
interrelationship between him and Long Island and of the Island's
influence upon him is proved by a selection in *Specimen Days*.
He wrote that there were three leading sources or "formative stamps" to his character: his maternal heritage from the
Netherlands; his paternal heritage from England; and his "Long
Island birth-spot." In the third he included New York and
Brooklyn, but emphasized eastern Long Island with its seashores
and rural scenes of childhood and youthful memories. He also
added that these three "formative stamps" influenced not only
his character, but also his literary outgrowth.[3]

He did his first writing on Long Island; in fact, the twelve

poems included in the first edition of *Leaves of Grass* were
written there.[4] Stretched out on the sand with the sound of the
surf in his ears, he composed his poems, often matching the
rhythm of the incoming breakers. He needed the solitude and
the freedom of such a retreat, and the ocean provided a natural
grave for discarded and unsatisfactory first drafts.[5] After the
first edition of *Leaves of Grass* was published, Dr. Moncure D.
Conway traveled out to Long Island to find the young author.
Later he described that first meeting:

> The day was excessively hot, the thermometer at nearly
> 100 degrees, and the sun blazed down as only on
> sandy Long Island can the sun blaze . . . I saw, stretched
> upon his back, and gazing up straight at the terrible
> sun, the man I was seeking.

Whitman was sunburnt and so was the grass, and — Conway
commented — he "was so like the earth upon which he rested that
he seemed almost enough a part of it for one to pass by without
recognition." Later in the meeting, Whitman told Conway that
this was his favorite place and position for the composing of
poems.[6]

Even the title of his great book, *Leaves of Grass,* has a possible source in an old Long Island tradition. Whitman himself
recounted this tradition in an article in the Brooklyn *Daily Eagle*
in 1847. He wrote: "An ancient Indian . . . more than a hundred
years ago, declared to one of the earliest inhabitants of Easthampton, that within his recollection the natives were as many as
the spears of grass."[7] The underlining is Whitman's own, and
it indicates, at the very least, that this image possessed a special
significance for him.

However, to talk of the influence of Long Island on Walt
Whitman is, in one sense, misleading; rather, one should talk of
the various ways in which Whitman *used* his knowledge of the
Island. He used it much as another writer might use a library.
It was his first encyclopedia of natural history and of country
living; it was a biographical dictionary populated with rural

"characters"; it was a source book of his country's early history, and an atlas in which he could locate towns, rivers, plains, and hills; it was a style book; and, finally, it was a microcosm of the United States. Each of these areas must be studied separately if one is to attain an accurate evaluation of Whitman's utilization of his Long Island experiences.

*   *   *   *

Natural History and Country Living

Whitman's intense and enduring attachment to nature began in his infancy in West Hills. Surrounded by farms, woods and ocean, he had an early opportunity to become familiar with nature through those five natural teachers, the senses. He could feel the friability of the soil, see the growth of flowers, and smell the freshly-ploughed earth; he could hear the song of the birds or the sound of the surf and taste salt in the air. This first-hand knowledge, acquired in childhood, gave him an attitude toward nature different from that of the Romantic poets. The result is an earthiness and a detail that were lacking in poetry in the middle 19th century. When Wordsworth looked at daffodils, he saw memories and their creative role in a man's life. When Whitman looked at lilacs, he saw lilacs. He saw also the miracle of birth, of life, and of death through the growth of the flower, but primarily he saw, quite simply, the lilac. He knew (and said in his poetry) that it was a perennial, that it was a tall-growing bush, had "heart-shaped leaves of rich green," and pointed blossoms. He knew that it had a strong perfume, that it bloomed in the spring, and that it grew so abundantly that one could fill one's arms with its laden, scented sprigs.[8] He knew the lilac so well because he had grown up with it; lilac bushes had grown just outside the door of his West Hills home.

Whitman also knew the calamus plant from first-hand experience. During his long rambles in the woods, he must often have seen this plant, three feet tall with long spiky leaves, growing in swamps and near pools. When he sought a symbol that would represent loneliness and love for one group of poems, he chose first the live oak of Louisiana, then changed to the native calamus. This change was a natural one since the calamus grows wild on Long Island even today, and in Whitman's time must have been still more prolific.[9]

This closeness to nature is common in Whitman's poetry. When he thinks of his birth, he thinks of his relationship to the earth: "My tongue, every atom of my blood, form'd from this soil, this air." When he mentions an incident of his early life, he places it in time by use of natural detail: "When the lilac-scent was in the air and Fifth-month grass was growing."[10] When he remembers his childhood, he equates it with singing birds, a house and barn, fields, an orchard, and old lanes.[11] Perhaps the best illustrations both of his use of detail and of his theories regarding the ties that bind man and nature occur in the poem, "There Was A Child Went Forth." The first lines clearly delineate the theory:

> There was a child went forth every day,
> And the first object he look'd upon, that object he
>   became,
> And that object became part of him for the day or
>   a certain part of the day,
> Or for many years or stretching cycles of years.

The following lines yield the details. From them one learns that a fish "suspends" itself in water and that water-plants have "graceful flat heads"; that field-sprouts grow in April and May, that corn is light-yellow, and that garden roots are often esculent. From them one learns of apple trees covered with blossoms and of wood-berries and of common weeds, of the mire by the pond and of the noisy brood in the barnyard. There are also March lambs, a sow's litter (pink-faint), a mare's foal, and a cow's calf; red and white morning-glories, red and white clover, a phoebe-bird and its song, colored clouds, and one "long bar of maroon-tint" solitary in the sky. Such a wealth of nature so extravagantly squandered in one poem suggests that these things were part of

him and of his life, and that he himself was the child who "went
forth every day."

He was also the child asking "What is the grass?" as he was
the adult answering that it is "the flag of my disposition," "the
handkerchief of the Lord," "the produced babe of the vegetation," "the uniform hieroglyphic," and most tenderly, "the
beautiful uncut hair of graves." Again the images are so prolific
and his affection for his subject so evident as to necessitate a
familiarity stretching back to childhood.

As a boy spending his summers on his Grandfather Van
Velsor's farm, he learned about farming and the charms of rural
life. His earliest poem, "Young Grimes," written in 1840, rhapso-
dizes about the tranquil life, far from "the wide city's noisy
din."[12]   The early tale, "The Tomb Blossoms," takes place in
a "pleasant, fair-sized country village — a village embosomed in
trees . . . a village with much grass and shrubbery, and no mortar,
no bricks, no pavements, no gas . . ." He catalogues the delights
of country living: "our pure air"; "our freedom from the sickly
vices that taint the town"; "our manners of sociality."[13]   In the
temperance novel, *Franklin Evans,* young Evans had been appren-
ticed to a farmer, and when he heads for the city (destruction)
leaving the farm (safety), he travels in a farm market-wagon.
Other early stories — "Death in a School-Room," "The Last
Loyalist," "Wild Frank's Return," "The Shadow and the Light
of a Young Man's Soul," and "An Incident on Long Island
Forty Years Ago" — all have their setting in small Long Island
towns and almost all contain numerous references to the salubri-
ous country air and to the "remarkable beauty" of peach blossoms, *et cetera, et cetera.*

The poems in *Leaves of Grass* reflect a more mature and practical attitude toward country life. One of the earliest examples
occurs in "Song of Myself," section nine:

> The big doors of the country barn stand open and
>   ready,
> The dried grass of the harvest-time loads the slow-
>   drawn wagon,

The clear light plays on the brown gray and green
    intertinged,
The armfuls are pack'd to the sagging mow.

I am there, I help, I came stretch'd atop of the load,
I felt its soft jolts, one leg reclined on the other,
I jump from the cross-beams and seize the clover and
    timothy,
And roll head over heels and tangle my hair full of
    wisps.

Here is a straight-forward, realistic account of a harvesting written by a man who had participated in many. From this time on,
Whitman's references to the rural life are of this order. They are
simple, almost photographic, possessing a new, stark beauty of
their own, immeasurably superior to the earlier, unassimilated
rhapsodies. He talks of the "darting swallow, the destroyer of
insects," and one is reminded of the orchard-owner, and of
Bryant who felt grateful to the English sparrow for helping to
protect his fruit trees. He describes the farmer's life, rising "at
peep of day" to plough the land, to train orchards, to graft
trees, and to gather apples.[14]
    During the 19th century, great compost heaps could be seen
scattered along the south shore of Long Island. They were composed of menhaden mixed with seaweed and kelp. The resulting
fertilizer was unusually effective in enriching the soil and in
producing outstanding crops.[15]   The paradoxical quality of these
compost heaps — their smell of death plus their ability to provide
nourishment — interested Whitman. In the poem, "The Compost," written in 1856, he considered the relationship between the
compost heap and the farm product as representative of the cycle
of life. How can the dead who are in the earth, he asks, furnish
health to the living who must draw their nourishment from this
same earth? He turns farmer for a moment: "I will run a furrow
with my plough, I will press my spade through the sod and turn
it up underneath,/ I am sure I shall expose some of the foul
meat." But all that is exposed is the earth, clean, sweet, and
purifying. From this earth the "bean bursts noiselessly," the

"delicate spear of the onion pierces upward," the "apple-buds cluster together," and the "resurrection of the wheat appears." The poem ends with a eulogy to the Earth which "grows such sweet things out of such corruptions." "The Compost" is an amazing mixture of disgust and delight, of death and of birth, of vileness and new innocence. It owes much of its power to its author's obvious knowledge of farming and of the processes of natural growth.

In 1881, after a forty years' absence (except for one brief visit) Whitman returned to West Hills for one week. The notes that he wrote at this time indicate that his eyes were still focused on the natural beauties, not on man-made changes. He noted the big oak, 150-200 years old, the well, and the sloping kitchen-garden; and nearby, "a stately grove of tall, vigorous black-walnuts, beautiful, Apollo-like." During this week, he visited the family cemeteries and found again "the gray and sterile hill, the clumps of chestnuts . . . the soughing wind." The visit revived early memories and stirred Whitman deeply:

> There is alway the deepest eloquence of sermon or poem in any of these ancient graveyards of which Long Island has so many; so what must this one have been to me? My whole family history, with its succession of links, from the first settlement down to date, told here — three centuries concentrate on this sterile acre.[16]

It was this aspect of nature that most fascinated Whitman: the cycle of life and death, and the continuity and unity that such a cycle implies. This was his major legacy from his birth-land. It shaped most of what he wrote and all that he thought.

During the Civil War years, while Whitman was surrounded by pain and death, his thoughts turned constantly to his beloved Paumanok with its memories of health and cleanliness. He dreamed "of buying an acre or two of land in some by-place on Long Island, and building for himself and his family a cheap house."[17] It was his anchor, his isle of permanency in a world ravaged by the violence and filth of war. But the dream remained unrealized. Paralysis and poverty stepped in, and his trip north from Washington stopped prematurely in Camden, New Jersey.

It may have been this forced absence in his late years that spurred Whitman into remembering some old Long Island habits. John Burroughs visited Whitman in Camden in August, 1887, and the two friends went for a drive. Whitman greeted every person they met. When Burroughs asked him if he knew them all, he answered that "he knew but few of those he spoke to, but that, as he grew older, the old Long Island custom of his people, to speak to everyone on the road, was strong upon him."[18] One wonders if this custom inspired the short poem, "To You."

> Stranger, if you passing meet me and desire to speak
>   to me, why should you not speak to me?
> And why should I not speak to you?

Certainly the custom was congenial to Whitman's personal philosophy, but it is also true that Whitman enjoyed using some of the old phrases "just for fun." When he was writing the preface to the English edition of *Specimen Days* in 1887, he said that he was sick "but in good heart." Then he added parenthetically — "to use a Long Island country phrase."[,19]

*   *   *   *

"Characters" on the Island

Whitman's predilection for following old Island customs in his speech habits may be related to his almost juvenile delight in chatting with "characters" found in out-of-the-way places on Long Island. In his first Letter from Paumanok written in June, 1851, he declared that the "best amusements in a country place, by the salt water, are the cheapest." Then he added, in a rather patronizing tone — "For I hugely like to accost the originals I see all around me, and to set them agoing about themselves and their neighbors near by. It is more refreshing than a comedy at any of the New York theatres. The very style of their talk is a treat.''[20]   This is a rather condescending attitude for a poet of the people, but at the time, Whitman was writing as a journalist, not as a poet.

A few days later in Letter # 2, he described a visit to Rocky Point (renamed Marion, now once again Rocky Point). While he was strolling through the village, he met an old man "with a pipe in his mouth, and a clam-basket and hoe in his hands." The old fellow was evidently on his way to get a basket of soft clams for bait. Whitman noted with amusement that he wore patched bright blue homespun trousers. After the old man had passed by, Whitman continued his walk. He concluded that strangers must have been rare in town since everybody rushed to their windows to stare at him. A little later the old man returned, and Whitman eagerly engaged him in conversation. The "character" turned out to be a retired businessman who owned over a hundred-acre farm, running from the turnpike to the Sound, and who had numerous sons and daughters. His apparent dejection was caused by the loss, twenty-eight months before, of his two eldest sons. They had set forth in a fine new sloop called the "Long Island," for a port near Florida, but they had sailed into a storm and had never been heard of again. When they reached the old man's house, Whitman joined his friend in a collation comprised wholly of fresh strawberries and then walked back to his own quarters.[21]   In this second letter, Whitman turned the trick on himself. The apparent hobo turned out to be a respectable citizen who did not ask for food, but who supplied it.

These two letters, considered jointly, provide a true index of Whitman's attitude toward his fellow Long Islanders. He found it easy to refer to them as "original characters...quaint... smacking of salt and sea-weed"[22]   when he referred to them *en masse,* but when he talked to an individual native, the "quaintness" disappeared and he found himself face-to-face with, quite simply, another human being.

For the most part, he found the patriarchal society of agricultural Suffolk County to his liking. He appreciated the simplicity, integrity, and independent attitudes of these people. He especially approved of the farmers' honesty—"Even the Railroad had not yet been able to eradicate it," he added cynically, a comment that might have come from the aristocratic Cooper.[23]

Whitman's interest in these people and their activities is important primarily as they influenced his early writing. He once wrote:

> On jaunts over Long Island, as boy and young fellow,
> nearly half a century ago, I heard of, or came across
> in my own experience, characters, true occurrences,
> incidents, which I tried my 'prentice hand at record-
> ing...and published during occasional visits to New
> York.[24]

Their influence on his early short stories is evident even from a cursory reading; their influence on his poetry is more difficult to assess. Probably these characters are most important when they are used anonymously in single-line descriptions of fishermen, whalemen, farmers, and clam-diggers as they are used in such poems as "A Song of Joys," "A Song for Occupations," and "Song of the Open Road." Only infrequently do they appear in greater detail. "Twenty Years" tells the story of one such "character" who went out to sea as "green-hand boy" and circled the globe for twenty years. Now he is returning to his home port to settle down. The description of the old tar—"the face all berry-brown and bearded—the stout-strong frame"— could describe any of the retired seamen Whitman had met and talked with in Greenport or the Hamptons; it could, incidentally, describe himself. One other poem in which there is possible direct use of a character he met in these early years is the third section of "I Sing the Body Electric." This stanza concerns a common farmer who has five sons. He is a man of "wonderful vigor, calmness, beauty of person"; he is six feet tall, over eighty years old, has black eyes and a white beard. He is clean-living, temperate, and skilled in hunting and fishing. His prototype could be the old man Whitman had met in Rocky Point just four years before he wrote this poem; but it could also be Whitman's own grandfather, or another farmer he had seen, or even a composite figure.

At any rate, the time he spent in country towns, watching the people and talking with them, provided a rich vein of ore for Whitman the writer. They were the "staples" of his early short stories and ·poems, and, universalized, they played a part (though a lesser one) in later great poems. After all, these were the people Whitman once called "the country's pride." [25] It is unlikely that he ever forgot them.

* * * *

The History of the Area

The Whitmans had been natives of Long Island for over two hundred years; when Walt Whitman visited the family cemeteries in 1881, he was impressed by the fact that three centuries of his family's history were concentrated in this soil. Through the gravestones he could trace his ancestors back to Joseph Whitman, the founder of the Long Island Whitmans, who had settled on the Island in 1660. Because this was true, because the Whitman roots were deep in Long Island earth, it was almost inevitable that Walt Whitman would eventually become interested not only in the history of his family but in the history of the Island itself.

In 1861, Whitman began writing the "Brooklyniana," a series of articles dealing with Long Island's past and present. His first chapter was devoted to the earliest Dutch settlement:

> So the first employees of the great Amsterdam Trading Association (the Dutch West India Company,) made their settlement here on the aboriginal Island of Paumanock (or *Paumanake,* as it is also sometimes spelt in the old Indian deeds). Here, on the west end of this said Paumanok Island, they found a beautifully rich country, sufficiently diversified with slopes and hills, well wooded, yet with open ground enough... And here they settled.[26]

This chapter shows an awareness of the Island's early settlement and Whitman's own pride in its long history.

Chapter eleven dealt with Long Island's role in the Revolu-

tionary War. This aspect of Whitman's interest in local history
has been extensively discussed earlier in this work.

Chapter thirty-six discussed eastern Long Island with an emphasis on Gardiner's Island. Whitman described the island as he
and his party on board a sloop approached it:

> Some miles ahead of us lay Gardiner's Island, like a
> big heart, with a bit of one of its edges sliced out.
> This fertile and "retired" little place (the Indian name,
> *Monchonock*), contains about 3,000 acres, mostly ex-
> cellent land, and was originally purchased at the fol-
> lowing price, according to the records:

> > One large black dog, one gun, a quantity (?) of
> > powder and shot, *some rum,* and a few Dutch
> > blankets. This was in 1630; it is now worth seventy
> > thousand dollars.

> This was in 1630; it is now worth seventy thousand
> dollars.

Whitman then summarized the history of Gardiner's Island,
pointing out that it was the first English settlement in New York
State. It was founded in 1639 by Lion Gardiner, a civil engineer
from Saybrook, Connecticut. Whitman was fascinated by this
man and by his probable way of life:

> Imagination loves to trace (mine does, anyhow) the
> settlement and patriarchal happiness of this fine old
> English gentleman on his island there all by himself,
> with his large farm-house, his servants and family, his
> crops on a great scale, his sheep, horses, and cows.
> His wife was a Dutch woman ... Imagine the Arcadian
> simplicity and plenty of the situation, and of those
> times ... [28]

Whitman added that he liked to imagine the mixture of whites
and Indians in the great hall or in the kitchen. This is a reasonable piece of guesswork, for Whitman knew about the unusually
close friendship between Wyandance (sic), the Indian chief of

East Long Island, and Lion Gardiner. Once, when the daughter
of Wyandance and thirteen other females were captured by a
hostile tribe, Gardiner was instrumental in having them restored
to their families. In performing this feat, Gardiner did, to some
extent, risk his life. Wyandance never forgot his white friend's
loyalty, and he proved his own great trust in his friend when
he wrote his will. In that document he made Mr. Gardiner the
guardian of his son and the advisor of his widow.[29]

The Gardiner-Wyandance relationship must have seemed a
welcome oasis to Whitman in the generally disgraceful story of
the white man's treatment of the Indians. Whitman's sympathy
usually lay with the "underdog," and this was especially true in
the white-Indian conflict. The aboriginal Indian had an empathy
with nature and with the natural life that appealed strongly to
Whitman. In fact, this aspect of local history is the only one
that remained of interest to Whitman throughout h¦s entire life,
and that entered into his prose and poetry of all periods.

He recognized that most of the Indians existent in his lifetime
were inferior to the aboriginals. At one time, he pointed out that
the Indian remnants near Easthampton were "degraded, shiftless
and intemperate," but they were also honest.[30]   He was in
Southold (one of the earliest settlements on Long Island) in 1847
and he noticed a *real* Indian. Tartly, he qualified the adjective:
"at least as far as there are any of that race now-a-days; that is,
perhaps, an Indian whose blood is only thinned by only two or
three degrees of mixture." The combination in one day of visiting
an early settlement and seeing a real Indian turned Whitman's
thoughts toward the aboriginal inhabitants who had dominated
this island before the coming of the white man:

A populous and powerful race! for such they once
were. Some authorities assert that, at the earliest
approach of the whites to this part of the continent,
and for a time after, the Indian inhabitants of Long
Island numbered a million and a half. This may be
an over-estimate; but the red race here was certainly
very numerous, as is evidenced by many tokens.[31]

He went on to explain that there had been on the Island thirteen separate tribes ruled by Wyandanch, who was of the royal tribe at Montauk. Montauk was the center of Indian civilization in that day, and it included the holiest of their burial places. At Montauk, too, were the remains of aboriginal fortifications, now called Fort Hill. Whitman described the fort in detail with some cynicism, then showed how it was one step in the movement that eventually resulted in the "end" of the Indian race on Long Island.

> It had ramparts and parapets, ditches around, and huge towers at each of four corners — and is estimated to have afforded conveniences for three or four hundred men, and to evince singular knowledge of warfare, even as understood by what we call civilized nations. Wars, indeed, added to pestilence, and most of all the use of the "fire-water," thinned off the Indian population from the earlier settlement of the whites, until there are hardly any remaining. I believe there are but two clusters of Indian families that can be called settlements, now on the island. One is at Shinnecock, and consists of some hundred and forty or fifty persons: the other is down on Montauk, and does not comprise a baker's dozen. Sad remnants, these, of the sovereign sway and the old majesty there! [32]

The type of Indian civilization Whitman knew was based on these "sad remnants." On the trip to Gardiner's Island, he and his friends passed the cave where an old Indian hermit lived. They didn't see the Indian, but one of the young men in the party knew him well and described him at length. Whitman commented: "From the young man's description, the old fellow must have been a pretty fair counterpart of Chingachgook, one of Cooper's Indian characters." [33] The outward descriptions of the two Indians may have been similar, but there was certainly an abysmal difference between the lone hermit living in his circumscribed cave as an object of tourist curiosity, and the noble Chingachgook who still had thousands of miles of woodland and

prairie in which to roam. There is a similar note of sadness in
one section of *Franklin Evans*. Young Evans, traveling to the
city, meets an old gentleman who has an antiquarian interest in
the history of old Long Island. He knows about the Indians
who had once lived there, and he tells his fellow passengers an
Indian legend.[34]   Whitman was apparently unconscious of the
pathos in this incident. It is an *old* man with an *antiquarian*
interest who tells an Indian story which is a *legend*. These three
elements indicate the author's true awareness that the Indians
were a dying race — that their present held no interest, their past
all. Whitman knew that past glory only through the most pathetic
evidence: the immense shell-banks along the shores of the island,
"some of them literally 'mountain high,'" and the exceedingly
large tract of land devoted to the fields of Indian corn.[35]

This is the Indian as Whitman knew him, and this is the
Indian who appears in a number of Whitman's poems. Occasionally he is wholly in the past, as he is in "Our Old Feuillage,"
and then the picture is a splendid one complete with the calumet,
the pipe of good-will, the sachem, the scalp-dance, the war-party,
the long march, the single file, the swinging hatchets, and cul-
minating in "the surprise and slaughter of enemies." But this is
rare; more often, he has outlived the glories of the past and has
merely survived into the present. Such is the case in "Yonnon-
dio," which means "lament for the aborigines." As a background, Whitman conjures up a swarm of "stalwart chieftains,
medicine-men, and warriors" against a setting of open woods and
free-flowing falls, but "unlimn'd they disappear." In a world of
cities, farms, and factories, the Indian way of life is anomalous
and hence doomed. Another poem, "Osceola," depicts a Seminole
who had been a leading brave in the Florida war. He had been
captured by United States troops and imprisoned in Fort Moul-
trie, South Carolina, where he had died of a broken heart.
Whitman describes his death-hour: how he had risen from his
bed, drawn on his war-dress, painted his face, neck, wrists, and
hands, and tightly grasped his tomahawk, before sinking slowly
to the floor. The poet adds: "And here a line in memory of his
name and death." Again the outstanding element in the poem is

the contrast between the past and the present, and the poignancy
of the Indian present.

Perhaps Whitman's finest handling of the Indian in his poetry
occurs in section six of the long poem, "The Sleepers." The
story is based on an actual incident experienced by his mother
while she was living on the Van Velsor farm.[36]   Whitman tells
the story as it was told to him. A red squaw came to the homestead one day; her hair was straight, shiny, coarse and black; her
step was free and her voice exquisite.

> My mother look'd in delight and amazement at the
>   stranger,
> She look'd at the freshness of her tall-borne face and
>   full and pliant limbs,
> The more she look'd upon her she loved her,
> Never before had she seen such wonderful beauty and
>   purity . . .

His mother made the squaw sit down to rest; she gave her food
and understanding through the long afternoon. Toward the
middle of the afternoon the squaw went away.

> All the week she thought of her, she watch'd for her
>   many a month,
> She remember'd her many a winter and many a
>   summer,
> But the red squaw never came nor was heard of there
>   again.

This poem, in many respects, both summarizes and symbolizes
Whitman's attitude toward Indians. The squaw in her purity and
simple beauty represents all the fine qualities of the ancient
Indian race. She is noble, dignified, and supremely healthy. She
is so magnificent that she stuns her white counterpart into love
and wonder. Then, still representing her people, she goes away
and is never "heard of there again." Thus the poem which
begins in the hope of meeting and develops in the growth of
friendship, ends in a final parting. Whitman had seen too many
"sad remnants." He could not disassociate, even when he wished,

the Indian and his ultimate disappearance. This, too, was part of his legacy from his birth-land.

* * * * * *

The Geography of the Area

In 1883, Richard M. Bucke wrote about Walt Whitman (with Whitman's full acceptance and approval) —

> The other main element[37] which has to be taken into account in the formation of the character of the poet, is that he was brought up on Long Island...indeed, there are few regions on the face of the earth better fitted for the concrete background of such a book as *Leaves of Grass*.[38]

On the same page of the biography, Bucke quoted William O'Connor, who also knew Whitman well, and who claimed "that no one can ever really get at Whitman's poems, and their finest lights and shades, until he has visited and familiarized himself with the freshness, scope, wildness and sea-beauty of this rugged island."

A look at the geography of 19th century Long Island confirms this view. The 120 miles that made up the island contained almost every possible geographical feature, from the highly-developed urban life in Brooklyn to the isolated rocky cliffs and sandy shores of Montauk. Between these two extreme limits were the Hempstead Plains, the high hills of Huntington (mountains, really, to a native Long Islander), the great wasted area in the central eastern section, the heavily wooded areas, the quiet shores on the north facing the Sound and the more tumultuous shores on the south facing the Atlantic, vast acres of tilled farmland and dozens of villages — some devoted to fishing, some to whaling, some to agriculture. This varied panorama was available to all, but few used the opportunity so well as Whitman who rambled all over the Island as a boy, as a youth, and as a mature editor of several Brooklyn newspapers. By culling selections from the many travel reports that he wrote, one can put together an annotated atlas-gazetteer of the region.

Whitman's favorite method of travel was the Long Island Railroad which began operation in 1834.[39]   Starting from Brooklyn, one first arrived in Bedford, "a pretty little hamlet" but one which had a "fever-and-aguish aspect." The next stop was East New York. A range of hills that ran through the village made it pleasant to the eyes, but unfortunately it was "devoid of that aspect of vitality which...denotes...a thriving and growing place." The train then passed the Union race course (famous in the 19th century) and pulled into Jamaica—"a charming place ...occupied by many intellectual and wealthy people." Whitman felt that it was rather citified, but noted with satisfaction that it had two flourishing newspapers, one democratic and one whig.[40]

The next stop was Hempstead, "an old village, mostly celebrated for its clams, (indeed, it is by some called Clamtown)." Whitman considered it a worthy village in a location good for trading. He waxed biblical in describing what must be the present Hempstead Turnpike: "To the southeast from it stretches the great turnpike that leads down along our island's 'sea-girt shore,' even through the gates of Jerusalem and into the recess of Babylon the Great." The biblical mood continued as they approached Hicksville: "Ah, how are the mighty fallen!" He added that Hicksville had been designed as a city, but had not quite made the grade.[41]   The first day's report ended with Farmingdale, once called Hardscrabble.

The second day began at Farmingdale and continued into eastern Long Island, an area for which Whitman had special affection. "After leaving Farmingdale, we trudged east with our steam steed through brush, plains, pines, scrub oak, and all the other peculiarities of those singular diggins..."[42]   Deer Park presented a dreary and barren appearance from the train window, but Whitman knew the area well and added that north and south of the railroad lay rich farms and the best soil on Long Island:

To the north are apple orchards and grass lands, so thrifty that the eye of an agriculturist might gloat for

hours in the mere seeing of them. The land is diversi-
fied into hills and valleys; and on the tops of the highest elevations are little lakes of the purest water, which
form brooks down the valleys, and irrigate many of the
neighboring fields. What is called the highest point of
land on the island is at West Hills, in the town of
Huntington; it was made much use of by Mr. Hassler,
the U.S. chief of engineers, in the great plan of coast
survey which has been going on for some years past.
The other part of Huntington, lying along the south
bay, is of a different character; it partakes of *fish,* both
on the land as well as water. Fish is one of the most
powerful manures known, and under its influence the
corn grows to an astonishing height and size. I have
thought, indeed, that the fault among the farmers here
was in putting too much of it, at a time, on their land.
Like Macbeth's ambition, it o'erleaps itself and falls
on the other side of fertility.[43]

There is obvious close knowledge of the area in the above account. Beyond Deer Park were some small stations. These made
Whitman think of the new habitations in the far west — "with
their cheerless looking houses, barefooted children, and general
slovenliness."[44]   The land in this area was of poor quality, and
the owners of little energy. From the train, all that could be
seen were dwarfed yellow corn and poor beans and potatoes.
Whitman was convinced, however, that a little knowledge of
agriculture and chemistry could transform the land and turn it
into an Eden. With his knowledge of the people of the area, he
added: "It is a pity that there is, among the farmers of Long
Island, an unusual share of the contempt of their craft for
'book-farming.' "[45]   The train pulled into Riverhead in the
middle of a "cold, dull, dark, blue-devilish, north-east rain," but
even the weather improved when Whitman heard the news of
Scott's victories in the city of Mexico: "Consider me as on the
top of the tallest pine tree in the present neighborhood, wafting
my gratified patriotism to you in the loudest sort of a 'holler.' "[46]
    The central interior of the Island possessed little beauty for
several reasons: first, as has already been noted, the soil needed

help which it did not receive; second, the trees in this section were stunted and only of medium growth, partly as the result of forest fires and partly as a result of charcoal-burning. In Whitman's day, this whole section was sprinkled with the huts of charcoal-burners, and for several decades this small industry flourished, much to the detriment both of the beauty and production of the land.[47]   Some of this interior land was also used as a common for cattle and sheep, "a great privilege for the poor man," Whitman noted.[48]   Only in late autumn did this section of the Island possess beauty. Then the scrub oak, birch, and sumac were at their loveliest, and the landscape was painted in "deep and pale red, the green of the pines, the bright yellow of the hickory." [49]

East of Riverhead, the Island breaks into two great tines, one to the north and one to the south. Whitman traveled both of them on different trips. On the northern tine one passes Mattituck and Southold before coming to Shelter Island:

> Shelter Island is another unknown, untraveled, but interesting part of Long Island, and is equally picturesque. It lies in the water of the Peconic, and is enclosed, as in the opened and half-embracing claws of a huge lobster, sheltering it all around; hence its name.[50]

Here Whitman makes the same mistake that Cooper had made earlier, for Shelter Island received its name not only from its sheltered location, but also from the fact that it provided shelter for Quakers during the Quaker persecution.

Just north of Shelter Island is Greenport, "a fine half-rural, half-marine village," popular with sportsmen and fishermen both as a summer and fall resort.[51]   One of Whitman's most enthusiastic articles concerns a "flying picnic" from Brooklyn to Greenport. This may have been a summer special offered by the Long Island Railroad. The participating group (of which Whitman was a member) had breakfast in Brooklyn, traveled by train one hundred miles to Greenport, spent the day in that village, then traveled the one hundred miles back, and suppered in Brook-

lyn.[52]   To Whitman, this "flying picnic" offered creditable proof
of American progress. He describes their arrival at Greenport:

> Going down with the L.I.R.R., you are dumped (the
> said R.R. going no farther,) on a long wharf, cluttered
> with rubbish of the most nondescript kind . . . you
> sweep your eyes around, and lo! a few rods to the
> south, a goodly habitation, of potent dimensions, and
> flags flying, a most christian looking house, and a
> satisfactory assurance, after fifty miles of "plains" and
> scrub oak, that you are *not* among heathen, but will
> surely get you a good civilized dinner.[53]

In 1846 when Whitman was there, Greenport had a population
of sixteen hundred. The houses were new and tidy, the gardens
filled with flowers. There were three churches. Industry in the
town revolved around shipbuilding and whaling, for eleven or
twelve whale ships were still leaving from Greenport each year.[54]
Five years later he again wrote about Greenport. (It was one of
his favorite towns, possibly because his sister Mary lived there
for years and he often visited her.)[55]   In 1851 he found the town
filled with summer boarders who did not know how to enjoy
themselves. They dressed for dinner, were afraid to get wet or
sunburnt. They might just as well have stayed in the city, Whitman reported. He himself had a wonderful time, bathing in the
salt water twice a day, fishing for porgy and blackfish, and
talking with the natives. He considered Greenport far more satisfactory than any fashionable watering place.[56]

Beyond Greenport, at the very point of the northern prong is
Orient (formerly Oysterponds). Whitman was acquainted with
this town, but did not know it well. He merely commented that
the road between Greenport and Orient was "pleasant and
thrifty-looking" and that there were many modest farm cottages.[57]   One of his notes in this article is interesting because it
reflects an opinion he shared with James Fenimore Cooper:

> Very great confusion arises on Long Island, from the
> numerosity of names, belonging to one and the same
> place. Hardly one fourth of the neighborhoods retain

the same names for twenty years in succession! Letters, packages, and even travelers are constantly getting lost, through this propensity.[58]

Both this statement (made in 1851) and Whitman's error regarding the naming of Shelter Island (made in 1859) parallel statements made by Cooper in *The Sea Lions,* written in 1849. Unfortunately there is no proof that Whitman ever read this novel, so the parallel may be completely coincidental.

Traveling along the southern prong of Long Island, one passes the Hamptons, and at length arrives at Montauk Point. This was one of Whitman's favorite places. He describes it most completely in an account written in the early 1860's. While visiting in Greenport, he hitched a ride on a sloop to Montauk. He was first delighted with the East Long Island girls whom he found to be "terraqueous." He admitted that they could give him a head-start and "beat me all hollow in matters connected with sailing."[59]   Navigation around Montauk Point was tricky, and his comments about keeping a sharp lookout for shallow places and sand bars again remind one of Cooper.[60]   About Montauk itself he grew lyrical: the soil was rich, the grass green and plentiful, and it had "the best patches of Indian corn and vegetables I saw last summer," all "within gun shot of the salt waves of the Atlantic."[61]   The Point itself is a high hill, Turtle Hill, on which is perched the lighthouse built in 1795. The lights are about two hundred feet above sea-level. The keeper and his family lived in a dwelling nearby. Whitman left his friends for a little while and took a walk along the coast:

> Even to my unscientific eyes there were innumerable wonders and beauties all along the shore, and edges of the cliffs. There were earths of all colors, and stones of every conceivable shape, hue, and destiny, with shells, large boulders of a pure white substance, and layers of those smooth round pebbles called "milk-stones" by the country children. There were some of them tinged with pale green, blue or yellow — some streaked with various colors and so on.[62]

He rejoined his friends and for the next few hours they jumped among the rocks, shouted at the waves, and wrestled happily. They cooked an impromptu supper on the sloop (six fat pullets bought from an owner unwilling to sell), and sailed west under the stars and a new moon.

Montauk Point stood alone in Whitman's affection. The solitude it offered and the incessant music of the ocean breaking on that lonely shore provided a background conducive to creation. It is the only Long Island town honored by its own poem, "From Montauk Point":

> I stand as on some mighty eagle's beak,
> Eastward the sea absorbing, viewing, (nothing but sea
>   and sky,)
> The tossing waves, the foam, the ships in the distance,
> The wild unrest, the snowy, curling caps — that in-
>   bound urge and urge of waves,
> Seeking the shores forever.

The last two lines suggest the cause of Whitman's fascination with Montauk: "the wild unrest" and the constant "seeking" were objective reflections of the poet's own unrest and seeking.

*   *   *   *

The "State" of Long Island

This was the Long Island of Walt Whitman. It was the land that, for the first forty years of his life, he knew best, indeed almost exclusively. He loved it so well, felt so much pride in it that he seriously considered the suggestion that Long Island should be separated from New York and set up as a sovereign state. There was a movement in the mid-19th century to do just this. It was sponsored by Colonel Spooner and supported by the local historians, Silas Wood, Gabriel Furman, and Benjamin Thompson.[63]   Whitman knew about this movement, and for a time almost believed in it.

> For thirty years past, there has been a suggestion made
> by spasms, sometimes in joke, sometimes in earnest,
> that Long Island should become a state in itself! The
> comparison is made between its extent of surface, the
> number of its population — and then in the comparison,
> Rhode Island and Delaware are brought in.[64]

He did not think the suggestion at all preposterous, but rather
enjoyed thinking about "The State of Paumanok," as he was
sure it would be called. One disadvantage of such a move occurred to him — he was afraid the necessary resultant taxes would
be too high.[65]   Evidently the disadvantage seemed a strong one
to Whitman, for he dropped the subject and never again mentioned it.

His interest in the name, "Paumanok," however, was not so
short-lived. Throughout his entire life he never used "Long
Island" when he could use "Paumanok" — an Indian word meaning "the island with its breast long drawn out, and laid against
the sea." "Long Island," he felt, was too common, and lacked
all significance or special associations, whereas "Paumanok"
occurred in all the aboriginal deeds and was used by the first
Dutch settlers. Actually, the Island had first been called "Sewant-
hackey" (the place of the shells) and sometimes "Mattowak" or
"Mattawake." But "Paumanok" too had a long and respectable
history; besides, calling it "Paumanok" would be an act of poetic
justice to the Lenni-Lenape, or Delawares, of which stock the
aborigines of Long Island were a part.[66]   On the occasion of
the one hundredth anniversary of the *Long-Islander*, Christopher
Morley, remembering Whitman's fondness for the Indian name,
re-named him "Paumanok, because I feel him especially in the
earth of Long Island, but he lives everywhere."[67]

*   *   *   *

Whitman's Long Island

It is the combination of these last two elements — that Whitman
was *in* the earth of Long Island, yet lived everywhere — that

makes a study of his Long Island background valuable. If his loyalty to the Island had been merely the result of local patriotism, he might well have become another Bloodgood Cutter, mentioned in Long Island histories but unknown to the rest of the world. In fact, in his earliest poems he seems to be treading just such a path. If, on the other hand, he had separated himself completely from his birth-place, he would have run the risk of becoming rootless, and this rootlessness, in turn, might have resulted in poems superficial and inert. Instead, he *used* Long Island, rather than letting the Island use him. He used it in two ways: as an exemplar for style, and as a microcosm of the great country that he wished to write about.

The influence of the ocean on Whitman's style has already been discussed; the earth influenced it, too. In his 1855 "Preface," he wrote: "One...need never be bankrupt while corn grows from the ground, or the orchards drop apples, or the bays contain fish." [68] The poet need never be bankrupt either, for corn, apples, and fish are more than mere foods: they are life; and as they grow, poems can grow. He explains this more clearly a few pages later:

> The rhyme and uniformity of perfect poems show the free growth of metrical laws, and bud from them as unerringly and loosely as lilacs and roses on a bush, and take shapes as compact as the shapes of chestnuts and oranges, and melons and pears, and shed the perfume impalpable to form. [69]

Here the earth, through the cycle of life and death and through the miracle of growth, becomes a teacher of versification. Poetry which hopes to indicate to other human beings "the path between reality and their souls" [70] must use the form and rhythm of natural life until the style becomes organic to the content. The earth also served as a warning to Whitman, reminding him that the wrong type of prudence results in "the loss of the bloom and odor of the earth, and of the flowers and atmosphere, and of the sea." [71] The poet's recognition of this warning may well account for the generous, almost overflowing quality of his poetry.

Whitman always freely acknowledged his debt to nature as a
teacher of style. Not to imitate nature, but to be one with nature
— to speak as she spoke, to grow as she grew — was Whitman's
aim. In the same "1855 Preface," he wrote:

> ... to speak in literature with the perfect rectitude and
> insouciance of the movements of animals, and the
> unimpeachableness of the sentiment of trees in the
> woods and grass by the roadside, is the flawless tri-
> umph of art.[72]

When asked by J. W. Wallace, an Englishman, about the origin of the idea behind *Leaves of Grass*, Whitman turned naturally
and easily to his own knowledge, from youth, of nature: "I
have felt to make my book a succession of growths like the
rings of trees."[73]   And, to a limited extent, *Leaves of Grass* is
just that — a series of tree-rings. As Schyberg has pointed out,
this is not *literally* true; for Whitman revised and rearranged his
poems many times, and the final *Leaves of Grass* is not a chron-
ological accumulation paralleling the various periods of Whitman's life, biologic or creative. In another sense, however,
Whitman's analogy is symbolically true of the book as a whole,
for it contains poems written in each period of his life, reflecting
the ideas and activities of that period.

*   *   *   *

Starting from Paumanok

Walt Whitman's use of Long Island as a microcosm of the
entire United States is still more interesting, and its study more
fruitful. Canby, in his biography of Whitman, was one of the first
critics to suggest this theory: "The chief geography of the imag-
ined America in that great symbolic poem (*Leaves of Grass*) is
curiously represented in this youth land of Whitman's memories."[74]   It should be remembered that the Long Island of the
19th century did include almost all the features of the country
as a whole: the great plains, agricultural lands, grazing lands,

beaches, waste lands, urban tracts, forests, bays, rivers, and lakes. It should also be remembered that when Whitman wrote his greatest poems, between 1850 and 1860, he knew well almost every foot of Long Island earth, and knew very little about the rest of the country. His travels to the Far West came many years later.

Whitman's use of Long Island as a microcosm may have been unconscious, but his use of the Island as a beginning, a starting place—this was conscious and deliberate. In "Starting from Paumanok" written in 1860, he composed a poem for all the states, beginning "Starting from fish-shaped Paumanok where I was born..." The song *is* for all the states, though Whitman knew them not. It was easy to depict the West by mentioning the buffalo, the plains, the sierras—things he had only heard about—but when he sought verisimilitude through detail, he chose (in Alabama) a pair of mockingbirds—birds with which he was thoroughly familiar from his long walks through the Long Island countryside.[75]   Thus, Alabama came alive. He used the same technique later in the poem, cataloguing "walking New England, a friend, a traveler" and "crossing the prairies, dwelling again in Chicago"; this time, these flat, almost factual statements are stirred into life by the insertion of a description that he knew with his heart as well as with his head: "Splashing my bare feet in the edge of the summer ripples on Paumanok's sands." The cataloguing of New England, Chicago, Pennsylvania, Virginia, Carolina, the Chesapeake, and the Arctic, give scope and range to the poem; the line about Paumanok adds humanity and warmth, vividly enough to make all the other areas familiar through it.

He used Paumanok as a starting point again five years later in "From Paumanok Starting I Fly Like a Bird." The title, which is also the first line of the poem, leads to California, Michigan, Wisconsin, Iowa, Minnesota, Ohio, and half a dozen other states like great branches extending from a single trunk. Here Paumanok acts as a familiar home base and also as a unifying agent for "the Western world one and inseparable."

This technique appears again and again in other poems. In

"Our Old Feuillage" he can only mention the Arkansas, the Rio Grande, the Tombigbee, and the Red River because he knew them by name only, but he ties them in with "some shallow bay of Paumanok" which he knows by heart and can describe in meaningful detail in the following ten lines of type. In "A Song of Joys," he lists the St. Lawrence, the Thousand Islands, the Chesapeake Bay, but writes at length about trailing for bluefish off Paumanok or spearing eels through the winter ice (which he did in the Great South Bay).

This microcosm theory becomes still more tenable if one relates to it all aspects of Long Island: the earth and the ocean, a birth-place, the background of his family and friends, the scene of his teaching and editing, the source of his knowledge of history and geography. Then, indeed, one finds that in almost every poem he wrote, Whitman made skillful use of his legacy.

There is no better way to close a discussion of Walt Whitman and Long Island than to quote his short poem, "Paumanok":

> Sea-Beauty! stretch'd and basking!
> One side thy inland ocean laving, broad, with copious
>   commerce, steamers, sails,
> And one the Atlantic's wind caressing, fierce or gentle
>   — mighty hulls dark-gliding in the distance.
> Isle of sweet brooks of drinking-water — healthy air
>   and soil!
> Isle of the salty shore and breeze and brine!

Notes and References

Abbreviations Used

CPP   *The Complete Poetry and Prose of Walt Whitman*, intro-
       duction by Malcolm Cowley, 2 vols. Garden City, 1954.

EPF   *The Early Poems and the Fiction of Walt Whitman*, ed.
       Thomas L. Brasher. New York, 1963.

GF   *The Gathering of the Forces: Editorials, Essays, Literary
       and Dramatic Reviews and Other Material Written by
       Walt Whitman as Editor of the Brooklyn Daily Eagle in
       1846 and 1847*, ed. Cleveland Rodgers and John Black,
       2 vols. New York and London, 1920.

ISL   *I Sit and Look Out: Editorials from the Brooklyn Daily
       Times*, ed. Emory Holloway and Vernolian Schwarz.
       New York, 1932.

PW   *Poetical Works of William Cullen Bryant*, introduction by
       R.H. Stoddard, Household Edition. New York and Lon-
       don, 1879.

PWB   *Prose Writings of William Cullen Bryant*, ed. Parke
       Godwin, 2 vols. New York, 1889.

UPP   *Uncollected Poetry and Prose of Walt Whitman: Much of
       Which Has Been But Recently Discovered with Various
       Early Manuscripts Now First Published*, ed. Emory Hollo-
       way, 2 vols. New York, 1932.

197

Chapter I

1. James Truslow Adams, *History of Southampton*, p. 160. Anna Mulford, in "A Sketch of Dr. John Smith Sage," p. 30, also places the challenge on Shelter Island. Thomas R. Lounsbury, in his biography of Cooper, places it at Scarsdale, and H.P. Hedges, in "Early Sag Harbor," p. 38, places it at Angevine, near Mamaroneck.
2. Susan Cooper, "Preface" to *The Sea Lions*, pp. xii-xiii.
3. All genealogical material is from Benjamin Thompson, *History of Long Island*, II, pp. 210-224.
4. Susan Cooper, "Preface" to *The Sea Lions*, p. xiii.
5. *Ibid.*, p. xvii.
6. *Ibid.*
7. Harry Sleight, *Sag Harbor in Earlier Days*, p. 260.
8. Adams, *History of Southampton*, p. 160.
9. Paul Bailey, *Early Long Island*, p. 69. See also Harry Sleight, *The Whale Fishery on Long Island*.
10. James F. Beard, *The Letters and Journals of James Fenimore Cooper*, I, p. 42.
11. *Ibid.*, p. 46.
12. *Ibid.*, p. 52.
13. *Ibid.*, p. 53.
14. *Ibid.*, p. 59.
15. Susan Fenimore Cooper, "Small Family Memories," in *Correspondence of James Fenimore Cooper*, I, p. 37.
16. Van Wyck Brooks, *The World of Washington Irving*, p. 224.

Chapter II

1. Roger W. McAdam, *Salts of the Sound*, p. 22.
2. *Ibid.*, p. 17.
3. *The Red Rover*, pp. 24-25.
4. *Jack Tier*, p. 35.
5. *Ibid.*, pp. 81-82.
6. McAdam, *Salts of the Sound*, p. 16.
7. *Jack Tier*, p. 59.
8. *Ibid.*, pp. 68-69.
9. *Ibid.*, p. 71.
10. McAdam, *Salts of the Sound*, p. 20.
11. *Jack Tier*, p. 93.
12. *Ibid.*, p. 99.
13. *Ibid.*, p. 100.
14. *Miles Wallingford*, p. 183.
15. *Ibid.*, p. 184.
16. *The Sea Lions*, p. 91.
17. *Ibid.*, p. 108.
18. *The Water-Witch*, pp. 42-43.
19. Warren Walker, *James Fenimore Cooper*, p. 75.

20. *The Pilot*, p. 11.
21. *Ibid.*, p. 13.
22. *Ibid.*, p. 14.
23. *Ibid.*, p. 187.
24. *Ibid.*, p. 188.
25. *Ibid.*, p. 190.
26. *Ibid.*, p. 191.
27. *Ibid.*, p. 193.
28. *The Water-Witch*, p. 161.
29. *The Pioneers*, p. 278.
30. *Home as Found*, p. 319.
31. *Ibid.*, p. 321.
32. *The Pathfinder*, p. 123.
33. *Afloat and Ashore*, p. 290.
34. *Jack Tier*, p. 83.
35. *The Sea Lions*, pp. 157-173.
36. *Ibid.*, p. 185.
37. *The Deerslayer*, p. 380.
38. *The Pioneers*, p. 117.
39. *Ibid.*, p. 187.
40. *Ibid.*, p. 188.
41. *The Pathfinder*, pp. 121-122.
42. *The Prairie*, pp. 14-15.

Chapter III

1. *The Spy*, p. 59.
2. *The Sea Lions*, pp. 2-3.
3. *Ibid.*, p. 4.
4. *Ibid.*, p. 61.
5. *Ibid.*, p. 7.
6. Mulford, "A Sketch," pp. 80-81.
7. *The Sea Lions*, pp. 10-11.
8. *Ibid.*, p. 9.
9. *Ibid.*, p. 5.
10. *Ibid.*, p. 8.
11. James F. Beard, *Letters and Journals*, I, p. 121.
12. *Jack Tier*, pp. 33-34.
13. *Ibid.*, p. 34.
14. *Afloat and Ashore*, p. 167.
15. *The Sea Lions*, p. 449.
16. *Ibid.*, p. 462.
17. *Ibid.*, p. 26.
18. *Ibid.*, p. 39.
19. This identification has been attested to by Anna Mulford, in "A Sketch of Dr. John Smith Sage," p. 36, and by James Truslow Adams in *History of the Town of Southampton*, p. 160. It has been accepted by Jacqueline Overton

in *Long Island's Story*, p. 218, and by Elizabeth Davis in "James Fenimore Cooper Lived Here," p. 254.

20. Thompson, *History of Long Island*, II, p. 198.
21. Mulford, "A Sketch," p. 7.
22. *Ibid.*, p. 62.
23. Thomas Philbrick, *James Fenimore Cooper and the Development of American Sea Fiction*, p. 299.
24. Mulford, "A Sketch," pp. 28-29.
25. Gardiner's Island has been owned by the Gardiner family since 1639. It is now leased as a shooting preserve for deer, pheasant, and wild ducks.
26. *The Sea Lions*, pp. 19-20.
27. *Ibid.*, p. 227.
28. Philbrick, *James Fenimore Cooper*, p. 213.
29. *The Sea Lions*, p. 463.
30. *Miles Wallingford*, p. 440.
31. Mulford, "A Sketch," p. 35.
32. *Ibid.*, p. 5.
33. Adams, *A History of Southampton*, p. 161.
34. This identification has been cited in Jacqueline Overton's *Long Island's Story*, p. 218; in James Truslow Adams' *History of the Town of Southampton*, p. 160; in Anna Mulford's "A Sketch of Dr. John Smith Sage," p. 35.
35. *The Pioneers*, pp. 21-22.
36. *Ibid.*, p. 26.
37. Reprinted in Cooper's "Preface" to *The Leatherstocking Tales* (D. Appleton and Co., 1872) pp. 3-4.
38. The *Wing-and-Wing*, p. 215.
39. Thomas Jones, *History of New York During the Revolutionary War*, p. 267.
40. *Ibid.*, p. 268.
41. *Ibid.*, in notes at end of volume.
42. Morton Pennypacker, *General Washington's Spies*, p. i.
43. *Ibid.*, p. 31.
44. *Ibid.*, pp. 12-16.
45. *Ibid.*, p. 8.
46. *Ibid.*, p. 44.
47. *The Spy*, p. 142.
48. *Ibid.*, p. 150.
49. *Ibid.*, p. 152.
50. Pennypacker, *General Washington's Spies*, p. 113.
51. *The Spy*, p. 459.
52. Pennypacker, *General Washington's Spies*, pp. 114-118.
53. *The Spy*, p. 354.
54. *Ibid.*, pp. 451-452.
55. Pennypacker, *General Washington's Spies*, p. 17.
56. *Ibid.*, p. 98.
57. *Ibid.*, p. 12.
58. *The Spy*, p. viii.
59. Pennypacker, *General Washington's Spies*, pp. 76-77.
60. *The Spy*, p. 141.

Chapter IV

1. *The Pathfinder,* p. 32.
2. *Ibid.,* p. 34.
3. Charles Glicksberg, "Cooper and Bryant," p. 1.
4. James F. Beard, *Letters and Journals,* I, p. 83.
5. Glicksberg, "Cooper and Bryant."
6. Parke Godwin, *Prose Writings of William Cullen Bryant*, I, pp. 299-331.
7. PWB, II, p. 329.

Chapter V

1. Parke Godwin, *A Life of William Cullen Bryant,* I, p. 406.
2. Newspaper article, Grist Mill Collection, Vol. I.
3. *Ibid.*
4. Item, Grist Mill Collection, I.
5. *Moore's Rural Life,* July 17, 1869, Grist Mill Collection, II.
6. James Grant Wilson, *Bryant and His Friends*, p. 97.
7. Item, Grist Mill Collection, II.
8. *Ibid.,* I.
9. *This Is Roslyn,* p. 8.
10. *Moore's Rural Life,* July 17, 1869, Grist Mill Collection, II.
11. Letter by Mrs. Simonson, *Long Island Forum*, March, 1955, p. 50.
12. Item, Grist Mill Collection, I.
13. *Bryant Memorial Meeting of the Century,* p. 40.
14. *The Story of Roslyn.*
15. Leggett, "Notes from the Leggett Diary," p. 10.
16. *The Story of Roslyn.*
17. *Ibid.*
18. Benjamin Thompson, *History of Long Island,* II, pp. 560-561.
19. Manuscript in Grist Mill Collection, I.
20. *This Is Roslyn.*
21. Godwin, *A Life,* II, p. 344.
22. *This Is Roslyn.*
23. *Nassau Daily Review-Star,* May 17, 1943.
24. Quotation from H.W. Loweree's *Historic Roslyn,* Grist Mill Collection, II.
25. Thompson, *History of Long Island,* II, pp. 563-564.
26. Wilson, *Bryant and His Friends,* pp. 75-76.
27. Godwin, *A Life,* II, p. 57.
28. *Ibid.,* p. 61.
29. *Ibid.,* pp. 31-32.
30. Mary Dewey (ed.), *The Life and Letters of Catharine M. Sedgwick,* 1871.
31. Godwin, *A Life,* II, p. 57.
32. *Nassau Daily Review Star,* May 17, 1943.
33. Godwin, *A Life,* II, p. 57.
34. Item, Grist Mill Collection, I.
35. The *New York Sun,* May 14, 1943.

36. James A. Briggs, *An Authentic Account . . .* , p. 4.
37. Robert Coles, "When Bryant Lived at Roslyn," p. 17.
38. James T. Adams, *Memorials of Old Bridgehampton*, p. 173.
39. Godwin, *A Life*, II, p. 54.
40. J.P.M., "Roslyn's Suicide Secret," p. 220.
41. Godwin, *A Life*, II, p. 74.
42. *The Roslyn News*, May, 1943, in Grist Mill Collection, I.
43. Tremaine McDowell, *Representative Selections*, p. v.
44. *The Roslyn News*, May, 1943, in Grist Mill Collection, I.
45. All dates of poems are those listed by Parke Godwin.
46. "To a Mosquito," *Poetical Works of William Cullen Bryant*, Household Edition, 1879, p. 89.
47. Godwin, *A Life*, II, pp. 198-199.
48. *Ibid.*, pp. 366-367. Also, in Wilson, *Bryant and His Friends*, p. 112.
49. Leggett, "Notes from the Leggett Diary," p. 14.
50. Wilson, *Bryant and His Friends*, p. 89.
51. Godwin, *A Life*, II, pp. 82-83.
52. Wilson, *Bryant and His Friends*, p. 62.

Chapter VI

1. PWB, I, p. 201.
2. *The Roslyn News*, Nov. 20, 1930, in Grist Mill Collection, I.
3. PW, p. 212.
4. *Ibid.*, pp. 226-228.
5. Godwin, *A Life*, II, p. 55.
6. *Ibid.*, p. 138.
7. PW, pp. 268-281.
8. *Ibid.*, pp. 212-213.
9. *Ibid.*, pp. 252-253.
10. *Ibid.*, pp. 344-348.
11. Item, Grist Mill Collection, I.
12. Godwin, *A Life*, II, p. 243.
13. PW, pp. 321-325.
14. Godwin, *A Life*, II, p. 374.
15. *Bryant Festival at "The Century."*
16. Wilson, *Bryant and His Friends*, p. 77.
17. PW, pp. 266-267.
18. *New Library of Poetry and Song*, p. lxvii.
19. PWB, I, pp. 194-202.
20. *Ibid.*, p. 196.
21. Tremaine McDowell, *Representative Selections*, p. 406.
22. Godwin, *A Life*, II, pp. 27-28.
23. PW, pp. 222-224.
24. Godwin, *A Life*, II, pp. 82-83.
25. Item, Grist Mill Collection, II.
26. Godwin, *A Life*, II, p. 196.

27. PW, pp. 321-325.
28. Item, Grist Mill Collection, I.
29. Godwin, *A Life,* II, pp. 52-53.
30. Godwin's edition of Bryant's poetry, II, pp. 303-304.
31. Thaddeus William Harris (1795-1856) was a naturalist and author of *A Treatise on Some of the Insects of New England Which are Injurious to Vegetation,* 1842. After Harris's death, the Massachusetts legislature ordered a new edition which was published in 1862, under the editorship of Charles L. Flint.
32. *Moore's Rural Life,* July 17, 1869, in Grist Mill Collection, II.
33. Godwin, *A Life,* II, pp. 52-53.
34. *Ibid.,* p. 345.
35. *Ibid.,* p. 274.
36. *Ibid.,* p. 304.
37. PW, p. 232.
38. *Ibid.,* p. 303.
39. *Ibid.,* p. 323.
40. *The Nassau Daily Review,* Nov. 22, 1928, in Grist Mill Collection, II.
41. PW, pp. 229-231.
42. PWB, I, p. 195.

Chapter VII

1. PW, p. 225-226.
2. *Ibid.,* pp. 297-306.
3. *Ibid.,* pp. 219-220.
4. *Ibid.,* pp. 266-267.
5. *Ibid.,* pp. 313-315.
6. *Ibid.,* pp. 310-312.
7. *Ibid.,* pp. 232-233.
8. *Ibid.,* pp. 231-232.
9. *Ibid.,* pp. 308-310.
10. *Ibid.,* pp. 327-329.
11. Godwin, *A Life,* II, p. 256.
12. *Ibid.,* p. 259.
13. *Ibid.,* p. 261.
14. *Ibid.,* p. 262.
15. *Ibid.,* pp. 263-264.
16. PW, pp. 325-327.
17. *Ibid.,* pp. 336-341.
18. "A Memory," in Godwin, *A Life,* II, pp. 318-319.
19. Item, Grist Mill Collection, I.
20. Wilson, *Bryant and His Friends,* p. 120.
21. Godwin, *A Life,* II, p. 402.

Chapter VIII

1. "Mr. Bryant," Brooklyn *Daily Eagle,* Sept. 1, 1846; reprinted GF, II, p. 261.

2. Gay Wilson Allen, *The Solitary Singer*, p. 43.
3. *Ibid.*, p. 73.
4. *Ibid.*, pp. 84-85.
5. UPP, I, p. 161.
6. "Mr. Bryant," Brooklyn *Daily Eagle*, Sept. 1, 1846; reprinted GF, II, p. 260.
7. *Specimen Days*, p. 110.
8. McDowell, *Representative Selections*, p. lxviii, footnote.
9. "Art and Artists," Brooklyn *Daily Advertiser*, April 3, 1851; reprinted UPP, I, p. 242.
10. *Specimen Days*, p. 180.
11. *Goodbye My Fancy*, p. 496.
12. *Specimen Days*, p. 111.
13. Katherine Molinoff, *Some Notes on Whitman's Family*, p. 25.
14. Allen, *The Solitary Singer*, p. 108.
15. Thomas Donaldson, *Walt Whitman, The Man*, pp. 239-240.

Chapter IX

1. *New York Herald Tribune*, May 12, 1963, Sec. 14, p. 6.
2. Verne Dyson, *Whitmanland*, p. 14. See also CPP, II, p. 5.
3. Charles Street, *Huntington Town Records*, II, p. 78.
4. Dyson, *Whitmanland*, p. 14.
5. Street, *Records*, II, p. 63.
6. Dyson, *Whitmanland*, p. 15.
7. Street, *Records*, II, p. 138.
8. *Ibid.*, p. 17.
9. *Ibid.*, p. 104.
10. *Ibid.*, p. 173.
11. Dyson, *Whitmanland*, p. 15.
12. Street, *Records*, II, p. 20.
13. Dyson, *Whitmanland*, p. 15.
14. Street, *Records*, II, p. 338.
15. Dyson, *Whitmanland*, p. 15.
16. *Ibid.*, p. 15. See also CPP, II, p. 8.
17. Street, *Records*, II, p. 293.
18. *Ibid.*, III, p. 36.
19. *Ibid.*, p. 5 (appendix).
20. Dyson, *Whitmanland*, p. 16.
21. Street, *Records*, III, p. 94.
22. Dyson, *Whitmanland*, p. 17.
23. Street, *Records*, III, p. 53.
24. *Ibid.*, p. 77.
25. *Ibid.*, p. 64.
26. Allen, *The Solitary Singer*, p. 14.
27. *Ibid.*, p. 13.
28. Babette Deutsch, *Walt Whitman*, p. 4.
29. Florence Freedman, *Walt Whitman Looks at the Schools*, p. 50.

30. "Song of Myself," section 1.
31. *Ibid.,* section 35.
32. Emory Holloway, "A Whitman Source," p. 24.
33. J.T. Headley, *Washington and His Generals,* pp. 342-347.
34. Phrase identical in both versions.
35. The change from 10:30 P.M. to midnight, for example, may have been deliberate. Ten-thirty is a prosaic time for a surrender; midnight, the closing of the day, is the "proper" time for a poetic surrender.
36. "How We Went Down to Fort Hamilton — and Other Matters," Brooklyn *Daily Eagle,* Aug. 14, 1847; reprinted GF, II, pp. 167-175.
37. Christopher Ward, *The War of the Revolution,* I, pp. 233-235. See also George O. Trevelyan, *The American Revolution,* I, p. 286.
38. "Brooklyniana," A Series of Local Articles on Past and Present, Chapter 11, Brooklyn *Standard;* reprinted UPP, II, p. 268.
39. *Ibid.,* p. 267.
40. "Fort Greene Park, Brooklyn," Brooklyn *Daily Eagle,* July 9, 1846; reprinted GF, II, p. 47.
41. "Ode — by Walter Whitman," Brooklyn *Daily Eagle,* July 2, 1846; reprinted GF, I, pp. 75-76. See also Peter Ross, *A History of Long Island* (1902), where it appears as a motto under the title of "Sons of Long Island."
42. EPF, pp. 34-35.
43. "Last Evening upon Fort Greene," Brooklyn *Daily Eagle,* July 8, 1846; reprinted GF, II, pp. 118-121.
44. "Shall We Have That Monument!'", Brooklyn *Daily Eagle,* Dec. 3, 1847; reprinted GF, II, pp. 50-52. A national tomb and shaft honoring the prison ship martyrs were erected at Fort Greene Park. The monument was designed by Stanford White and dedicated by President Taft in 1908.
45. ISL, p. 15.
46. "The First Independence Days," Brooklyn *Daily Times,* July 3, 1857; reprinted ISL, p. 57.
47. *Ibid.,* p. 58.
48. Cf. "Song of Myself," section 35; "The Centenarian's Story"; "Ode on Fort Greene."
49. "The Last Loyalist," *Democratic Review,* May, 1842; reprinted EPF, pp. 101-107.
50. "Song of Myself," section 44.
51. "Thanks in Old Age."
52. "Twenty Years." See also "Wild Frank's Return" and "The Last Loyalist."
53. "The Shadow and the Light of a Young Man's Soul," *Union Magazine of Literature and Art,* June, 1848; reprinted UPP, I, pp. 229-234.
54. "Death in the School-Room," *Democratic Review,* August, 1841; reprinted CPP, II, pp. 351-355.
55. "Wild Frank's Return," CPP, II, pp. 366-371.
56. *Ibid.*
57. Richard Chase, *Walt Whitman, Reconsidered,* p. 24.
58. "As I Ebb'd with the Ocean of Life," section 3.
59. Molinoff, *Some Notes on Whitman's Family,* p. 11.

60. Molinoff, *Some Notes...*, p. 10, quoting a letter from the Jacob Schwartz catalogue of Bucke Whitmaniana, Anderson Galleries (New York, April 1936), p. 57.
61. "Faces," section 2.
62. Allen, *The Solitary Singer*, p. 318.
63. "Song of Myself," section 15.
64. *Specimen Days*, p. 7.
65. *Ibid.*, p. 8, quoted from John Burroughs' Notes.
66. *November Boughs*, pp. 469-487.
67. *Ibid.*, p. 479.
68. *Ibid.*, p. 469.
69. Horace Traubel, *With Walt Whitman in Camden*, II, p. 19.
70. "Song of Myself," section 33.
71. "Faces," section 5.
72. *November Boughs*, p. 471.
73. *Ibid.*, p. 485.
74. *Ibid.*
75. *Specimen Days*, p. 7.
76. Molinoff, *Walt Whitman at Smithtown*, p. 183.
77. *Specimen Days*, p. 193.
78. "Song of Joys."
79. *Specimen Days*, p. 13.

Chapter X

1. Bliss Perry, *Walt Whitman*, p. 299.
2. UPP, II, p. 86.
3. Katherine Molinoff, *Whitman's Teaching at Smithtown, 1837-1838*, pp. 14-15.
4. "The Shadow and the Light of a Young Man's Soul," *Union Magazine of Literature and Art*, June, 1948; reprinted UPP, I, pp. 230-232.
5. *Ibid.*
6. *Ibid.*
7. Parallels suggested by Holloway, UPP, I, footnote, p. 232.
8. UPP, II, pp. 86-87.
9. "Long Island Schools and Schooling," Brooklyn *Daily Times*, April 27, 1858; reprinted UPP, II, p. 13.
10. Molinoff, *Whitman's Teaching*, p. 7.
11. *Ibid.*, p. 11.
12. *Ibid.*, p. 16.
13. Molinoff, "Walt Whitman at Smithtown," p. 179.
14. Molinoff, *Whitman's Teaching*, pp. 19-20.
15. Freedman, *Walt Whitman Looks at the Schools*, p. 29.
16. EPF, pp. 18-19., editor's footnote.
17. *Ibid.*, pp. 18-19.
18. "An Hour in One of the Brooklyn Public Schools," Brooklyn *Daily Eagle*, Mar. 4, 1847; reprinted GF, I, p. 131.
19. Molinoff, *Whitman's Teaching*, p. 20.

20. Freedman, *Schools,* p. 29.
21. "An Hour in One of the Brooklyn Public Schools," Brooklyn *Daily Eagle,* Mar. 4, 1847; reprinted GF, I, pp. 121-133.
22. CPP, pp. 351-355.
23. "Long Island Schools and Schooling," Brooklyn *Daily Times,* April 27, 1858; reprinted UPP, II, p. 13.
24. *Specimen Days,* p. 11.
25. "The Shadow and the Light . . . "; reprinted UPP, I, p. 232.
26. "Eastern Long Island," Brooklyn *Daily Eagle,* June 27, 1846; reprinted UPP, I, pp. 120-121.
27. *Ibid.*
28. GF, I, p. 121.
29. "Our Venerable Contemporary of the *Star,*" Brooklyn *Daily Eagle*, Sept. 27, 1847; reprinted GF, II, pp. 17-18.
30. "A Song of the Rolling Earth," section 2.
31. "A Song of Myself," section 47.
32. *Ibid.*
33. *Ibid.*
34. "Song of the Open Road," section 15.
35. "To a Western Boy."
36. "Song of the Open Road," section 6.
37. "A Song for Occupations," section 4.
38. "Prayer of Columbus."
39. "The Sleepers," section 5; "The Wallabout Martyrs;" "The Dying Veteran."
40. "Eighteen Sixty-one;" "Beat! Beat! Drums;" *Drum-Taps.*
41. "Year of Meteors;" "I Sing the Body Electric," section 7.
42. "The Sleepers," section 6; "Red Jacket;" "Yonnandio;" "Osceola."
43. "Pioneers! O Pioneers!"
44. "To a President."
45. "Election Day, November, 1884."
46. "Mannahatta;" "Paumanok."
47. "Our Old Feuillage;" "O Magnet South;" "Starting from Paumanok."
48. "Salut au Monde!"; "Passage to India."
49. "Mannahatta;" "City of Orgies;" "Broadway."
50. "Song of the Open Road;" "A Farm Picture;" "There Was a Child Went Forth."
51. "Roaming in Thought;" "Continuities;" "The Base of All Metaphysics."
52. "Soon Shall the Winter's Foil Be Here;" "Song of Myself," section 9.
53. "Song of Myself," section 34; "I Sing the Body Electric," section 9.
54. "Song of Myself," section 2; "Miracles."
55. *Ibid.*
56. *Ibid.*
57. "An Old Man's Thought of School."
58. *Specimen Days,* p. 11.
59. Molinoff, *An Unpublished Whitman Manuscript,* p. 5.
60. *Ibid.,* p. 6.
61. *Ibid.*
62. *Ibid.,* p. 5.

63. *November Boughs,* p. 428.
64. *Ibid.*
65. "Song of Myself," section 10.
66. *Ibid.,* section 33.
67. Molinoff, *Whitman Ms.,* p. 5.
68. *Ibid.*
69. "By Blue Ontario's Shore," section 13.
70. *A Backward Glance,* pp. 473-474, esp.
71. *Ibid.*
72. *Ibid.,* p. 479.
73. Molinoff, *Whitman Ms.,* pp. 5-6.

Chapter XI

1. "As I Ebb'd with the Ocean of Life," section 1.
2. *Specimen Days,* p. 7.
3. *Ibid.,* pp. 91-92.
4. *Ibid.,* p. 92.
5. Listed by Edgar Lee Masters in *Walt Whitman,* p. 317.
6. "Out of the Cradle Endlessly Rocking."
7. "As I Ebb'd with the Ocean of Life," section 1.
8. "On the Beach at Night Alone."
9. "Song for All Seas, All Ships."
10. "With Husky-Haughty Lips, O Sea!"
11. *Ibid.*
12. "Song at Sunset."
13. Traubel, *With Walt Whitman,* I, p. 5.
14. *Specimen Days,* p. 182.
15. "Brooklyniana," Chapter 36, Brooklyn *Standard;* reprinted UPP, II, p. 318.
16. *Specimen Days,* p. 9.
17. *Ibid.,* p. 10.
18. "A Song of Joys."
19. "More Hottentot Ignorance," Brooklyn *Daily Eagle,* Aug. 27, 1846; reprinted GF, II, p. 224.
20. "A Song of Joys."
21. *Ibid.*
22. "Brooklyniana," Chapter 36, Brooklyn *Standard;* reprinted UPP, II, p. 313.
23. "A Song of Joys."
24. "Sun-Down Papers," No. 10, *Long Island Farmer,* July 20, 1841; reprinted UPP, I, p. 50.
25. "Brooklyniana," Chapter 13, Brooklyn *Standard;* reprinted UPP, II, p. 278.
26. "Sun-Down Papers," No. 10, *Long Island Farmer,* July 20, 1841; reprinted UPP, I, p. 50.
27. "A Song of Joys."
28. "Ride to Coney Island, and Clam-Bake There," Brooklyn *Daily Eagle,* July 15, 1847; reprinted GF, II, p. 154.
29. "Song of Myself," section 10.

30. *Ibid.*, section 27.
31. "To Be at All."
32. "Sun-Down Papers," No. 10, *Long Island Farmer*, July 20, 1841; reprinted UPP, I, p. 50.
33. "Song of Myself," section 15.
34. *Ibid.*, section 33.
35. "The World Below the Brine."
36. Richard M. Bucke, *Notes and Fragments*, pp. 117-118. This volume includes a brief listing by Whitman of whaling lore gleaned from a conversation with Mr. Maher, an old whaleman.
37. *Specimen Days*, p. 8.
38. *Ibid.* (Italic is mine.)
39. "Thought."
40. "As I Ebb'd with the Ocean of Life," section 2.
41. "To the Man-of-War-Bird."
42. "Aboard at a Ship's Helm."
43. "Song of Prudence."
44. "Letters from Paumanok," No. 1, New York *Evening Post*, June 27, 1851; reprinted UPP, I, pp. 248-249.
45. *Specimen Days*, p. 182.
46. "Bathing," Brooklyn *Daily Times*, June 27, 1857; reprinted ISL, p. 101.
47. EPF, pp. 319-320.
48. "Bathing," Brooklyn *Daily Times*, June 27, 1857; reprinted ISL, p. 101.
49. "When I Heard at the Close of the Day."
50. "Out of the Rolling Ocean the Crowd."
51. "As I Ebb'd with the Ocean of Life."
52. "Song of the Open Road," section 10.
53. "Ths Ship Starting."
54. "Patroling Barnegat."
55. "On the Beach at Night Alone."
56. "Song for All Seas, All Ships."
57. "The World Below the Brine."

Chapter XII

1. Hugh Fausset, *Walt Whitman, Poet of Democracy*, pp. 17-18.
2. Richard M. Bucke, *Walt Whitman*, p. 51.
3. *Specimen Days*, p. 16.
4. Bucke, *Walt Whitman*, p. 24.
5. O.L. Triggs, *Selections*, xxiii, as quoted by Leon Bazalgette, *Walt Whitman, The Man and His Work*, pp. 127-128.
6. William Gay, *Walt Whitman, the Poet of Democracy*, p. 8. Whitman later denied the truth of this story. See G.W. Allen, *Walt Whitman Handbook*, p. 16.
7. "East Long Island Correspondence," Letter III, Brooklyn *Daily Eagle*, Sept. 20, 1847; reprinted UPP, I, p. 180.
8. "When Lilacs Last in the Dooryard Bloom'd," sections 1, 3, and 16.

9. Kenneth P. Neilson, "Calamus: Search and Discovery," in *Walt Whitman Birthplace Bulletin,* October, 1960, pp. 13-19.
10. "Out of the Cradle Endlessly Rocking."
11. "A Song of Joys."
12. "Young Grimes," *Long Island Democrat,* Jan. 1, 1840; reprinted EPF, pp. 2-4.
13. "The Tomb Blossoms," *Democratic Review,* January, 1842; reprinted EPF, p. 88.
14. "A Song of Joys."
15. Sidney Forman, *The Story of the Five Towns,* pp. 25-26.
16. *Specimen Days,* pp. 5-6.
17. Burroughs, *Walt Whitman,* p. 48.
18. *Ibid.,* p. 54.
19. *November Boughs,* p. 446.
20. "Letters from Paumanok," No. 1, New York *Evening Post,* June 27, 1851; reprinted UPP, I, p. 248.
21. "Letters from Paumanok," No. 2, New York *Evening Post,* June 28, 1851; reprinted UPP, I, pp. 250-254.
22. "Long Island Is a Great Place," Brooklyn *Daily Times,* July 30, 1857; reprinted ISL, p. 167.
23. Cf. Cooper re: railroads, Chapter III.
24. *Collect,* CPP, p. 207.
25. "Eastern Long Island," Brooklyn *Daily Eagle,* June 27, 1846; reprinted UPP, I, p. 120.
26. "Brooklyniana," Chapter I, Brooklyn *Standard,* June 8, 1861; reprinted UPP, II, p. 224.
27. "Brooklyniana," Chapter 36; reprinted UPP, II, p. 314.
28. *Ibid.,* p. 315.
29. *Ibid.* The preferred spelling of the Indian chief's name is *Wyandanch,* which Whitman used in later articles. Here he seemed to prefer a variant spelling, *Wyandance.*
30. "Brooklyniana," Chapter 38; reprinted UPP, II, p. 317.
31. "East Long Island Correspondence," Letter III, Brooklyn *Daily Eagle,* Sept. 20, 1847; reprinted UPP, I, p. 180.
32. *Ibid.,* p. 181.
33. This quotation is of special interest because it proves that Whitman knew Cooper's novels and probably had read some of them.
34. *Franklin Evans,* or The Inebriate, *New World,* II (No. 10, Extra Series, November, 1842); reprinted EPF, p. 132.
35. "East Long Island Correspondence," Letter III; reprinted UPP, I, pp. 180-181.
36. Frederick Schyberg, *Walt Whitman,* p. 125.
37. The first main element was Whitman's family.
38. Bucke, *Walt Whitman,* p. 18.
39. Whitman is unique in that he is the only writer of his time, or of subsequent times, to write kindly of this railroad! The Long Island Railroad was incorporated in 1834, completed to Hicksville in 1837, and to Greenport in 1844.
40. "East Long Island Correspondence," Letter I, Brooklyn *Daily Eagle,* Sept. 16, 1847; reprinted UPP, I, pp. 174-175.
41. *Ibid.,* p. 176.

42. *Ibid.*, p. 177.
43. "East Long Island Correspondence," Letter II, Brooklyn *Daily Eagle,* Sept. 18, 1847; reprinted UPP, I, p. 178.
44. This is a rather amazing "memory," since in 1847 Whitman had never visited the Far West.
45. "East Long Island Correspondence," Letter II, Brooklyn *Daily Eagle,* Sept. 18, 1847; reprinted UPP, I, p. 179.
46. *Ibid.*, pp. 179-180.
47. "Long Island Is a Great Place," Brooklyn *Daily Times,* July 30, 1857; reprinted ISL, p. 166.
48. "Brooklyniana," Chapter 13, Brooklyn *Standard;* reprinted UPP, II, p. 276.
49. "Brooklyniana," Chapter 36, Brooklyn *Standard;* reprinted UPP, II, p. 311.
50. "Long Island Is a Great Place," Brooklyn *Daily Times,* July 30, 1857; reprinted ISL, p. 167.
51. "Brooklyniana," Chapter 36, Brooklyn *Standard;* reprinted UPP, II, p. 312.
52. "Eastern Long Island," Brooklyn *Daily Eagle,* June 27, 1846; reprinted UPP, I, p. 118.
53. *Ibid.*, p. 119.
54. *Ibid.*, p. 120.
55. Molinoff, *Some Notes on Whitman's Family,* pp. 3-6.
56. "Letters from Paumanok," No. 1, New York *Evening Post,* June 27, 1851; reprinted UPP, I, pp. 248-249.
57. "Letters from Paumanok," No. 2, New York *Evening Post,* June 28, 1851; reprinted UPP, I, p. 250.
58. *Ibid.*
59. "Brooklyniana," Chapter 36, Brooklyn *Standard;* reprinted UPP, II, p. 313.
60. *Ibid.*, p. 315.
61. "Brooklyniana," Chapter 38, Brooklyn *Standard;* reprinted UPP, II, p. 317.
62. *Ibid.*, p. 318.
63. Jesse Merritt, "Walt Whitman 'The Long Islander,'" in *Essays on Whitman and the West Hills Country* (pages not numbered).
64. "Long Island Is a Great Place," Brooklyn *Daily Times,* July 30, 1857; reprinted ISL, pp. 165-166.
65. "Brooklyniana," Chapter 13, Brooklyn *Standard;* reprinted UPP, II, p. 277.
66. *Ibid.*, pp. 274-275.
67. Merritt, "Walt Whitman, 'The Long-Islander.'"
68. "Preface, 1855," p. 269.
69. *Ibid.*, p. 271.
70. *Ibid.*
71. *Ibid.*, p. 278.
72. *Ibid.*, p. 273.
73. Schyberg, *Walt Whitman,* p. 12.
74. Henry S. Canby, *Walt Whitman,* p. 9.
75. That the mockingbird did exist on Long Island in the 19th century is proved conclusively in *Birds of Long Island* (1843). The author, J.P. Giraud, was a member of the Lyceum of Natural History and based his study on personal observation and confirmed reports. Giraud states clearly that the mockingbird sometimes spent the breeding season on Long Island and that it preferred

"the dry sandy beaches in the immediate vicinity of the sea" (p. 83). A comparative study of Giraud's description of the mockingbird with Whitman's description of the same bird in "Out of the Cradle Endlessly Rocking" suggests that Whitman, although personally familiar with the bird, may have turned to Giraud for specific details. For example, Giraud writes that "the eggs, from four to six in number, are light green, spotted with brown"; Whitman — "four light-green eggs, spotted with brown." Other examples: Giraud — the nests are placed "among the briars"; Whitman — "in some briars." Giraud — that it sang "on calm, bright nights"; Whitman — "under the fall of the moon, in calmer weather." Giraud — that its voice blended "with the subdued voice of the ocean"; Whitman — that its voice could be heard "over the hoarse surging of the sea."

Bibliography

Adams, James Truslow, *History of the Town of Southampton* (Empire State Historical Publications Series). Port Washington, 1962 (copyright 1918).
——, *Memorials of Old Bridgehampton* (Empire State Historical Publications Series). Port Washington, 1962 (copyright 1916).
Bailey, Paul, *Early Long Island*. Westhampton Beach, 1962.
——, *Long Island — A History of Two Great Counties, Nassau and Suffolk*. New York, 1949.
Bayles, Richard, *Historical and Descriptive Sketches of Suffolk County* (Empire State Historical Publications Series). Port Washington, 1962 (copyright 1873).
Brooks, Van Wyck, *The World of Washington Irving*. New York, 1944.
Brooks, Van Wyck and Otto L. Bettmann, *Our Literary Heritage*. New York, 1956.
Duvall, Ralph G., *The History of Shelter Island*. New York, 1932.
Eberlein, Harold D., *Manor Houses and Historic Homes of Long Island and Staten Island*. Philadelphia, 1928. (Reissued by Ira J. Friedman, Inc. Empire State Historical Publications Series.)
Foerster, Norman, *Nature in American Literature*. New York, 1923, revised 1950.
Forman, Sidney, *The Story of the Five Towns* (Inwood, Lawrence, Cedarhurst, Woodmere, Hewlett). American Guide Series, 1941.
Giraud, J.P., Jr., *Birds of Long Island*. New York, 1843.
Jones, Thomas, *History of New York During the Revolutionary War*, 2 vols. New York, 1879.
Long Island Forum, Vols. I-XXVI (1938-1963). Bayshore, Long Island.
McAdam, Roger Williams, *Salts of the Sound*. New York, 1939, 1957.
Overton, Jacqueline, *Long Island's Story*. Garden City, 1929. (Reissued Ira J. Friedman, Inc., Port Washington, N.Y. Empire State Historical Publications Series.)
Rattray, Jeanette Edwards, *Ship Ashore!* New York, 1955.
Smith, Mildred, *Early History of the Long Island Railroad*. Uniondale, Long Island, 1959.
Thompson, Benjamin F., *History of Long Island*, 3 vols., revised by Charles J. Werner, 1918. (Reissued Ira J. Friedman, Inc., Port Washington, N.Y. Empire State Historical Publications Series.)
Trevelyan, George O., *The American Revolution*, 6 vols. London, 1909-1914.
Ward, Christopher, *The War of the Revolution*, 2 vols. New York, 1952.

JAMES FENIMORE COOPER

Primary Sources

Cooper, James Fenimore, *Afloat and Ashore*. New York, 1861 (copyright 1844).
———, *The Chainbearer*. New York, 1861 (copyright 1845).
———, *The Deerslayer*. New York, 1861 (copyright 1841).
———, *Home As Found*. New York, 1860 (copyright 1838).
———, *Jack Tier*. New York, 1860 (copyright 1848).
———, *Miles Wallingford*. New York, 1861 (copyright 1844).
———, *The Pathfinder*. New York, 1860 (copyright 1840).
———, *The Pilot*. New York, Leatherstocking Edition (copyright 1823).
———, *The Pioneers*. New York, 1859 (copyright 1823).
———, *The Prairie*. New York, 1859 (copyright 1827).
———, *The Red Rover*. New York, 1859 (copyright 1828).
———, *The Sea Lions*. Boston, 1884 (copyright 1849).
———, *The Spy*. New York, 1859 (copyright 1821).
———, *The Water-Witch*. New York, 1860 (copyright 1830).
———, *The Wing-and-Wing*. New York, 1860 (copyright 1842).
———, *The Letters and Journals of James Fenimore Cooper*, ed. James Franklin Beard. 2 vols. Massachusetts, 1960.
———, *Representative Selections*, ed. Robert E. Spiller. New York, 1936.

Secondary Sources

Bailey, Paul, "Island's Great Whaling Era," *Long Island Forum*, XX, 11 (November, 1957), pp. 207-208, 213-215.
Davis, Elizabeth, "James Fenimore Cooper Lived Here," *Long Island Forum*, III, 12 (December, 1940), pp. 253-254.
Grossman, James, *James Fenimore Cooper*. William Sloane Associates (American Men of Letters Series), 1949.
Glicksberg, Charles G., "Cooper and Bryant: A Literary Friendship," *The Colophon*, Part 20 (1935).
Hedges, H.P., "Early Sag Harbor — An Address," (delivered before the Sag Harbor Historical Society). New York, 1902.
Howell, N.R., "Long Island Whaling," *Long Island Forum*, IV, 9 (September, 1941), pp. 210-212, 215-216.
Lounsbury, Thomas R., *James Fenimore Cooper*. Boston, 1882.
Mulford, Anna, "A Sketch of Dr. John Smith Sage of Sag Harbor," (Hofstra University Special Collection). Sag Harbor, 1897.
Pennypacker, Morton, *General Washington's Spies on Long Island and In New York*. Brooklyn, 1939.
Philbrick, Thomas, *James Fenimore Cooper and the Development of American Sea Fiction*. Cambridge, 1961.
Ringe, Donald A., *James Fenimore Cooper*. New York, 1962.
Sleight, Harry, *Sag Harbor in Earlier Days*. Bridgehampton, 1930.
———, *The Whale Fishery on Long Island*. Bridgehampton, 1931.
Walker, Warren S., *James Fenimore Cooper*. New York, 1962.

BIBLIOGRAPHY 215

WILLIAM CULLEN BRYANT

Primary Sources

Bryant, William Cullen, ed., *A New Library of Poetry and Song.* New York, 1877.
——, *Poetical Works.* New York, 1879 (copyrights 1854, 1871, 1878).
——, *Prose Writings of William Cullen Bryant,* ed. Parke Godwin, 2 vols. New York, 1889.
——, *Representative Selections,* ed. Tremaine McDowell. New York, 1935.

Secondary Sources

——, *Bryant Centennial, Cummington,* August 16, 1894. Springfield, Massachusetts, 1894.
——, *The Bryant Festival at "The Century."* New York, November 5, 1864.
——, *Bryant Memorial Meeting of the Century.* New York, November 12, 1878.
——, *The Story of Roslyn.* Roslyn, 1925.
——, *This Is Roslyn.* Roslyn, 1958.
Briggs, James A., *An Authentic Account of Lincoln Being Invited to Give an Address in Cooper Institute.* New York, 1860.
Coles, Robert R., "When Bryant Lived at Roslyn," *Long Island Forum,* XVIII, 1 (January, 1955), p. 7.
Glicksberg, Charles G., "Cooper and Bryant: A Literary Friendship," *The Colophon,* Part 20 (1935).
Godwin, Parke, *A Life of William Cullen Bryant,* 2 vols. New York, 1883.
J.P.M., "Roslyn's Suicide Secret," *Long Island Forum,* XXI, 11 (November 1958), p. 220.
Jackson, Birdsall, "Bryant and the Art of Poetry," *Long Island Forum,* IV, 9 (September, 1941), pp. 217-218.
Leggett, Eliza Seaman, "Notes from the Legget (sic) Diary," unpublished. Presented to the Roslyn Library by Jesse Merritt. Typed copy.
Simonson, Marjorie, "Letter," *Long Island Forum,* XVIII, 3 (March, 1955), p. 50.
Wilson, James Grant, *Bryant and His Friends.* New York, 1885.
Grist Mill Collection, Bryant Library, Roslyn. Two vols. of clippings, photographs, pamphlets, and manuscripts.

Specific Works Cited

Bryant, William Cullen, "James Fenimore Cooper," *Prose Writings,* I, pp. 299-331.
——, "Our Native Fruits and Flowers," *Prose Writings,* II, pp. 194-202.

WALT WHITMAN

Primary Sources

Whitman, Walt, *The Complete Poetry and Prose,* 2 vols. Garden City, 1954.
——, *Correspondence of Walt Whitman,* ed. Edwin Miller, 2 vols. New York, 1962.

———, *The Early Poems and the Fiction,* ed. Thomas L. Brasher, New York, 1963.

———, *The Gathering of the Forces* (articles from the Brooklyn *Daily Eagle,* 1846-47), ed. Cleveland Rodgers and John Black, 2 vols. New York, 1920.

———, *I Sit and Look Out* (articles from the Brooklyn *Daily Times*), ed. Emory Holloway and Vernolian Schwarz. New York, 1932.

———, *Notes and Fragments:* Left by Walt Whitman and now edited by Dr. Richard Maurice Bucke. Printed for private distribution only, 1899.

———, *The Uncollected Poetry and Prose,* ed. Emory Holloway, 2 vols. New York, 1932.

Secondary Sources

———, *Huntington-Babylon Town History.* Huntington, 1937.

Allen, Gay Wilson, *The Solitary Singer.* New York, 1955.

———, *Walt Whitman Handbook.* Chicago, 1946.

Bailey, John C., *Walt Whitman.* New York, 1926.

Bazalgette, Leon, *Walt Whitman, The Man and His Work* (translated from the French by Ellen Fitzgerald). Garden City, 1920.

Bucke, Richard M., *Walt Whitman.* Philadelphia, 1883.

Burroughs, John, *Whitman, A Study.* Boston, 1896.

Canby, Henry S., *Walt Whitman, an American.* Boston, 1943.

Chase; Richard, *Walt Whitman, Reconsidered.* New York, 1955.

Deutsch, Babette, *Walt Whitman, Builder for America.* New York, 1941.

Donaldson, Thomas, *Walt Whitman, The Man.* New York, 1896.

Dyson, Verne, *Whitmanland.* Brentwood, Long Island, 1960.

Fausset, Hugh, *Walt Whitman, Poet of Democracy.* London, 1942.

Freedman, Florence B., *Walt Whitman Looks at the Schools.* New York, 1950.

Gay, William, *Walt Whitman, The Poet of Democracy.* Melbourne, 1893.

Headley, J.T., *Washington and His Generals,* 2 vols. New York, 1847.

Holloway, Emory, "A Whitman Source," *Walt Whitman Newsletter,* September, 1956.

Jackson, Birdsall, "Walt Whitman and Paumanok," *Long Island Forum,* III, 11 (November, 1940), pp. 231-232.

MacLachlan, C.H., "Whitman as a Newspaper Editor," *Long Island Forum,* XXVI, 11 (November, 1963), pp. 249-250, 266.

Masters, Edgar Lee, *Whitman.* New York, 1937.

Merrill, Stuart, *Walt Whitman.* Toronto, 1922.

Merritt, Jesse, *Essays on Whitman and the West Hills Country.* Huntington, 1940.

———, "Whitman 'The Long Islander,'" *Long Island Forum,* I, 7 (September, 1938), pp. 7, 18-19.

Molinoff, Katherine, *Some Notes on Whitman's Family.* Brooklyn, 1941.

———, "Walt Whitman at Smithtown," *Long Island Forum,* IV, 8 (August, 1941), pp. 179-180, 182-184.

———, *An Unpublished Whitman Manuscript: The Record of the Smithtown Debating Society, 1837-38.* Brooklyn, 1941.

———, *Whitman's Teaching at Smithtown, 1837-38.* Brooklyn, 1942.

Morris, Harrison S., *Walt Whitman*. Cambridge, 1929.

Neilson, Kenneth P., "Calamus: Search and Discovery," *Walt Whitman Birthplace Bulletin*, IV, 1 (October, 1960), pp. 13-19.

Perry, Bliss, *Walt Whitman: His Life and Work*. Boston, 1906.

Rubin, Joseph J. and Charles Brown, *Walt Whitman of the New York Aurora*. Pennsylvania, 1950.

Sammis, Romanah, "Walt Whitman," *Long Island Forum*, III, 5 (May, 1940), pp. 93-94, 98.

Schyberg, Frederik, *Walt Whitman* (translated from the Danish by Evie Allison Allen). New York, 1951.

Street, Charles R., ed., *Huntington Town Records*, 3 vols. Huntington, New York, 1888-89.

Turrell, Guy H., "The Evolution of a Library," *Long Island Forum*, XV, 2 (February, 1952), pp. 23-25.

Traubel, Horace, *With Walt Whitman in Camden*, Vol. I, Boston, 1906; II, New York, 1908; III, Mitchell Kennerly, 1914; IV, Philadelphia, 1953.

Specific Works Cited

A Backward Glance, in *CPP (Complete Poetry and Prose)*, I, pp. 469-482.

Collect in *CPP*, II, pp. 207-391.

"Death in the School-Room," in *CPP*, II, pp. 351-355.

"Elias Hicks," in *CPP*, II, pp. 469-487.

"A Fact-Romance of Long Island," in *The Early Poems*, pp. 319-320.

Franklin Evans, in *The Early Poems*, pp. 124-239.

Goodbye My Fancy, in *CPP*, II, pp. 492-538.

"The Last Loyalist," in *CPP*, II, pp. 361-366.

November Boughs, in *CPP*, II, pp. 392-491.

"Ode to Be Sung on Fort Greene," in *Gathering*, pp. 75-76.

"Preface, 1855," in *CPP*, II, pp. 269-281.

"Preface to the English Edition," in *CPP*, II, pp. 445-446.

"The Punishment of Pride," in *The Early Poems*, pp. 18-19.

"The Shadow and the Light of a Young Man's Soul," in *UPP (The Uncollected Poetry and Prose)*, I, pp. 229-234.

Specimen Days, in *CPP*, II, pp. 3-206.

"The Tomb Blossoms," in *The Early Poems*, pp. 88-94.

"Wild Frank's Return," in *CPP*, II, pp. 366-371.

"Young Grimes," in *The Early Poems*, pp. 2-4.

Index

219